THE
PLAINS
POLITICAL
TRADITION

VOLUME 3

• • •

THE PLAINS POLITICAL TRADITION

. . .

ESSAYS ON SOUTH DAKOTA POLITICAL CULTURE

VOLUME 3

EDITED BY

JON K. LAUCK, JOHN E. MILLER,

AND PAULA M. NELSON

SOUTH DAKOTA

HISTORICAL SOCIETY PRESS

PIERRE

This book is funded, in part, by the Great Plains Education Foundation, Inc.,
Aberdeen, S.Dak.

Library of Congress Cataloging-in-Publication Data available

The paper in this book meets the guidelines for permanence and
durability of the committee on Production Guidelines for Book Longevity
of the Council on Library Resources.

Text and cover design by Rich Hendel

Cover photograph by Chad Coppess, South Dakota Department of Tourism

Please visit our website at www.sdhspress.com

Printed in the United States of America
18 17 16 15 14   1 2 3 4 5

In honor of James David McLaird, 1940–2017,
Historian of South Dakota

CONTENTS

JON K. LAUCK,

JOHN E. MILLER, AND PAULA M. NELSON

INTRODUCTION

. . .

After more than a decade of research and preparation, we are proud to present the third volume of *The Plains Political Tradition: Essays on South Dakota Political Culture* series. We consider this three-volume project an important part of the recent revival of American political history. Several decades ago, political history, along with diplomatic history, constituted the widely accepted and essential core of historical studies. The decade of the 1960s, however, brought a spectacular rise in social and cultural history in the United States, the infusion of quantitative research techniques, an explosion of feminist studies, and the introduction of a whole menu of "new" histories, including the New Social History, the New Economic History, the New Western History, and others. As expanded emphases on race, class, gender, and other themes flowered, attention paid to "old standbys," including political history, lagged. That steep downward trend, however, has reversed course in recent years. Political history is now enjoying a major and much-needed revival, although critics are right to point out the continuing weaknesses in the field.[1]

When two of the editors of this volume joined geographer Edward P. Hogan in 2004 to write an exploratory essay on South Dakota political culture for *South Dakota History*, we were immediately motivated by an inquiry from the *New York Times* about how to best describe the political culture of South Dakota.[2] This question generated some quick discussion and answers. But it also motivated us to develop a longer-term strategy for answering the question in greater detail and to address the frayed condition of the state's political history. While not exactly moribund, the field had large gaps in coverage that needed attention. The field operates at a disadvantage because of the state's low population density, scarce resources, a small number of historians employed at universities in the state, and what might be termed an underdeveloped historical infrastructure. The state, for instance,

1

has never had a PhD program in history, which often serves as the spark for graduate theses on state and local history: theses that become books and thus the building blocks of a state historiography. South Dakota also has no public university press, relatively few bookstores, and fewer think tanks, institutes, and other cultural institutions that might boost both the writing and reading of state and local history. The establishment and growth of the South Dakota Historical Society Press (SDHSP), now an affiliate member of the Association of University Presses, and its publication of volumes like this one on South Dakota political history thus are wildly exciting developments for those who have been toiling in the lonely vineyard of South Dakota political history for decades. The Press, as represented by the three-volume series *The Plains Political Tradition*, has been essential to the recent burst of energy in the field of South Dakota political culture and South Dakota history more generally, as evidenced by the runaway success of its works on Laura Ingalls Wilder.

While the SDHSP has been essential to reviving South Dakota political history, the larger enterprise of reinvigorating the historical study of politics has raised key questions about the importance of state history in academia. The search for a "new history" in recent decades has led some to reject the significance of state boundaries and policies shaped by state citizens. Instead, some believe, the basic unit of investigation should be broadly defined groups, e.g., workers, women, specific racial and ethnic groups, and economic classes. To these scholars, states and nations have lost their former importance. We disagree. History is the analysis and interpretation of what happened in the past—the institutions people fashioned, the organizations they established, the laws they passed, the political choices they made, their economic exchanges, and their family structures—in sum, their changing worlds. States and nations have served as the organized center of life and the driving force behind many consequential movements. While time may sweep them away, they have been and remain vital units of human organization. In them, individuals have their private lives, their families and friends, and their neighborhoods and communities, all of which, in the best cirumstances, command loyalty and commitment. The most public of identities is as citizens of a state and nation. Some things are possible in some states but not in others; some states possess characters or identities that others do not share; and some states develop political cultures that function better or worse than those in neighboring states. Our focus in this series of books has been on the history of South Dakota, which possesses its own unique narrative. Thus, while its institutions, practices, ideas, and values overlap considerably with those of other states, it has developed its own peculiar political culture that sets it apart from them. It is not Massachusetts, Oregon, or Texas. Place matters; state boundaries matter.

Understanding the particularities of South Dakota has been the goal of all three volumes of *The Plains Political Tradition,* and we have found it particularly useful to draw upon ideas developed in the more general and loosely-defined field seeking to understand varying political cultures. This field of study attempts not only to record the stated goals of political leaders or the results of elections but also to explain the broader social dynamics, cultural forces, language, and symbols inherent in the political systems that shape the sociocultural landscape, determine election and policy outcomes, and generally provide a "key to understanding the nature of power and how one acquires it."[3] In this way, we join other historians in "rejecting the separation between culture and politics" and in embracing the mission of explaining how a certain set of cultural circumstances leads to a particular sociopolitical order, a corresponding set of political conditions, and a resulting set of policies.[4]

After more than a decade of working on this three-volume project, we continue to believe that "agrarian conservatism" is the best way to characterize the political culture of South Dakota. This characterization takes into account how South Dakota was, for most of its history, dominated by a rural and small-town culture that tended toward conservatism and generally supported the Republican Party (GOP), although it could deviate from this norm during times of economic stress in farm country. While this characterization is true in the main, our goal is to add complexity and nuance to this generalization by way of the more detailed accounts provided in the chapters of this volume, as well as volumes one and two.

The essays included in this collection highlight these nuances and give added texture to the South Dakota political landscape. The essays suggest, for example, that while the majority of South Dakotans hold conservative attitudes and beliefs and tend to support the GOP, there has always been a Democratic opposition that, given the right conditions and strong candidates, could break through. For instance, progressive or liberal inclinations have manifested themselves occasionally in the form of certain elements of populism and progressivism and during times of agricultural depression, such as during the 1930s or, less acutely, during the 1970s and 1980s. Despite South Dakota's conservative reputation, women, Jews, American Indians, members of various religious denominations, and other cultural groups have successfully brought their issues and perspectives into the public eye at different times and in a variety of ways. In a low-population state such as South Dakota, individual leadership and personal networks are also important, as evidenced by the success of personalities such as Henry L. Loucks, Coe I. Crawford, Karl E. Mundt, and Bill Janklow. These individuals all operated, however, within constraints and limits created by the state's political culture, and all were careful to navigate these cultural and ideological dynamics on their path to political success.

The role of particular individuals and the experiences that shaped them is on full display in this collection's first chapter about the Civil War veterans who settled South Dakota. This chapter also helps to correct some misunderstandings created by earlier historical works. The Dakotas were both blessed and cursed to have an eminent Yale historian write the history of their early territorial days. Howard Lamar's interpretation, set forth in *Dakota Territory, 1861–1889: A Study of Frontier Politics*, argued that territorial politics was dominated by personal feuds, factionalism, self-interested economic deals, and patronage, which was dished out of federal monies under the control of appointed politicians, and that few higher ideals influenced the scene. In the first chapter, however, Kurt Hackemer finds high-mindedness and laudable intentions motivating Civil War politicians as they focused on important war-related issues, especially the idea of the Union, during these formative years. Those active in politics were aware of the dangerous developments in Washington, maintained their faith in the continued existence of the Union once the war broke out, and stated their ideals through editorials, in campaign debates and territorial conventions, and through their display of shared national symbols, banners, the flag, and general expressions of patriotism. Hackemer builds his case for the existence of broader patriotic principles in territorial politics through careful examination of each of these elements, providing examples of Union that appear again and again. This intense national interest and patriotic faith lays the foundation for South Dakota's post-Civil War political culture.

If we needed any further proof that not all politics is party politics, Linda M. Clemmons's chapter on the implementation of President Ulysses S. Grant's Peace Policy in Dakota Territory during the 1870s illustrates the truth of the notion. She compares the political maneuverings of the Presbyterian/Congregationalist American Board of Commissioners for Foreign Missions (ABCFM) with those of the Episcopalian missionary establishment, finding the latter to have been much more effective. Numbers alone do not explain the Episcopalians' relative success (they administered around twenty-five thousand American Indians in the territory; the Catholics, seven thousand; and the ABCFM, fifteen hundred). Denominational activity on the reservations established an early connection between church and state — one that carried over into the twentieth century. Ironically, Grant's Peace Policy did little to promote peace among the denominations or between American Indians and whites. Despite denominational differences, most white Dakotans shared the assumption that their American Indian neighbors lacked knowledge and sophistication and needed outside help to manage their affairs and control their lives.

The last fifteen years of the nineteenth century witnessed an agricultural depression and, not coincidentally, a spasm of third-party politics in the state. South Dakotans played an important role in the populist revolt in farm country aimed at bolstering the agricultural economy and restoring the influence and the place of farm families in American life. The Farmers' Alliance and the Populist Party brought influential Dakotans into the national spotlight, where they helped create the dynamic but short-lived Populist movement aimed at reining in the power of increasingly monopolistic industry. Jeff Wells pictures the Populists as modernizers who used new tools in their fight to win political office and promote economic and political reforms in the state. Focusing his attention on the South Dakota Reform Press Association, Wells highlights key individuals, including Henry Loucks, who journeyed from Republican politics and Farmers' Alliance activities to Populism and back to the GOP after the Populists decided to fuse with Democrats to win political power. Some of the editors, especially those in the Black Hills, became advocates of socialism, while others, like Loucks, returned to their Republican roots.

Kenneth L. Smith's chapter on the relationship between William M. Blackburn and Coe I. Crawford illustrates how effective political leadership often includes deeply rooted Christian convictions about mission and purpose. It also indicates how fundamental values ought to shape relations between citizens and how they can be passed on from one generation to the next. Crawford was the first governor of South Dakota to place himself firmly in the center of the burgeoning progressive movement. Later, in the United States Senate, he added his voice to a growing contingent of midwestern progressive innovators with national stature. William M. Blackburn, a widely respected Presbyterian minister, historian, and college president, was Crawford's neighbor, pastor, and colleague on the Pierre College board between 1885 and 1898, which were formative years in the younger man's political career and civic consciousness. "That old philosopher," as Crawford fondly referred to Blackburn, did not directly shape his policy stances or political strategy, but helped form his sense of mission, encouraged his reformist zeal, and gave him a model of broad-minded leadership that was crucial to his success in public service. The cases of the ABCFM and the early Episcopalians, the Populists, and the relationship between Crawford and Blackburn also indicate the pervasiveness of Christianity in early South Dakota political culture.

The strength of the Christian tradition in South Dakota did not preclude the political success of other groups, however. Combining work from several larger studies of South Dakota Jewish history, Eric Steven Zimmer, Art Marmorstein, and Matthew Remmich survey patterns of Jewish settlement in the late nineteenth and early twentieth centuries before exploring the political and civic contributions carried out by this small—and relatively understudied—minority of South Dakotans. Historically, the state has been home to few Jews and has the lowest population of them in any state today. Yet, from the synagogues they founded in Aberdeen, Sioux Falls, and Rapid City, Jews celebrated the things that made them different—their heritage, history, customs, and beliefs—while weaving themselves into the fabric of the broader South Dakota community. Serving as judges, state legislators, party officials, active members of civic clubs, and more,

Jewish people took advantage of South Dakota's accessible and intimate political culture, becoming champions of myriad causes and, in a few cases, influential players in political circles.

From the earliest years, South Dakota political leaders have been concerned with building and developing the state's economy, but not until Joe Foss's governorship during the 1950s did the goal become concrete and practical. During this era, United States Senator Karl Mundt made economic development one of his top priorities and worked to implement it in a variety of ways. During the postwar period, the loss of farms through consolidation, the outmigration of young people, small-town population loss, and declining numbers of small businesses brought attention to the subject. Ryan Burdge discusses Mundt's efforts to promote Missouri River development projects, to build the interstate highways, and to enhance small-town viability. He argues that the senator's sponsorship of resolutions and bills to promote balanced rural and industrial development provided superior alternatives to the programs advanced by Presidents Lyndon Johnson and Richard Nixon. In the process, South Dakota politics became more focused on the cause of economic development and recruiting new businesses to the state, a cause that endures.

These same decades also brought the disruptions of the cultural revolution. Matthew Pehl provides a window on these cultural changes by examining women's activism in the state during this era and explaining how the South Dakota Commission on the Status of Women (CSW), an advisory board for women's issues, rethought rights and gender norms while promoting what he refers to as "knowledge activism." Begun in 1963 as a fact-finding commission, the CSW sought fairer treatment of women in the economic sphere, especially with regard to credit and wages. By the early 1970s, the CSW also supported the Equal Rights Amendment (ERA), promoted second- wave feminism (which argued that women were entitled to full access to the public sphere), and encouraged "consciousness raising," later turning its attention to sexual abuse and domestic violence, which resulted in laws to protect women from family violence. The CSW became more controversial over time, as the Supreme Court's *Roe* v. *Wade* decision and conflicts over the ERA helped stimulate an organized backlash, causing the group to lose popular support as conservative activists criticized its agenda. The legislature defunded and disbanded the

CSW in 1979. According to Pehl, the CSW's brand of moderate feminism made possible some modest gains for a short period of time, but by 1980, conservative views and values returned to a position of dominance and still hold sway in the state.

In his chapter on liberalism in South Dakota during the early 1980s, Cory M. Haala traces the reorganization of the South Dakota Democratic Party from the time of George McGovern's defeat in 1980 to Tom Daschle's reclaiming of McGovern's United States Senate seat in 1986. He argues that Daschle and other prominent Democrats focused on economic issues, especially relating to agriculture, used populist rhetoric, and downplayed divisive social issues in order to rebuild a winning electoral coalition. On the local level, the party struggled due to financial instability and the popularity of Republican Governor Bill Janklow, but Haala details how Democratic Party chairs like Loila Hunking and Bob Williams rebuilt the party's finances and encouraged grassroots participation in party activity. The strategy paid dividends in the 1986 statewide elections, as candidates like Daschle, Tim Johnson, and Lars Herseth ran competitively as Democrats in a state often dismissed as conservative.

Emily O. Wanless's chapter explores how South Dakota's political culture can be examined through the lens of the state's most-elected governor, William Janklow. Wanless analyzes how Janklow reflected the political beliefs and values of the South Dakotans electing him to the office four times, in 1978, 1982, 1994, and 1998. Specifically, she focuses on Janklow's 1994 election and explores his campaign strategy in order to understand what issues resonated with voters and what candidate characteristics they responded to when in the voting booth. South Dakota's political culture is revealed through content analysis of Janklow's campaign advertisements, campaign archives, internal public opinion polling, and interviews with campaign staffers and political observers at the time of the 1994 election. Wanless demonstrates how campaign strategies were crafted to emphasize Governor Janklow's authenticity and effectiveness as a problem solver. Ultimately, this case study affirms that Janklow's campaign tactics were successful because they embodied the moralistic-individualistic political values of the state.

Lastly, in the interest of promoting future research into the broader meaning and particular nuances of South Dakota political culture, this volume includes a master list of all of the state's elected governors and United States senators and representatives, as well as the location of their personal papers and a description of the contents of these collections. Compiled by Michele Christian, Daniel L. Daily, Lisa E. Duncan, and Chelle Somsen, all archivists at South Dakota institutions, this master list will prove to be an essential guide for the next generation of scholars who will tackle topics related to South Dakota political history. We believe we are on the path toward the launch of many such research projects. We hope the three volumes of *The Plains Political Tradition* will provide guidance and context for future scholars as they head to the archives.

NOTES

1. Fredrik Logevall and Kenneth Osgood, "Why Did We Stop Teaching Political History?," *New York Times*, 29 Aug. 2016, nytimes.com.

2. Jon K. Lauck, John E. Miller, and Edward Hogan, "The Contours of South Dakota Political Culture," *South Dakota History* 34, 2 (Summer 2004): 157–78.

3. Michael Kazin, "Hofstadter Lives: Political Culture and Temperament in the Work of an American Historian," *Reviews in American History* 27 (June 1999): 337.

4. Lawrence B. Glickman, "The 'Cultural Turn,'" *American History Now,* ed. Eric Foner and Lisa McGirr (Philadelphia: Temple University Press, 2011), p. 234.

KURT HACKEMER

1 | MORE THAN FACTION AND ECONOMIC INTEREST

A REEXAMINATION OF DAKOTA TERRITORY'S POLITICAL CULTURE DURING THE CIVIL WAR

. . .

Two years after Dakota Territory was formally opened to Anglo settlers, the Yankton *Weekly Dakotian* defined the personal characteristics of those who came West. "We must claim for the West," the writer opined, "a preeminence in those traits of character which are best calculated to elevate man to his legitimate standard, and to uphold and perpetuate our present form of government." While disparaging neither the East nor the South, the author stated those "who move to and settle in the West, soon lose those peculiar characteristics, marking the society from whence they came, and become more liberal, generous and unsuspecting; . . . in soul, body and spirit they become *Western men*." The end result was "a high standard of National, social, and moral worth."[1] Like most frontier newspapers, the *Weekly Dakotian* regularly published boosterish articles, but this particular piece reflects a larger attachment to and understanding of national politics during the American Civil War, one that historians of Dakota Territory have too readily discounted. Period sources reveal that the territory's residents were quite aware of the Civil War's ideological underpinnings and that their efforts to grapple with republican ideology in turn affected Dakota Territory's political culture.

Politics in Dakota Territory was raucous, unabashedly partisan, and fluid. Legislators and political appointees who nominally labeled themselves as Democrats, Republicans, or simply as Union men, fought and schemed with reckless abandon, forming factions of convenience that reflected the cause of the moment. When the next great issue emerged, new factions would appear, often composed of erstwhile political enemies. This description of Dakota Territory politics, initially articulated in firsthand accounts authored by George Kingsbury, Moses Armstrong, and George Batchelder, and later appearing in works by Doane Robinson and other historians, became an essential component of Howard Lamar's thesis in *Dakota Territory 1861–1889: A Study in Frontier Politics*.[2] Lamar argued that the vagaries of the plains environment called Dakota Territory's long-term economic viability into question. As a result of this uncertainty, the federal government became the territory's primary economic engine, which had a direct impact on territorial politics. Those who best manipulated the local political process for personal gain thrived, while those who failed sank into political and economic oblivion. Federal and local government, therefore, became essential to the successful settlement of Dakota Territory.[3]

In Lamar's interpretation, the economic self-interest associated with local politics explained the early political milieu of the territory. Factions were dominated exclusively by local rather than national concerns, and those who "wished to present a harmonious front for a few weeks [did so] by adopting the name of a national party and paying lip service to its platform." It was the patronage subsidies associated with national political parties, not their ideology, that explained all that happened, and it was all motivated and facilitated by economic dependency.[4]

Lamar's argument fails to account for the power of ideas and political ideology during a pivotal moment in American history. As political institutions in Dakota Territory took shape, the Civil War threatened the survival of the Union itself. At its core, the war was about ideology, especially the future form of republican government in the United States. In the North, Republicans and Democrats actively engaged in ideological debate within their parties and with political opponents from the other party locally, regionally, and nationally.[5] The war "clarified issues, identities and enemies" even as it simultaneously drew clear lines between patriotism and partisanship.[6] The reform movements of the preceding decades demonstrated a "pattern of locally based, nonpartisan civic activism" linked more to republican ideals than specific political parties.[7] Republicanism in the Civil War era had come to mean a reverence for civic virtue driven by collective action rather than individual self-interest. The liberty that guaranteed representative government and civic order was to be preserved at all costs. It was those republican ideals, specifically unionism, that took center stage when the war broke out, and Americans became more politically engaged in the public sphere even as they relied less on traditional party organizations to mediate their understanding of exactly what "political" meant. That does not mean that party politics disappeared, or became any less vicious, as confirmed by local studies of midwestern states and communities. However, it was often subordinated to nonpartisan expressions of republican ideals, such as unionism.[8]

At all levels, the debate organized itself around national issues and identities. Those conversations became particularly important within the Republican Party as different national factions vied for control of policy and thus the conduct of the war. Republicans believed that unionism was a key element of republicanism that trumped traditional partisan issues, and they deliberately stressed a nonpartisan approach to the war that appealed to more than just their party. In effect, they made nonpartisanship into a political tool that benefitted the party even as it preserved the Union, and their "propaganda was designed to persuade habitual non-Republicans with flattery and threats." Parties became important conduits for information, but a closer examination of contemporary political language reveals "voters' rejection of the concept of partisanship even while they cheered for their party's candidates."[9] Republican ideology was not the exclusive preserve of the Republican Party, and its essentially conservative nature appealed to Democrats, even those who ultimately opposed the war. The result was that republicanism, not partisanship, emerged triumphant and remained an important part of public discourse throughout the war, but the Republican Party more effectively integrated its precepts in support of their larger agenda. Republicanism, and especially unionism, affected both state and national elections in 1862 and 1864 and ultimately determined how Americans understood the conflict.[10]

President-elect Abraham Lincoln's personal political philosophy, which was reflected in the political philosophy of the Republican Party, strongly linked republicanism to the very existence of the Union, leading Alexander Stephens to famously note that Lincoln's dedication to "the Union rose to the sublimity of religious mysticism."[11] Lincoln's stance was articulated in a newspaper article that was reprinted across the country in January 1861. The first wave of southern states had seceded, others were considering secession, and the country breathlessly watched as multiple attempts at last-minute compromise took shape. A correspondent reported Lincoln's observation, "Whatever I might think of the merit of the various propositions before Congress, I should regard any concession in the face of menace the destruction of the government itself, and a consent on all hands that our system shall be brought down to a level with the existing disorganized state of affairs in Mexico."[12] Preserving the Union as it currently existed was paramount.

President Lincoln never wavered from his focus on unionism. It remained his primary goal from the moment he assumed office, and it was consistently embedded in his public pronouncements throughout the war. For example, his first inaugural address declared "that in contemplation of universal law, and of the Constitution, the Union of these States is perpetual." With some optimism, he hoped that "the mystic chords of memory . . . will yet swell the chorus of the Union, when again touched, as surely they will be, by the better angels of our nature."[13] As the fortunes of war ebbed and flowed over the next four years, Lincoln's devotion to preserving the Union was at the core of every major policy decision and regularly appeared in his public messages. More important, that devotion to the Union unified the Republican Party even as it transcended party lines.

As the war went on, the rhetoric of Union was always present, most notably when the party renamed itself the Union Party for the 1864 election and used republican values to appeal to civic-minded individuals of all political persuasions, a stratagem it also adopted in Dakota Territory.[14] Lincoln confirmed the primacy of unionism in his short but powerful second inaugural address, pointing out, "Both parties deprecated war; but one of them would make war rather than let the nation survive; and the other would accept war rather than let it perish."[15] He clearly intended to make reunion (and therefore union) the basis of postwar policy, but assassination removed his steady hand from a process otherwise fraught with peril.[16]

Historians have consistently underestimated the extent to which those living in Dakota Territory engaged with the larger issues that defined the Civil War. In territorial histories, the war appears sporadically but almost always as unconnected to the events and experiences that defined life in the area. However, a closer reading of the sources suggests that Dakotans kept a close eye on the war and its impact on the country at large. Engagement with the war meant engagement with ideological questions, and discussions and debates about unionism affected the conduct of politics in the territory. That is not to say that self-interest did not play an important role in territorial politics or that federal patronage was not eagerly sought by territorial politicians, for avarice and greed clearly affected political culture in the territory. However, the impact of ideological questions of national significance has been undervalued by historians who have written about the territory's early political history. Territorial politicians and their newspaper surrogates consistently invoked the language of republicanism, especially unionism, in pushing their political agendas because that language resonated so deeply with the electorate.[17]

That historical oversight is surprising, for republican ideology that stressed unionism was pervasive in the territory. First, it was touted in gubernatorial speeches, legislative resolutions, and local newspapers as a sacred principle that defined the territory, its residents, and their relationship to the rest of the country. Second, as political factions formed in Dakota Territory, they defined themselves using the rhetoric of unionism. This rhetoric was so powerful, and its antithesis held so little appeal, that Dakota Territory's Civil War experience would be characterized by a factionalized one-party system loosely organized around the Republican Party rather than the two-party system found elsewhere throughout the Union. Finally, those factions attempted to differentiate themselves based on their measure of devotion to unionism while simultaneously decrying their opponents' lack of devotion to the same ideals. Much of what they fought over met Lamar's definition of economic self-interest, and many legislators benefitted personally as a result, but when those factions reconciled near the end of the war, they did so because of unionism.

In the first few months of Anglo settlement, it was clear that unionism was of paramount importance to Dakotans. Sioux Falls residents agitated for an organic act that would organize a territorial government, for "Dakota is destined, we believe, to form another link in the great chain which Time is forging to bind the Atlantic and Pacific states."[18] Their only concern was partisan politics, which delayed the passage of an organic act for just over another year. In the meantime, settlers began pouring into the territory. The 1860 census recorded 2,128 Anglo residents, with the majority located along the Missouri and Big Sioux rivers in the southern half of the territory.[19] They could not vote for electors in that year's contentious national election, but their sentiments were well known. *The Register* of Sioux City, Iowa, which identified politically with the Democratic Party, was the only newspaper publishing on a regular basis in or near the Dakota frontier. Its editor noted "a great change in public sentiment . . . throughout the country." The recent election forced the question in many minds. The editor suggested, "When a practical test is made of the choice of the people whether they are for Union or disunion— prosperity or bankruptcy—blessings or misery, there is found really but one voice in the country, and that is for the government and all its attending blessings as our Fathers made it under the Constitution."[20] As the country lurched toward open conflict, Dakotans were likely asking themselves where they stood on this pressing national question.

Towns up and down the Missouri River Valley soon sported familiar American institutions like churches, local governments, and newspapers. The first permanent newspaper in Dakota Territory began printing in June 1861 in Yankton as *The Dakotian*. Although it lured potential settlers with the promise of removal "from the immediate troubles that unfortunately hang around our beloved country," *The Dakotian* actually reflected the centrality of unionist thinking.[21] The newspaper's masthead proclaimed, "Where the Flag of our Country Leads, we will Follow," and its locally written articles declared secession to be an outrage, advocated for the use of force to restore the Union, affirmed local support for the Union and its cause, and celebrated the fact that newly appointed territorial officials were closely tied to the Lincoln administration.[22] The *Dakota Republican*, which began publishing regularly in Vermillion in 1862, also editorialized frequently about the importance of union. Its masthead, "Our country if right, if wrong, God forgive, but our country still," was decidedly national and pro-Union, and although it, too, entered the political fray with gusto, editor John Glaze stressed "the perpetuity and welfare of the government," as well as the patriotism and devotion to the Union shared by both local and territorial residents.[23]

The Dakotian and the *Dakota Republican* would become partisan mouthpieces for different territorial political factions, with the invective and name-calling that typified political culture at the time, but both were unwavering in their support for the Union through the darkest days of the war. *The Dakotian* directly linked "self-preservation" of the territory to the preservation of the Union, noting that "we are unconditionally for the Union, believing that our liberties, our free institutions, . . . our greatness and our prosperity, are dependent on its perpetuity."[24] Even when it became clear that the Emancipation Proclamation linked the ending of slavery to preservation of the Union, *The Dakotian* steadfastly supported the Lincoln administration and its plan to end the war. That devotion to the Union remained solid even when it appeared that President Lincoln might lose his reelection bid.[25] The *Dakota Republican* likewise remained staunchly pro-Union throughout the war, chastising "Tories" and "Peace Men" alike who suggested that any other outcome might be acceptable. Union supporters were urged to be true to the cause even when the war was not going well.[26]

The temptation, of course, is to dismiss this kind of language as being unrepresentative of the views of the larger population. That, however, underestimates the power of political ideology and the role it played in defining and stabilizing nineteenth-century American society. Parties and political factions were "part of, not remote from, political experience," and politics itself "was not a separate sphere, isolated from the socioeconomic, even personal concerns of most Americans."[27] Instead, political ideology provided order, structure, and language that defined the parameters of social interaction and discourse. The Republican Party proved particularly adept at bridging the gap between politics and ideology, and "effectively equated Unionism with dynamic capitalist growth and the opening of economic opportunity for ordinary American farmers, workers and small manufacturers of modest wealth."[28] This resonated well in Dakota Territory and supports Lamar's observation about the importance of personal gain to the territory's settlers. Newspapers became the primary means of popularizing unionist discourse, but they were also businesses that survived only with a critical mass of subscribers. Adopting viewpoints not representative of those held by the general population meant closing up shop and ceasing publication. If anything, newspapers played an outsized role in defining public opinion by amplifying and distorting local, regional, and national events. The fact that Dakota Territory's two most prominent newspapers were ardently pro-Union suggests that the majority of the population shared a similar predilection.[29]

That predilection was also reflected in the official trappings of territorial government. The territorial seal, adopted in the fall of 1862, proudly proclaimed "Liberty and union; one and inseparable; now and forever." *The Dakotian* opined that this "convey[ed] a good idea of 'out west'."[30] Similar sentiments could be found every year in the governor's annual message. William Jayne stressed the importance of union and the righteousness of the Union cause in two separate sections of his first annual message, delivered on 17 March 1862. The majority of his second annual message, read before the legislature just nine months later, focused on American Indian affairs, but Jayne still extolled the virtues of union, anticipating the benefits that increased migration and a transcontinental railroad would bring to the territory once the war was over.[31]

Governor Newton Edmunds similarly understood the relationship between the concept of union and territorial affairs. He devoted part of his first annual message to the Civil War, efforts to preserve the Union, and what that meant for the citizens of Dakota Territory, stressing the necessity of "preserv[ing] our institutions and republican form of government."[32] *The Dakotian* noted the connections drawn between unionism and life in Dakota Territory, commenting "that loyalty to the Government, the actual wants of the people, and the consciousness of the responsibilities resting upon the chief director of our Territorial affairs, are plainly manifest in every matter taken into consideration."[33] Governor Edmunds's second annual message, delivered after Abraham Lincoln's reelection, reiterated the importance of preserving the Union and linked that concept to the general well-being of Dakota Territory. Edmunds devoted approximately a quarter of his message to national affairs, a measure of its importance to those on the frontier.[34]

The territorial legislature, despite its fractious nature and tendency to make decisions based on the economic self-interest of its members, also acknowledged the ideological importance of union at multiple points in the war. Lengthy joint resolutions about the war and the importance of preserving the Union were passed and forwarded to national authorities in 1862 and 1864. The 1862 resolution was particularly direct, declaring "that the present war is prosecuted for the integrity of the union, the preservation of the constitution, and the supremacy of the government." The legislators starkly suggested "that the plain, simple, stern alternative is now presented to the people of crushing out treason, or yielding the national existence." Legislators also connected preservation of the Union to territorial events, arguing that Dakota Territory should "receive the highest commendation from every citizen" for fulfilling its obligation to raise troops for the war effort.[35] Those soldiers would never leave the territory, but they served the Union cause nonetheless.[36]

The 1864 resolution was equally direct. While legislators preferred a timely end to the war, they affirmed, "We are opposed to a cessation of this conflict . . . until the rebellion [is] effectually put down, and the authority of the government in full force and vigor, is fully established and acknowledged in every State and Territory of the United States." At a time when the war was not going well and muted criticism of President Lincoln's leadership could be heard across the country, these Dakotans made a point of articulating their support for the president, his conduct, and his policies. Lincoln's continuous rhetoric about the importance of preserving the Union had clearly resonated with them. They valued "the co-operation of the pure and patriotic men" who set aside individual differences and "the trammels of party organization" to fight for higher ideals.[37] Perhaps they sensed that they, too, would have to make similar choices in the coming year, and perhaps they wondered if they were capable of similar high-minded action.[38]

Historian Herbert Schell described the early territorial period of Dakota politics as one where "personalities rather than party principles" dominated, noting that the Republican Party did not formally organize until 1866 and the Democratic Party until 1868.[39] Strong personalities certainly made their presence known in Dakota Territory throughout the Civil War, but factions professing a strong adherence to principles were also a fixture of the political scene. Howard Lamar suggests that those factions consisted of a "Democratic frontier element in Dakota" that set itself in opposition to "those recently arrived from the East" who came from both Democratic and Republican backgrounds. The former, Lamar argues, did not overtly support the Confederacy but "cared little for the principles upon which the abolitionists and Republicans had taken their stand."[40] His interpretation

18   PLAINS POLITICAL TRADITION

is based on one trial for alleged disloyalty in which the defendant was ultimately acquitted.

A closer reading of the political pronouncements generated by Dakotans vying for control of the territory reveals different ideological motivations, however, with both dominant factions professing strong support for unionism. The Organic Act of 2 March 1861 that created Dakota Territory, coupled with President Lincoln's subsequent appointment of William Jayne as the first territorial governor, triggered the first organized political activity. At stake was the election of the territory's delegate to Congress, a position valued widely for its influence on patronage appointments. Factions began organizing around several individuals, including A. J. Bell, Charles P. Booge, and John B. S. Todd, and those factions sought to legitimize themselves by holding local political conventions.[41]

The first convention met in Vermillion on 1 June 1861 to support Bell's candidacy. Howard Lamar dismisses their platform, noting that it was the only one to come out of what was otherwise a personality-driven political process.[42] That dismissal, unfortunately, makes it easier to overlook genuine interest in national affairs. The platform's first resolution affirmed unanimity "in favor of maintaining inviolate the Constitution of the United States and the enforcement of all the laws of Congress and the perpetuity of the Union." After pledging to support the democratic process in Dakota Territory and declaring Dakotans' support for a national homestead law, the platform returned to the issue of union, resolving "that we fully and frankly endorse the policy of the present administration in relation to our national difficulties, believing that it is both patriotic and just."[43] Bell's Vermillion supporters were most explicit in linking their cause to unionism through formal proceedings, but Todd's supporters also felt compelled to establish his sincerity of commitment by stressing his devotion to the Union cause. They reminded readers of the *The Dakotian* just how important the next Congress would be in prosecuting the war effort and preserving the Union, implying that Todd's presence would somehow enhance that effort.[44]

These sentiments were not unique. Another convention, meeting in Yankton in late August to nominate legislative candidates for the upcoming territorial elections, also felt compelled to link its actions with preservation of "the Constitution and union of states." George

Kingsbury, the partisan editor of *The Dakotian*, later noted that this convention's labors resulted in a pro-Todd "ticket composed entirely of democrats and while there were a number of staunch republicans in the convention and in the town, they were not recognized on the ticket."[45] Historian Norman Thomas suggests that Todd's victory was due in part to an effort by his supporters to play up the fact that none of his opponents lived in Dakota Territory when it was created. In an environment where all claimed some allegiance to republican ideals built on civic virtue, an appeal to republicanism might not work as well for candidates who only recently arrived in the territory. Todd supporters adopted similar tactics just a few months later in an election for the territorial delegate to Congress, pointing out that Todd's opponents and their supporters rarely set foot in the territory and were therefore unfit to govern.[46]

Writing decades later, Kingsbury took great pains to point out that all involved "affirmed staunch loyalty to the Union," declaring, "The restoration and preservation of the Union was the only question of importance."[47] This statement suggests a wider worldview that was fully engaged with national politics and the ideology of unionism. It also explains the relative dominance of the Republican Party in Dakota Territory politics both during and after the war. Wilbur Zelinsky's Doctrine of First Effective Settlement suggests that the strong unionist sentiment that characterized its first Anglo settlers affected "the later social and cultural geography of the area."[48] Despite their relatively small numbers, those first migrants defined the political landscape for all those who followed. The fact that so many came from Republican strongholds in Wisconsin, Minnesota, Iowa, Ohio, and New York made single-party domination of local politics and a strong attachment to republicanism and union almost inevitable, a trend that continued well after the war, reinforced by the Lincoln administration's consistent appointment of radical Republicans to key political posts affecting the territory. The differences between the factions, it seems, were partially defined by their perceived devotion to republican ideals.[49] William Beadle suggested that the importance of republicanism was missed by Dakota Territory's earliest chroniclers, who "sometimes followed a partisan record and have magnified and belittled individuals at the cost of the general movement of popular opinion, development and public service," and he charged them with failing to "see the life, civic and moral, of the people."[50]

Identification with unionism was evident in 1862, when voters went to the polls for the first elections held under territorial law. The event was in September, but factions began organizing formally in early July around John B. S. Todd and Governor William Jayne. Todd was associated with the Democrats, while Jayne identified with the Republicans, but their supporters avoided party affiliation when describing themselves, and it was not unusual to find avowed Republicans supporting Todd who thought Governor Jayne should have stayed out of the race. Todd, for his part, could not count on there being enough ardent Democrats in Dakota Territory to back his candidacy, so he instead played upon his social standing in Yankton and his kinship ties with Mary Todd Lincoln. Supporters of both men avoided national party labels and instead went to great lengths to link themselves and their causes to unionism, mirroring trends in national politics.[51]

Even as territorial residents prepared for Fourth of July celebrations that reinforced their devotion to the Union, large-scale organizing efforts for both Jayne and Todd were well underway. Jayne supporters announced that a "Republican and Union" territorial convention would be held in Vermillion on 16 July and urged citizens to elect delegates for that meeting at county-level conventions on 5 July. Todd supporters announced a "People's Union" convention to be held in Vermillion on 24 July, with county-level conventions also held in advance.[52] Both political factions appropriated the rhetoric of unionism in an attempt to seize the political high ground, an indication of the power of that ideology. The Jayne faction's announcement had only one criterion for those attending its convention:

> All citizens, without regard to former party differences, who support the administration of Abraham Lincoln and approve its policy and principles, and who are in favor of the vigorous prosecution of the present war until the rebellion is crushed out and the supremacy of the Constitution and Laws completely established in every State and Territory of the Union, are earnestly requested to participate in the primary meetings for the election of Delegates.[53]

The full text of the call for the "People's Union" convention lacked the same direct appeal, but political opponent George Kingsbury later observed, "The title declared that the party was a 'Union' party, which at that time was the dominating issue in national and territorial political affairs."[54] Even in an electoral contest driven by personalities, unionism still held sway.

The extent to which unionism pervaded political culture in Dakota Territory is evident in the resolutions generated by the local conventions that met in July to choose delegates for the territorial convention that would nominate a candidate for the Congressional delegate election. The Yankton County Republican convention's three resolutions stressed "the perpetuity of the American Union," called for the "vigorous prosecution of the present war," and declared that its delegates would only support a candidate "who shall be a known and recognized endorser of these sentiments." Likewise, the Minnehaha County Republican and Union convention "fully and cordially endorse[d] the policy of the administration of Abraham Lincoln." Conventions organized under the auspices of the People's Union did not generate resolutions at the county level, but the same kind of language could be seen in the documents generated by both groups' territorial gatherings. The Republican and Union territorial convention reiterated the county-level resolutions and "cheerfully extend[ed] an invitation to every Union man in Dakota, without the least reference to his past political connections, to join us in our pledges and our labors." When the People's Union territorial convention met eight days later, they, too, expressed their support for "restoring the Union as it was, and for the preservation of the Constitution as it is," decrying partisan politics as something to be avoided "until our national difficulties are settled—the Union restored."[55] Clearly, both factions chose to define themselves politically using the language of unionism, suggesting that this ideology resonated even on the frontier.

Despite the high-minded language offered by both factions and claims of being "strangers to that sort of political warfare which invokes little nasty personal animosities . . . with our political opponents," partisanship was alive and well, and it only grew worse over time.[56] Elections always generated a fair amount of name-calling. A description of potential People's Union delegates as "worn-out politicians, sore-headed office seekers, rag tag, bob tail, Billy Patterson, sod corn whiskey" drinking citizens was typical. Nonetheless, even the invectives hurled about by both factions used the language of unionism, or rather, language that pro-Unionists nationally used to describe their political opponents as pro-Confederate collaborators.[57] These rhetorical excesses occurred with enough frequency and stridency to convince a few historians that Dakota Territory was home to a significant number of Southern sympathizers during the war. Historian Will Robinson, for example, argued "There is no way that the Southern sympathizers could be determined, but there were many."[58]

The 1864 territorial election was notable for the extent to which local disagreements were defined and then resolved using the rhetoric of unionism. At stake, once again, was the selection of Dakota Territory's delegate to Congress. Walter Burleigh, a Jayne confidant who assumed the editorial helm of *The Dakotian* in 1863, emerged as a leading candidate. His opponent was Philemon Bliss, the territory's chief justice and a longtime Jayne critic. During the rough and tumble 1862 elections, Bliss had already been labeled as a Copperhead sympathizer, an epithet reserved at the national level for those who were disloyal to the Lincoln administration and its devotion to unionism and who preferred a negotiated settlement to the war with the Confederacy.[59] The rhetoric of implied treason grew more strident in the fall of 1863, leading Bliss advocate Moses Armstrong to anonymously (and sarcastically) point out that Burleigh's supporters "are already making the Copperhead party in Dakota too large to be manageable."[60] By 1864, battle lines were clearly drawn, and both factions sought to demonize the other as traitors to the cause of unionism.

With Burleigh firmly in control of *The Dakotian* and Vermillion's *Democratic Republican* not publishing issues on a regular basis, Bliss supporters needed a public mouthpiece. They got it with the creation of the *Dakota Union* on 21 June 1864. Also headquartered in Yankton, the *Dakota Union* was published by George Kingsbury, who until this point had been associated with *The Dakotian*, and Moses Armstrong.[61] Kingsbury and Armstrong went on the offensive, explaining that *The Dakotian* existed only to serve the "selfish ends" of its owners and that the *Dakota Union* was such a strong supporter of Lincoln and his administration that they "desire[d] to see it renewed too eagerly to allow the officers of his appointment to betray the trust he has confided to them—and bring disgrace upon his Administration."[62] The "officers of his appointment," of course, were Jayne and, by extension, Burleigh.

Burleigh fired back with charged rhetoric of his own, quickly linking Kingsbury to the national Republican insurgency led by John C. Frémont and alleging "Copperhead support, their only hope of success." He then denounced "every one of the renegades from the Republican party, who today form the nucleus around which Copperheads and Democrats concentrate for the purpose of forming this new 'Union' party."[63] Charges and countercharges continued in subsequent issues of *The Dakotian*, all intended to undermine political enemies claiming a pro-Union pedigree by linking them to those seen nationally as enemies of the republic.[64] The editor of the nearby *Sioux City Register* struggled to make sense of it all for his readers, finally deciding, "The truth of it is both sides are made up of shrewd men and honest men, but the trouble is, the honest men are not shrewd, and the shrewd ones are not honest."[65]

Kingsbury and Armstrong drew no such distinctions and quickly defended themselves. Appealing to the court of public opinion, they replied, "The body of Dakota's people is thoroughly loyal, and the many representations that have been made to the President that there was a formidable copperhead party in this Territory, have been manufactured by a few designing politicians who have desired to make Mr. Lincoln believe that *they* had accomplished a Herculean task by electing Union men against a terrible combination of frontier rebels."[66] The implication, of course, was that Kingsbury and Armstrong represented unionist sentiment in Dakota Territory and that Burleigh and his followers were opportunists who could "profess great loyalty to the Union" while trying to manipulate the political process for their own gain. "We have traitors at home," warned the *Dakota Union*, "who walk in the garb of loyalty, and are clothed with official power."[67] These "traitors" properly declared their support for unionism and republican government, but "their action at home has been directly inimical to the institutions peculiar to our government."[68]

The sniping continued for the rest of the summer, with both factions explicitly questioning each other's loyalty and devotion to the Union. Local sins, such as alleged voter fraud in the 1862 election and the quest for personal gain, were sporadically mentioned, but alleged malfeasance was generally described using the language of unionism and republicanism. At the same time, each faction repeatedly affirmed its allegiance to the Union and its ideals. Imagine, then, the surprise of the territory's residents as they opened the 3 September edition of *The Dakotian* to find that these mortal enemies who had excoriated each other all summer had resolved their differences and joined forces to counter John B. S. Todd, who entered the race late and posed a real political threat to both factions. The new fusion party now presented itself as a National Union Party representing all unionist supporters in the territory.[69]

The sudden rapprochement may not have been all that surprising to Dakotans, especially if one accepts the idea that politics in Dakota Territory was driven as much by unionist ideology as it was by personal avarice and greed. Events in Dakota Territory mirrored almost exactly what was happening nationally in the spring and summer of 1864. The war was not going well, which opened the door to challengers for the Republican nomination for president. Secretary of the Treasury Salmon P. Chase launched an abortive bid for the nomination in early 1864, but President Lincoln outmaneuvered him by playing political hardball with patronage. At the end of May, General John C. Frémont, the Republican presidential nominee in 1856, launched a third-party bid that threatened to siphon off enough Republican votes to hand the election to the Democrats. Party leaders undermined the insurgency by calling a National Union convention in early June designed not only to lure disaffected Republicans back into the fold but also to provide a haven for pro-Union Democrats.[70] When Dakotans opened *The Dakotian* of 3 September to find a National Union movement declared in the territory, they saw yet another example of local politics defined using national language, practice, and ideology.

The rapprochement between the two self-described unionist factions drew on that national context. *The Dakotian* declared that "personal bitterness between the friends of the Administration in Dakota has at length given away to Common Sense," acknowledged public dissatisfaction with the feuding factions, and suggested "this division has, in its effects, been more detrimental to the prosperity of our Territory, than all the drouths [sic], grasshopper raids and Indian scares we have ever had among us." The long-term goal for all involved was statehood, and the best way to reach that goal was "*together* keeping step to the music of the Union."[71] To that end, the newly reconciled factions proposed a mass convention to reaffirm their support for the Union, following the example set by national leaders just a few months earlier.[72]

The final act of reconciliation came in mid-November with the first edition of the *Union and Dakotian*, "the consolidated and official organ of the National Union Party Dakota." This continuation of *The Dakotian* incorporated the sensibilities of the now-defunct *Dakota Union* and explained its current incarnation almost entirely using the language of unionism. Both of its predecessors "appeared to be laboring for the same commendable purpose, by sustaining the National Administration, and the War for the Union." Their disagreements, however, meant that the territory, "for the last two years, has been drifting towards political ruin." The good of the territory, and especially the importance of "united Union sentiment," led to reconciliation. Even John B. S. Todd, the clear loser of this partisan squabble, was declared "a true gentleman."[73]

The inaugural *Union and Dakotian* promised readers, "We now, once and for all, place ourselves above and beyond the baneful influences of any political warfare, save that arising from a high-toned, fair and fearless vindication of the Administration, the Territory and the Union."[74] An optimist might see this declaration as the beginning of a new political culture in Dakota Territory, but it most certainly was not. The greed, avarice, and personal motivations that defined territorial politics were still there. Indeed, as Howard Lamar suggested so long ago, they never really left. However, the rhetoric and actions of Dakota Territory legislators and politicians simultaneously point to an engagement with the unionism that dominated the national political scene, an engagement that would continue in the postwar years, especially as veterans migrated west and assumed leadership roles in their communities and the territorial government. In the end, the rhetoric of republicanism that permeated wartime Dakota Territory was more than the "lip service" claimed by Lamar, for Dakotans could have waged their political battles on purely local and personal terms.[75] They chose not to, however, drawing instead upon the ideology of unionism that formed the core of their political beliefs. In doing so, they demonstrated a sophisticated and nuanced political culture that would be reflected in territorial and state politics for the rest of the nineteenth century.

NOTES

1. "Western Characteristics," *Weekly Dakotian*, 13 July 1861 (emphasis in original).

2. George W. Kingsbury, *History of Dakota Territory*, and George Martin Smith, ed., *South Dakota: Its History and Its People*, 5 vols. (Chicago: S. J. Clarke, 1915); Moses K. Armstrong, *History and Resources of Dakota, Montana and Idaho* (1866; repr. ed., Fairfield, Wash.: Ye Galleon Press, 1967); George Alexander Batchelder, *A Sketch of the History and Resources of Dakota Territory* (1870; repr. ed., Pierre, So. Dak.: Hipple Printing Co., 1928); Doane Robinson, *History of South Dakota*, 2 vols. (n.p.: B. F. Bowen & Co., 1904); Herbert S. Schell, *History of South Dakota*, 4th ed., rev. John E. Miller (Pierre, S. Dak.: South Dakota Historical Society Press, 2004); Elwyn B. Robinson, *History of North Dakota* (Lincoln: University of Nebraska Press, 1966); Harry F. Thompson, ed., *A New South Dakota History*, 2nd ed. (Sioux Falls: Center for Western Studies, 2009).

3. Howard Lamar, *Dakota Territory, 1861–1869: A Study in Frontier Politics* (New Haven: Yale University Press, 1956). Lamar popularized the thesis, but Herbert Schell had offered a similar analysis two years earlier in his *Dakota Territory during the 1860s* (Vermillion, S. Dak: Governmental Research Bureau, 1954), pp. 72–74.

4. Lamar, *Dakota Territory*, p.75, 98–99.

5. Public interest in national issues and ideology at all levels of the political process preceded the war and had been a fixture of the political scene since the 1830s. *See* Joel H. Silbey, *The American Political Nation, 1838–1893* (Stanford, Calif.: Stanford University Press, 1991), pp. 86–88.

6. Adam I. P. Smith, "Beyond Politics: Patriotism and Partisanship on the Northern Home Front," in *An Uncommon Time: The Civil War and the Northern Home Front*, ed. Paul A. Cimbala and Randall M. Miller (New York: Fordham University Press, 2002), p. 159.

7. Ibid., p. 149.

8. Ibid., pp. 162–63; Jean Baker, "From Belief into Culture: Republicanism in the Antebellum North," *American Quarterly* 37 (Autumn 1985): 543–49. Subordination of party politics to republican ideals might not hold up over time. Nicole Etcheson, *A Generation at War: The Civil War Era in a Northern Community* (Lawrence: University Press of Kansas, 2011), pp. 47–49, 122, notes several Union meetings in Putnam County, Indiana, during the secession winter that were held "irrespective of party," but local parties were so split by 1863 that they held separate Fourth of July celebrations.

9. Smith, "Beyond Politics," pp. 166, 169.

10. Michael S. Green, *Freedom, Union, and Power: Lincoln and His Party during the Civil War* (New York: Fordham University Press, 2004), pp. 6–7; Smith, "Beyond Politics," pp. 164–69; Jennifer L. Weber, *Copperheads: The Rise and Fall of Lincoln's Opponents in the North* (New York: Oxford University Press, 2006), pp. 19–20; J. Matthew Gallman, *Defining Duty in the Civil War: Personal Choice, Popular Culture, and the Union Home Front* (Chapel Hill: University of North Carolina Press, 2015), pp. 252–55.

11. Joseph R. Fornieri, "Lincoln's Reflective Patriotism," *Perspectives on Political Science* 39 (Apr.-June 2010): 110–11.

12. "Remarks Concerning Concessions to Secession," 19-21 Jan. 1861, in *The Collected Works of Abraham Lincoln*, ed. Roy P. Basler, 9 vols. (New Brunswick, N.J.: Rutgers University Press, 1953), 4:176.

13. "First Inaugural Address—Final Text," 4 Mar. 1861, ibid., pp. 264, 271.

14. Gary W. Gallagher, *The Union War* (Cambridge: Harvard University Press, 2011), pp. 48–74; Lucas E. Morel, "Lincoln and the Constitution: A Unionist for the Sake of Liberty," *Journal of Supreme Court History* 35, no. 3 (2010): 216–18; Green, *Freedom, Union, and Power*, pp. 58–85; Martha Watson, "Ordeal by Fire: The Transformative Rhetoric of Abraham Lincoln," *Rhetoric and Public Affairs* 3 (2000): 33–49.

15. "Second Inaugural Address," March 4, 1865, in *Collected Works of Abraham Lincoln*, 8: 332.

16. Merrill D. Peterson, *Lincoln in American Memory* (New York: Oxford University Press, 1994), pp. 38–39.

17. For a more detailed discussion, *see* Kurt Hackemer, "Finding Dakota Territory's Civil War: A Call for Further Research," *South Dakota History* 43 (Summer 2013): 147–67.

18. "The Present and Future of Dakota," *Dakota Democrat*, 18 Feb.1860.

19. Schell, *History of South Dakota*, p. 93; Kingsbury, *History of Dakota Territory*, 1:176–77.

20. "Revulsion of Sentiment," *Sioux City Register*, 15 Dec. 1860.

21. "Come to Dakota," *The Dakotian*, 6 June 1861.

22. *See*, for example, "A Rotten Sympathy" and "Our Rulers," 20 June 1861, "The Next Congress," 27 June 1861, and "Our Views Exactly," 20 July 1861, all ibid.

23. Editorial, *Dakota Republican*, 5 Apr. 1862. *See also* 5 July 1862.

24. "Position of the Dakotian," *The Dakotian*, 15 Sept. 1863.

25. "The Situation as We View It," 10 Nov. 1863, "Revolution," 26 Apr.1864, and "The Government, Not Men," 3 Sept. 1864, all ibid.

26. "Tory Humbug" and "A Rebuke to Peace Men," *Dakota Republican*, 14 Feb. 1863. *See also* "Be Men," *Dakota Republican*, 21 Mar. 1863.

27. Silbey, *American Political Nation*, pp. 127–28.

28. Richard Cawardine, *Lincoln: Profiles in Power* (Edinburgh, Scotland: Pearson Education Publishing, 2003), p. 230.

29. Barbara Cloud, *The Business of Newspapers on the Western Frontier* (Reno: University of Nevada Press, 1992), pp. 35–38; Edward L. Ayers, *What Caused the Civil War: Reflections on the South and Southern History* (New York: W. W. Norton, 2005), pp. 140–41; Richard Cawardine, "Abraham Lincoln and the Fourth Estate: The White House and the Press during the American Civil War," *American Nineteenth Century History* 7 (Mar. 2006): 2–4; Cawardine, *Lincoln: Profiles in Power*, pp. 230–31.

30. "Territorial Seal," *The Dakotian*, 28 Oct. 1862.

31. "Governor Jayne's First Message," in Kingsbury, *History of Dakota Territory*, 1:197–204; "Second Annual Message of Governor William Jayne, Delivered to the Legislative Assembly of Dakota, Thursday, Dec. 18, 1862," *The Dakotian*, 23 Dec. 1862.

32. "Address of His Excellency, Governor Edmunds, to the Legislature of Dakota, in Joint Convention Assembled, December, 1863," *The Dakotian*, 8 Dec. 1863.

33. "The Governor's Message," ibid., 8 Dec. 1863.

34. "Governor's Message," *The Union and Dakotian*, 10 Dec. 1864. These annual addresses also appear in Kingsbury's *History of Dakota Territory*, but he edited them, removing much of the language devoted to national issues.

35. "Joint Resolutions Relative to the Rebellion," in D.T., *General Laws, and Memorials and Resolutions of the Territory of Dakota, Passed at the First Session of the Legislative Assembly, Commenced at the Town of Yankton, March 17, and Concluded May 15, 1862* (Yankton: D. T.: Josiah C. Trask, 1862), p. 513.

36. Schell, *History of South Dakota*, pp. 84–85.

37. "Joint Resolution on the State of the Union," in D.T., *General and Private Laws, Memorials and Resolutions, of the Territory of Dakota, Passed at the Third Session of the Legislative Assembly, Commenced at the Town of Yankton, December 7, 1863, and Concluded January 15, 1864* (Yankton, D. T.: G. W. Kingsbury, 1864), p. 117–18

38. For an insider's view of challenges to Lincoln's leadership, *see* William E. Gienapp and Erica L. Gienapp, eds. *The Civil War Diary of Gideon Welles, Lincoln's Secretary of the Navy: The Original Manuscript Edition* (Urbana: Knox College Lincoln Studies Center & the University of Illinois Press, 2014), pp. 491–92.

39. Herbert S. Schell, "Politics—Palaver and Polls," in *Dakota Panorama*, ed. J. Leonard Jennewein and Jane Boorman (n.p.: Dakota Territory Centennial Commission, 1961), p. 190.

40. Lamar, *Dakota Territory*, p. 87.

41. Schell, *History of South Dakota*, pp. 93–94; Lamar, *Dakota Territory*, pp. 74–75.

42. Lamar, *Dakota Territory*, p. 75.

43. Kingsbury, *History of Dakota Territory*, 1:184–85.

44. "The Coming Campaign—Delegate to Congress," 6 June 1861; and "The Next Congress," both in *The Dakotian*, 27 June 1861.

45. Kingsbury, *History of Dakota Territory*, 1:224.

46. Norman Thomas, "John Blair Smith Todd, First Dakota Delegate to Congress," in *South Dakota Historical Collections* 24 (1949): 194–8.

47. Kingsbury, *History of Dakota Territory*, 1:224.

48. Wilbur Zelinsky, *The Cultural Geography of the United States,* rev. ed. (Englewood Cliffs, N.J.: Prentice-Hall, 1992), p. 13.

49. Schell, *History of South Dakota*, p. 79; Jon K. Lauck, *Prairie Republic: The Political Culture of Dakota Territory, 1879–1889* (Norman: University of Oklahoma Press, 2010), pp. 30–32; Vincent Tegeder, "Lincoln and the Territorial Patronage: The Ascendancy of the Radicals in the West," *Mississippi Valley Historical Review* 35 (June 1948): 78–81.

50. William Henry Harrison Beadle, "Memoirs of General William Henry Harrison Beadle," *South Dakota Historical Collections* 3 (1906):113.

51. Schell, "Politics—Palaver and Polls," p. 190; Green, *Freedom, Union, and Power*, pp. 268–71.

52. "Fourth of July" and "What's Next," *Dakota Republican*, 5 July 1862.

53. "Republican and Union Congressional Convention; To the Electors of Dakota Terr.," ibid.

54. Kingsbury, *History of Dakota Territory*, 1:221. The call for the People's Union convention can be found in "By Request," *The Dakotian*, 1 July 1862.

55. Kingsbury, *History of Dakota Territory*, 1: 219–20, 223.

56. "'Many Citizens' County Convention, *The Dakotian*, 22 July 1862.

57. "What's Next?," *Dakota Republican*, 5 July 1862.

58. Will G. Robinson, "Dakota's Own Civil War," in *Dakota Panorama,* ed. Jennewein and Boorman, p. 279. *See also* Kenny L. Brown, "Dakota and Montana Territories," in *The Western Territories in the Civil War,* ed. LeRoy Fischer (Manhattan, Kans.: Journal of the West, 1977), pp. 12–15.

59. Schell, *History of South Dakota*, pp. 105–7; Schell, *Dakota Territory during the 1860s*, pp. 78–79; James McPherson, *Battle Cry of Freedom: The Civil War Era* (New York: Oxford University Press, 1988), pp. 228–30; Weber, *Copperheads*, pp. 20–22, 157–59.

60. Moses Kimball Armstrong, *The Early Empire Builders of the Great West, Compiled and Enlarged from the Author's Early History of Dakota Territory in 1866* (St. Paul, Minn.: E. W. Porter, 1901), p. 131. Armstrong was writing anonymous columns about Dakota Territory politics for the *Sioux City Register* under the pseudonym "Logroller."

61. Maxine Wiseman, "Pioneers with Presses," in *Dakota Panorama*, ed. Jennewein and Boorman, pp. 151–52.

62. "To the People of Dakota," *Dakota Union*, 21 June 1864.

63. "The Dakota Election," *The Dakotian*, 2 July 1864. Secretary of the Navy Gideon Welles nicely captured the national party's evaluation of Frémont in a June 1864 diary entry, declaring him for "Frémont first and country after" (Gienapp and Gienapp, *Civil War Diary of Gideon Welles*, p. 420).

64. For example, *see* "A Vindication," 16 July 1864, "True and False Loyalty," 23 July 1864, "Blissful Emotion," 30 July 1864, and "Political Trappers," 6 Aug. 1864, all in *The Dakotian*.

65. Editorial, *Sioux City Register*, 28 May 1864.

66. "Territorial Politics," *Dakota Union*, 12 July 1864.

67. "True and False Loyalty," ibid., 19 July 1864.

68. "Queer Politics," ibid., 9 Aug. 1864.

69. Lamar, *Dakota Territory*, pp. 95–97.

70. McPherson, *Battle Cry of Freedom*, pp. 713–17; Green, *Freedom, Union, and Power*, pp. 273–79; Heather Cox Richardson, *To Make Men Free: A History of the Republican Party* (New York: Basic Books, 2014), pp. 48–49.

71. "United We Stand," *The Dakotian*, 3 Sept. 1864 (emphasis in original).

72. "Platform of the Republican and Union Party of Dakota," *The Dakotian*, 3 Sept. 1864.

73. "Dakota Redeemed and United," *Union and Dakotian*, 19 Nov. 1864.

74. Ibid.

75. Lauck, *Prairie Republic*, pp. 34–38; Lamar, *Dakota Territory,* p. 75.

LINDA M. CLEMMONS

2 | "BUSINESS IS BUSINESS EVEN IF
WE ARE CHRISTIANS"
THE POLITICS OF GRANT'S PEACE POLICY
IN DAKOTA TERRITORY, 1870–1880

• • •

I n 1871, Thomas Riggs wrote to his brother Alfred—both were missionaries affiliated with the Presbyterian/Congregationalist American Board of Commissioners for Foreign Missions (ABCFM)—complaining that the Episcopalians had taken over "their" mission field in Dakota Territory. Thomas Riggs bluntly informed his brother, "Business is business even if we are Christians." He grumbled that the ABCFM's leadership "has not done enough 'blowing' . . . in regard to what we have done among the Indians. The result is you and father and others do all the work and the Episcopalians get all the credit and hold the places of Govt. power."[1] Prior to the Civil War, ABCFM missionaries to the Dakota people, as well as the ABCFM governing board, attempted to distance themselves from government agents and the politics of American Indian affairs. With the advent of President Ulysses S. Grant's "Peace Policy," however, missionary organizations competed for control of American Indian agencies. The Episcopalians expertly participated in the political process by developing a strong lobbying presence in Congress and creating networks of supporters at the local and national level. While ABCFM missionaries complained bitterly in their private correspondence about the success of the Episcopalian missionaries, their national leadership only reluctantly (and belatedly) engaged in the political fight for control of Indian agencies, which kept them from coveted access to potential Indian converts in Dakota Territory during the 1870s.[2]

Despite the intensity of opinion expressed by ABCFM missionaries, few historians studying American Indian policy during this era have highlighted conflicts between Protestant religious organizations.[3] Indeed, many historians argue that all Protestant denominations shared "a 'canopy' of common sensibilities" with regard to Indian policy during this era.[4] Henry Fritz called Grant's Peace Policy "a Protestant crusade."[5] Historians have assumed, like politicians of the time, that Christians would "forget doctrinal differences" in the service of Indian reform.[6] Those historians who highlight religious tension, such as R. Pierce Beaver and Peter J. Rahill, focus on conflict between Catholics and Protestants but conclude that between Protestant denominations, "there was little rivalry."[7] Likewise, historian Jon Lauck discusses tensions between Protestant and Catholic settlers within Dakota Territory in general but minimizes conflict between Episcopalians and Presbyterian/Congregationalists, noting that Protestant groups shared political power in the territory based on their common "Yankee Protestant heritage."[8]

Protestant denominations amiably shared political power in white-occupied regions of Dakota Territory, but the same did not hold true on reservations. Episcopalians, and especially Presbyterian/Congregationalists, maneuvered for control of Indian agencies throughout the 1870s. From the beginning, Episcopalians at both the local and national level proved adept at influencing the political process to their advantage. In contrast, the ABCFM's governing board and its missionaries adhered to their longstanding policy of remaining disengaged from politics. As the Episcopalians received control of agencies across Dakota Territory, however, ABCFM missionaries in the field argued that their leadership in Boston needed to play the political game if they wanted access to American Indians. The board reluctantly agreed, although too late to change the distribution of agencies in their favor. A study of the politics of Grant's Peace Policy in Dakota Territory thus highlights the methods, tactics, and political posturing used by Protestant missionary organizations to gain control over Indian agencies. The political lessons learned during the 1870s lasted beyond Grant's Peace Policy and allowed missionary organizations, eventually including the ABCFM, to continue to exert control over Indian affairs in South Dakota into the early twentieth century.

The conflict between missionaries in Dakota Territory also illustrates the expanded role religious organizations played in federal Indian policy under President Grant. Since colonial times, Indian affairs officials believed that "churchmen were honest and capable of 'elevating' Indian tribes" and would help the government to achieve its goals of "civilizing" and Christianizing American Indians.[9] Beginning in the early nineteenth century, missionary organizations received government funds that defrayed the cost of their schools, farms, and churches on reservations across the United States. In 1872, President Grant formalized the government's partnership with churches by turning over control of Indian agencies to religious denominations. Grant promised that missionary societies would "Christianize and civilize the Indian, and . . . train him in the arts of peace."[10] Dakota Territory, home to over thirty-three thousand American Indians—second only to Oklahoma in the late nineteenth century—thus serves as an important case study of the unparalleled partnership between church and state that occurred in the post-Civil War period.

In spite of Protestant control and conflicts over federal Indian policy in Dakota Territory, American Indians had their own opinions about the religious organizations they wanted assigned to their reservations. However, government officials never asked Indians whether they preferred a certain denomination, or if they wanted Christian missionaries at all. Despite the government's indifference to Indian sovereignty, leaders on reservations across Dakota Territory fought to have their political and religious preferences taken into account, repeatedly requesting Catholic missionaries or agents over the strong objections of Protestant missionaries and anti-Catholic politicians.

The political maneuverings of Protestant denominations in Dakota Territory in the 1870s cannot be separated from the historical context of the era, specifically President Grant's so-called Peace Policy. Following the Civil War, politicians and religious leaders harshly criticized United States Indian policy for many reasons. The 1864 Sand Creek Massacre in Colorado was especially shocking to the eastern public. In addition to the immorality of killing innocent Cheyenne at Sand Creek, many argued that such military clashes were prohibitively expensive. Some members of Congress complained that it cost the government nearly one million dollars for every American Indian killed and approximately one to two million dollars per week to defend the frontier population.[11] At a purely material level, these politicians argued that peace was more cost effective than war.

In addition to the high price of warfare, the cost of running American Indian agencies also came under attack. An "Indian Ring," characterized by fraud, graft, and a host of illegal activities, purportedly controlled agencies across the United States. Lurid examples of fraud filled newspaper articles, congressional reports, and missionary writings. Episcopal Bishop Henry Whipple called Indian agents "a disgrace to a Christian nation . . . [who] follow all the evils of bad example, of inefficiency, and of dishonesty."[12] Some Indian agents allegedly received an annual salary of only fifteen hundred dollars but could retire with a fortune after only three years of service; indeed, agents reportedly paid hefty bribes in order to procure lucrative appointments. Traders also profited from schemes to defraud Indians by providing substandard products at exorbitant prices. Courts rarely, if ever, punished Indian officials for fraud or abuse of their positions.[13]

Even before Grant took office, Congress took steps to investigate the so-called Indian Ring, the Sand Creek Massacre, and other problems on reservations. In March 1865, Congress formed a special joint committee, led by Senator James R. Doolittle, to report on the condition of American Indian tribes and their treatment by civilian and military authorities. The resulting "Doolittle Report," published in January 1867, contained a brief commentary and over five hundred pages of documents and harshly criticized the management of Indian affairs, pointed out examples of corruption, and condemned the actions of Colonel John Chivington at Sand Creek.[14]

The Doolittle Report also included testimony about Crow Creek in Dakota Territory, a reservation that would become a site of contention between the ABCFM, Episcopalians, and Catholics in the 1870s. Following the Dakota War of 1862, the United States relocated mainly Dakota women and children from Minnesota to the isolated and undeveloped Crow Creek Indian Reservation in Dakota Territory. According to testimony gathered by the Doolittle Commission, Dakota families at Crow Creek suffered starvation, illness, and graft at the hands of the agent, other Indian employees, the military, and traders. For example, instead of ordering goods from the closest settlement at Sioux Falls, the agent contracted to have supplies sent from Mankato, Minnesota. Provisions thus traveled hundreds of miles out of the way and reached Crow Creek depleted, spoiled, or not at all. The lack of goods led to starvation. Dakota families resorted to desperate measures to survive, including scavenging corn that government workers had dropped while feeding their horses, eating poisoned wolves, and cooking rancid food provided by the agent.[15]

Because of the Doolittle Report, government officials and the public knew about the terrible conditions at reservations like Crow Creek by the time Grant was elected in November 1868. Representatives of various churches approached Grant prior to his inauguration offering solutions to the "Indian problem." For instance, a delegation of Quakers met with Grant and suggested that he put agents from religious groups such as the Quakers in charge of the "administration, education, and evangelism" of reservations.[16] The Quakers argued that religious agents would end the graft and violence endemic at reservations like Crow Creek; more important, they also would help to "civilize" and Christianize native peoples.

Grant took the oath of office in March 1869. In his short inaugural address, he made only one passing reference to American Indians, despite his meeting with the Quakers. He stated that he would "favor any course toward them [Indians] which tends to their civilization and ultimate citizenship."[17] Although this statement was vague, after taking office Grant quickly began implementing what historians have since called his Peace Policy. He dismissed most of the agents (who managed reservations) and the superintendents (who watched over several Indian agents), replacing them with Quakers. He turned the rest of the agencies over to military officers who had recently served in the Civil War.[18]

On 15 July 1870, Congress passed a bill forbidding military personnel from holding civil offices, leading Grant to expand his Quaker program and award all agencies to Christian denominations.[19] Grant justified his new policy in two ways: first, missionaries would contribute to the "moral and religious advancement of the Indians"; and second, the policy would take politics out of the nomination of Indian agents by assigning agencies to individual with no political agendas.[20] Indeed, the missionary nominees did not need to have any practical administration experience; religious character was more important than expertise in Indian affairs. After confirmation by the United States Senate, the agents would be paid by the government but supervised by their own missionary board. The church-affiliated agents would carry out all government business, including the hiring of reservation employees. They also would set up programs to Christianize and educate all Indians within their jurisdictions.[21]

In his 1872 message to Congress, Grant ordered that control of agencies be distributed "to such religious denominations as had heretofore established missionaries among the Indians."[22] It fell to Vincent Colyer, an Episcopalian and secretary of the Board of Indian Commissioners, to carry out Grant's order. Based on Grant's message to Congress, missionary organizations expected to receive control of agencies where they already had established mission stations. Colyer's final list, however, was often idiosyncratic and did not always reflect a denomination's previous work with a tribe. For instance, southern churches did not receive any agencies due to Reconstruction politics. Colyer frequently overlooked Catholic and Mormon agents because of the virulent anti-Catholicism and anti-Mormonism of the era. Protestant groups eventually gained exclusive jurisdiction to sixty-four out of seventy-two reservations, although the denominations represented varied. For example, Colyer assigned control of fourteen agencies to the Methodists, ten to the Orthodox Quakers, six to the Hicksite Quakers, nine to the Presbyterians, eight to the Episcopalians, and five to the Baptists.[23]

In Dakota Territory, the ABCFM received management of one station (Sisseton), while the Catholics controlled the Devil's Lake (now known as Spirit Lake) and Grand River (now known as Standing Rock) agencies. The Episcopal church received all of the other appointments in Dakota Territory. In total, the Episcopalians administered 25,194 Indians in the territory; the Catholics, 7,120; and the ABCFM, 1,496.[24]

In addition to appointing missionaries to head agencies, Grant implemented several other programs designed to reform Indian affairs. While some historians have focused on the conservative ideology that linked all of the disparate parts of the Peace Policy, most scholars call these additional programs haphazard, incoherent, piecemeal, and even "vacuous."[25] First, in 1869, Congress created the Board of Indian Commissioners (BIC), comprising ten wealthy philanthropists, to oversee Indian policy. The commissioners served without pay and would "supervise the whole work of the Indian Department."[26] Initially, the wealthy Episcopalian merchant and philanthropist William Welsh (an appointment much maligned by the ABCFM), headed the board, but he left over financial issues after only one month. By 1874, the other original board members also had resigned because the BIC did not have any authority to enforce its decisions.[27]

Second, in 1871, Congress ended treaty making with tribes for their lands. Instead, Indian officials would negotiate "agreements" that

Fort Bethold
(Episcopal)

Devil's Lake
(Catholic)

DAKOTA TERRITORY

Grand River
(Catholic)

Sisseton
(American Board)

Cheyenne River
(Episcopal)

WYOMING

Upper Missouri
(Episcopal)

Whetstone
(Episcopal)

Red Cloud
(Episcopal)

Yankton
(Episcopal)

Santee Sioux
(Friends)

NEBRASKA

would be ratified by both houses of Congress instead of only the Senate. Third, although moving Indians to reservations had been central to Indian policy for decades, there was a renewed focus on relocating all tribes to reservations where they would become "civilized Christians." Fourth, there was an extended and time-consuming debate from 1876 to 1879 over whether to transfer control of the Indian Bureau from the Department of the Interior to the War Department. While Grant supported the transfer, missionary groups actively opposed it. The Department of the Interior ultimately retained control over the Indian Bureau, where it resides today.[28]

Finally, and ironically, throughout Grant's two terms as president the United States consistently waged war "amid a policy of peace."[29] The military fought over two hundred military engagements with American Indians; indeed, the era may have seen the most intense fighting with Indians in the nation's history, especially in Dakota Territory.[30] As historian David Sim noted, "the Peace Policy manifestly did not bring peace."[31]

The Peace Policy also created tension between missionary organizations. After Vincent Colyer had assigned churches to run agencies, several reservations operated under competing denominations—one missionary organization officially in charge of an agency, and another operating a separate mission, supported by its mission board but with no political power. Such was the case in Dakota Territory, where the ABCFM had established (or planned to establish) missions on reservations across Dakota Territory, while political control of most of the reservations rested with the Episcopalians. Publicly, ABCFM missionaries denied any tension with the Episcopalians. Stephen Riggs, in his memoir *Tah-Koo Wah-Ka* , wrote, "Friendly relations and kindly intercourse have ever prevailed between that [Episcopalian] mission and ours."[32] Likewise, Episcopalian William Welsh promised, "Perfect harmony and cordiality . . . have always existed there between the Missionaries of the American Board of Commissioners for Foreign Missions and those of the Episcopal Church."[33]

Private missionary correspondence tells another story. Martha Riggs, Stephen's daughter, wrote to her brother that she was "quite disgusted" that an Episcopalian clergyman was appointed to run the Fort Wadsworth Agency, the location of "her" ABCFM mission.[34] Samuel Hinman, an Episcopalian missionary, also spoke ill of his ABCFM peers in a private letter. He informed fellow missionary Joseph Cook: "Our Presbyterian friends are trying to make up for their lethargy by being unusually active just now. They are bringing new men and reorganizing generally. But they can't succeed—their system is bad and not all designed for Indians."[35] Both letters illustrate—despite public claims to the contrary—the tense battle that arose for Indian souls among Protestant missionaries in Dakota Territory.

The ABCFM's conflict with the Episcopalians actually began a decade before Grant formulated his Indian policy. In 1835, the ABCFM established two mission stations among the Dakotas of Minnesota. Over the next three decades, ABCFM-affiliated missionaries opened and closed nine additional stations across southern Minnesota and employed dozens of workers, most prominently members of the Riggs and Williamson families. Although their churches and schools remained small, the ABCFM claimed the Dakota field by virtue of their organization's monetary commitment and lengthy devotion to the Dakotas. ABCFM missionaries also invested considerable time and resources in turning the Dakota language into a written one and then translating thousands of pages of religious texts and hymns; the missionaries believed that these translations would eventually play a key role in converting the Dakotas to Christianity.

In 1860, Bishop Henry Whipple established an Episcopal mission headed by Reverend Samuel Hinman on the Lower Sioux Agency. The appearance of the rival Episcopalians in Minnesota did not sit well with ABCFM missionaries. ABCFM Corresponding Secretary Selah B. Treat stated, "The Board regarded the commencement of the Episcopalian mission as a clear departure from what is sometimes called 'missionary comity'. . . . The field was ours."[36] The ABCFM missionaries also complained that the Episcopalians "used books prepared by our missionaries," sang hymns translated by them, and read "our translations of the Scriptures" to potential converts. However, "in their publications and public speeches, [the Episcopalians] altogether ignored our work among the Dakotas."[37] For their part, the Episcopalian missionaries defended their new Minnesota mission, stating that the ABCFM did not have a "mission of any kind" near the majority of Dakota villages.[38]

At the same time he founded his Dakota mission, Bishop Whipple became nationally known as an Indian reformer. He wrote numerous letters, petitions, and memorials to the president, members of Congress, and cabinet officials demanding changes in Indian policy. For example, in November 1862, Whipple presented a memorial to President Abraham Lincoln—signed by eighteen Episcopal bishops—calling for reforms in the administration of Indian affairs. In 1871, following Whipple's lead, the Episcopal church created a Standing Committee on Indian Affairs, chaired by William Welsh.[39] Welsh's committee worked in Washington to "aid in promoting legislation and executive action favorable to Christian civilization among the Indians."[40] Later, the Episcopal church paid a director to live in Washington, D.C., to keep an eye on Indian affairs; it also created a subcommittee headed by Senator John W. Stevenson of Kentucky to lobby Congress on behalf of the Episcopalians. Because of all its political efforts, religious historian R. Pierce Beaver noted, "No other denomination in this period was so well organized to work for Indian rights as the Episcopal Church."[41]

While Bishop Whipple and the Episcopalians adeptly established political contacts and organizations, ABCFM leadership in Boston actively eschewed political engagement. Throughout much of the nineteenth century, Rufus Anderson, the ABCFM's chief policymaker and administrator, ordered all of the governing board's missionaries to "carefully refrain from intermeddling with politics." Its missionaries needed "to fully resolve not to meddle with their political relations."[42] This policy stemmed in large part from the ABCFM's earlier experiences with Andrew Jackson's Indian removal policies, especially with regard to the Cherokees. In the late 1820s, ABCFM missionary Jeremiah Evarts led a national campaign against the Cherokees' removal from Georgia. One week after Congress enacted the Indian Removal Act of 1830, Secretary of War John Eaton terminated ABCFM's allotment of nearly three thousand dollars for proselytizing to the southern Indians, stating that the loss of funds stemmed directly from the board's opposition to the Cherokees' removal.[43] This experience led the board to reject all "sordid" political entanglements through the post-Civil War period.

At first, the ABCFM's missionaries in Dakota Territory echoed their board's strict policy of political disengagement. Like their leaders in Boston, the Dakota missionaries viewed politics, and especially lobbying, as distasteful, unsavory, and even counterproductive as it distracted from their main goal of proselytizing. Stephen Riggs sniffed, "The business [of politics] is to me very unpleasant." His son, Thomas Riggs, agreed, writing, "It was not pleasant for all men to talk of what they do" or to promote their own political agenda.[44]

Their desire to separate from politics, however, did not mean that the ABCFM missionaries remained quiet about their Episcopal rivals. In 1863, shortly after the Dakota people's arrival at the Crow Creek Agency, ABCFM missionaries accused Reverend Hinman of "stealing" their converts. ABCFM missionary John Williamson wrote that the Episcopalians "*work things sharper*' at Crow Creek." He charged Hinman with actively attempting to "steal" Paul Mazakutemani, Simon Anawanmani, and Antoine Renville, three of the first members of his church.[45] Williamson, of course, denied any agency on the part of the three men to choose whether to affiliate (or not) with a particular church.

According to ABCFM missionaries, the Episcopalians used underhanded methods to lure Indians away after decades of toil on the part of ABCFM missionaries. In 1866, Stephen Riggs reported: "Some thirty or forty of the men . . . have gone off to the Episcopalians. [Hinman] was over there a few weeks ago and [gave] money largely it is said. In this kind of work we do not profane to compete with him."[46] According to John Williamson, Paul Mazakutemani confirmed that Hinman "had told him he would give him money" to join his church.[47] Several years later, Episcopalian missionaries allegedly "compensated Wizi," a Yanktonai leader at Crow Creek, for joining their church with a "check for 100 dollars to purchase a wagon."[48] The ABCFM believed that such bribes worked against a true acceptance of Christianity; indeed, it taught Indians the wrong values, morals, and ethics. ABCFM missionaries vowed to take the "high ground" with such matters. Stephen Riggs wrote that if the Episcopalians could afford to pay for converts, ABCFM missionaries "can afford to stand aside and let the procession pass. . . . I would rather let their work fall to the ground of its own weight than attempt to throw it off their shoulders."[49]

ABCFM missionaries also criticized their Episcopalian rivals for building overly elaborate churches and other mission structures, contrasting what they called the superficial extravagance of the Episcopalians with their own simplicity. They criticized Bishop William Hobart Hare for building a "large and elegant mission" at the Yankton

Agency, "which it is expected will cost eight or ten thousand dollars."[50] Likewise, Stephen Riggs condemned Hinman for buying a "large hotel" near the Santee reservation for about one thousand dollars. "The Episcopal mission must be very expensive," Riggs informed his wife. "I should judge it would not cost less than ten thousand dollars this year."[51]

In this case, however, Episcopalians backed up Riggs's critique of Hinman's expensive construction. Joseph W. Cook, an Episcopalian missionary on the Yankton reservation, complained that Hinman built a home and church with "turrets, gables, corners, pinnacles, tower and nooks which was the wonder of the Indians . . . and in which was sunk an untold sum of money." He noted that the extravagant building showed a "sad lack of judgment" and that the money would have been better spent helping the mission in general.[52] Even Hinman himself acknowledged he overspent on his mission buildings. "We are in the midst of the perplexities of building," he wrote. "The work goes on more slowly than we anticipated and will cost twice as much as was proposed. I am at my wits end and have the horror of bankruptcy before me. . . . I find the anxiety and doubt and fear of debt a hard load to bear."[53] In March 1878, church officials temporarily stripped Hinman of his mission post, due in part to his "dishonest and unfaithful use of money entrusted to him for work of the mission."[54]

Although both missionary organizations criticized each other, they also found some common ground, at least throughout the 1860s. In August 1867, the Episcopalian missionaries at the Santee reservation (just over the South Dakota border in Nebraska) invited Stephen Riggs and John Williamson for tea. By all accounts, they had a pleasant and civil social visit.[55] At times, ABCFM missionaries also shared some of their translations with the Episcopalians. Stephen Riggs noted that, while the ABCFM was not "under any obligation to give an account of our work to the Episcopalians, . . . if any of them in a brotherly way desire to cooperate with us in the work of giving the copy of the Bible to the Dakotas we can."[56] ABCFM missionary Thomas Williamson went beyond sharing materials and actively collaborated with Episcopalian Joseph Cook on religious translations.[57]

This tentative détente, however, ended when Grant fully implemented his Peace Policy in 1872. ABCFM missionaries assumed they would receive control of reservations across Dakota Territory due to their longstanding and continued missionary work with all portions of the Sioux nation. Since the Dakota people's removal to Crow Creek in 1863, the ABCFM had worked at "enlarging" and "increasing" its presence throughout the territory. By 1871, the ABCFM had mission stations at the Santee Agency (Dakota/Nebraska) and the Yankton Agency (Yankton/Dakota Territory), as well as missions near Good Will (Lakota/Dakota Territory) and Choteau Creek (Yankton/Dakota Territory).[58] Unfortunately for them, the ABCFM learned that the Quakers would be placed in charge of the Santee reservation. Although they lost Santee, the ABCFM missionaries believed that they would be given "control of the Yankton Agency" and "the nomination of agents for Whitestone and Crow Creek and Fort Sully" in Dakota Territory. They especially hoped to establish a political presence among the Lakota people due to their new mission at Good Will. Stephen Riggs bluntly stated that these agencies "belong to us of course."[59] For their part, the Episcopalians downplayed the presence of the ABCFM's missions. Hinman called Dakota Territory "large and unoccupied" by other Christian missionaries.[60]

At first, the ABCFM missionaries seemed to have the support of Interior Secretary Jacob Cox, who wrote a letter promising them that they would be able to nominate agents for reservations where they currently had mission stations.[61] Despite the secretary's assurances, however, when Vincent Colyer actually divvied up the agencies, he ignored the ABCFM's claim to the Dakota field and instead gave the Episcopalians control of most of the territory's reservations. In their private correspondence, ABCFM missionaries strongly protested these nominations. They even accused the Episcopalians of using underhanded methods to "steal" agencies, just as they had allegedly stolen converts over the last decade. Stephen Riggs blamed Episcopalian Bishop Whipple for these "unfair" appointments, charging that the government was "evidently beholden by Bishop Whipple's money."[62]

The ABCFM missionaries' barrage of charges against the Episcopalians increased over time. The missionaries angrily asserted that "an Episcopalian ring" controlled the Indian Department. This ring acted "unchristianly," "whitewashed" information about the ABCFM missions, and "hoodwinked" the government into keeping the ABCFM from receiving its rightful control of agencies.[63] Stephen Riggs complained that the Episcopalians' "interference is very real" and alleged they had "done many things that seem to me *unchristian, unmanly, and mean.*"[64] Although the ABCFM missionaries confined their harshest critique to private letters, their anger certainly leaked out, leading an Episcopalian agent to refuse Riggs bricks to build his mission "due to affronts." For his part, Riggs claimed that he "was as innocent as a child."[65] The Episcopalians dismissed Riggs's protestations of innocence, calling him "insane" and accusing him of having a "porcupine's propensities," always "shooting off his quills."[66] Episcopalian William Welsh also called Riggs "scandalous," "contemptible," and filled with "rascality."[67]

While ABCFM missionaries certainly disliked the criticism from their rivals, behind the scenes they begrudgingly respected the Episcopalians' political astuteness. In one letter, Stephen Riggs admitted (albeit in a sarcastic way) that the Episcopalians adeptly promoted their agenda to Congress and other government officials. He wrote his son Alfred: "I think it is fortunate that there are Episcopalians otherwise this world would be poorly run. So it would seem from Whipple's letter" to the Secretary of the Interior. Without Episcopalian agents, Whipple implied the Indians would "go back to barbarianism!!"[68] Stephen Riggs complained that the Episcopalians succeeded because they excelled at "that which is . . . political" while the ABCFM "preferred to do evangelistic work."[69]

Thus, despite their misgivings, ABCFM missionaries pressed their governing board to become more like the Episcopalians and engage in politics on the national level. Stephen Riggs noted that, while politics was unpleasant, "it is necessary [to] go through it as a kind of crucifixion."[70] Thomas Riggs made the same point to his brother Alfred, writing, "The fact is the ABCFM has not enough political foresight on the front of the Secretaries. . . . And if we cannot wake up those very respectable Secretaries to some sense of the situation of Indian Affairs, sooner or later all will go into the hands of the Episcopalians."[71]

ABCFM missionaries penned dozens of letters to governing board members demanding that they lobby for control of agencies in Dakota Territory. Stephen Riggs wrote Secretary Treat, "urging that the Board claim the right to nominate a man to displace the [Episcopalian agent]. If the Board cannot accomplish that, then we must see what can be done to secure a proper connection of our mission with the government schools." The same year, Riggs asked Treat to "let the government know what our rights are, and to obtain them as soon as may be."[72] ABCFM missionaries also requested that the board inform government officials that no other "Christian mission among the aborigines of this country has been more successful than" the ABCFM Dakota mission. Riggs stated, "It is not too much to claim, that, in the first twenty-five years of our missionary work among the Sioux, we had prepared the way for the effective working of our Episcopal friends." The exclusion of the ABCFM from Dakota Territory "was manifestly unjust to the Presbyterian and American Boards of missions, who had done so much to uplift the Sioux Indians, that they should now be confined to a single Agency."[73]

Despite the missionaries' pleas for the ABCFM to engage politically, its board members were slow to act. For example, in January 1872, Stephen Riggs suggested to Secretary Treat that the board lobby for Andrew Williamson's appointment as Indian agent to the Cheyenne Agency. Treat wrote that he would "keep in mind the matter," but Riggs quickly realized "that he is not disposed to push it."[74] Thomas Riggs continued to write letters to Treat begging him to press for Williamson's nomination. Thomas Riggs protested that the board's lack of political advocacy forced the missionaries "to be their own political backers," which took them away from proselytizing. He demanded that the board back its missionaries politically, as the Episcopalians did, or "give up and withdraw" from the mission field.[75]

When the board still failed to act at the national level, the missionaries took matters into their own hands and engaged in political maneuvering on the local level. For instance, ABCFM missionaries heard a rumor that the Episcopalians wanted to replace the Quaker agent at Santee with one of their own.[76] While ABCFM missionaries had "fundamental differences" with the Quakers, they decided to support their agent to keep the Episcopalians from taking control of the Santee Agency.[77] Stephen Riggs urged his son Alfred to back the Quaker agent, writing, "With things as they now stand at Washington, if you oust the Quakers. . . . you will have an Episcopal agent. . . . My advice is, keep on as good terms as you can with the Quakers, for the present."[78] With the help of the Quakers, he maintained, the ABCFM "will surely break the Episcopalian ring—or at least get some sort of equitable arrangement. [If] this looks like a conspiracy—So it may be."[79] Certainly, ABCFM missionaries wished that they had outright control of the Santee Agency, but they decided that the Quakers were the lesser of two evils.

When they failed to wrest control of agencies from Episcopalians on the national or local level, ABCFM missionaries switched tactics. They asked the government to end the Peace Policy entirely. In 1877, ABCFM's bilingual newspaper, the *Iapi Oaye*, printed an article stating that it was "high time" that the "present ecclesiastico-political arrangement of President Grant . . . was displaced. It has done a good work, but it is by no means the ideal of an Indian Civil Service. And were it continued much longer it might . . . breed disorders which would bring shame and loss of reputation to the great missionary cause."[80] In 1880, Stephen Riggs also wrote that the policy "of giving the nomination of Indian Agents to the religious denominations should now be abandoned . . . it has built up *a wall of exclusion* around the agencies . . . which is entirely inconsistent with the ideas of religious liberty."[81]

While the ABCFM's calls to end the Peace Policy probably had little effect, the practice of assigning missionaries to administrative positions slowly ended at the national level. When he took office in 1877, President Rutherford B. Hayes appointed only a few missionary agents to run reservations. By 1882, churches no longer officially controlled Indian agencies. Although the Peace Policy eventually ended, it left a legacy of distrust among missionaries in Dakota Territory. For over a decade, ABCFM missionaries filled their private letters and official correspondence to their board with angry references to the Episcopalians. The Episcopalians devoted less ink to their rivals but still noted religious tension in Dakota Territory. In his journal, Rev. Hinman obliquely referenced being "made continually sad by the opposition and jealously that our work provokes . . . the words that do reach our ears are unkind and full of mis-judgment."[82] While Hinman did not specify to whom he was referring, it certainly would not be a stretch to assume ABCFM missionaries were the subject of his remarks, given the decades of religious conflict that followed Grant's Peace Policy.

Despite their differences, ABCFM and Episcopal missionaries, as well as government officials, all shared the view that American Indians did not have the knowledge or sophistication to choose agents or control their political affairs. Administrators in Washington, D.C., made decisions for native peoples across Dakota Territory without asking them for input regarding the religious affiliation of their agents or, more importantly, whether they wanted missionaries at all. Although they lacked official political power, American Indians across Dakota Territory expressed strong opinions about the issue, often requesting Catholic rather than Protestant missionaries. For example, at the same time that ABCFM and Episcopalian missionaries waged a war of words over control of the Yankton Agency, the Yanktonai themselves repeatedly asked for Catholic priests instead of Protestant missionaries. ABCFM missionary John Williamson noted that the Yanktonai "requested [their agent] to tell the Great Father that they wanted him to send them a Catholic missionary." The agent tried to convince them to work with the ABCFM, "but they were set . . . *they* wanted a Catholic."[83] In 1866, Stephen Riggs again complained that the Yanktonai at the Yankton Agency requested a Catholic priest. Likewise, Lakotas at the Red Cloud and Spotted Tail agencies asked for Catholic missionaries.[84]

Yanktonai on the Crow Creek reservation also requested Catholic priests rather than Protestant missionaries. Historian Robert Galler argues that several reasons influenced their desire for Catholic missionaries. First, "Crow Creek leaders sought [Catholic] allies to help them defend themselves against further land loss and a federal policy (mainly led by Protestants) that enabled it." Second, Galler contends that Catholic religious and cultural adaptations influenced some tribal members to choose Catholic priests over Protestant missionaries.[85] Many historians have argued that Catholic missionaries were somewhat more accepting of native culture and religion than their Protestant counterparts; Catholics tended to advocate a more "pluralistic approach." While Catholic missionaries still supported the Christianization and civilization of Indians, they recognized "to a much greater degree the need of the Indians to accept on their own both American culture and Christianity rather than have it imposed upon them by an external force."[86] At the same time that some requested Catholic missionaries, they also made clear their expectations that priests follow strict guidelines and not overstep boundaries set by the Yanktonai themselves. At Crow Creek reservation, Standing Elk bluntly told Father Boehm Pius, a Catholic priest, "If you come for our land, we will kick you out."[87]

Interestingly, while the ABCFM never successfully challenged

Episcopalian hegemony in Dakota Territory, they effectively used what they had learned from their Episcopal rivals to contest Catholic agents. For instance, although the Catholics received few agencies in Dakota Territory, they oversaw the Devil's Lake reservation (Spirit Lake) in present-day North Dakota. The ABCFM sent a Dakota minister named Daniel Renville to Devil's Lake. When Renville arrived, however, the Catholic agent refused to give him rations, reported his presence to the Indian Bureau, and demanded that he leave the reservation. Initially the commissioner of Indian affairs allowed the agent to banish Renville from the reservation. After his expulsion, however, the ABCFM's board immediately flew into action, writing numerous letters and petitions to the commissioner of Indian affairs, the secretary of interior, and even to the president. By 1880, when faced with these appeals, the commissioner of Indian affairs reversed his decision and allowed Renville to preach at the reservation.[88] The ABCFM's appropriation of Episcopalian political tactics to challenge Catholic control of Spirit Lake was a clear demonstration of the increased political engagement the ABCFM had undertaken by the late nineteenth century.

Despite the official end of the Peace Policy in the 1880s, missionaries continued to play a prominent role on reservations across Dakota Territory.[89] Most important, missionary organizations administered federally funded boarding schools into the late nineteenth century and beyond. The Episcopal church managed boarding schools at the Yankton, Rosebud, and Standing Rock agencies. Some of these schools remained open into the twentieth century, including Saint Elizabeth's (Standing Rock) and Saint Mary's for Indian Girls (Rosebud).[90] The ABCFM, under Thomas Riggs, headed the Oahe Industrial School (north of present-day Pierre) and superintended schools on the Cheyenne River, Standing Rock, and, for a time, Rosebud reservations. Just across the state border with Nebraska, Thomas's brother Alfred ran the Santee Normal Training School, which remained open until 1937. Catholic missionaries also established boarding schools, including the Holy Rosary Mission on the Pine Ridge Indian Reservation.

In addition to running schools and churches on reservations, missionaries from Dakota Territory influenced Indian affairs at a national level into the early twentieth century. After Grant's religious experiment ended, the BIC held a yearly conference comprising mainly representatives from missionary societies. This meeting eventually transformed into the Lake Mohonk Conference of the Friends of the Indians. Each year, religious attendees at the Lake Mohonk Conference met with government policy makers and offered suggestions for reforming the Indian office and for "civilizing" and Christianizing native peoples. Historians argue that religious participants at the Mohonk conference helped to create federal American Indian policy, especially the Dawes Act of 1887, which allotted reservation lands in severalty and led to millions of acres of land loss.[91]

Thomas and Alfred Riggs and John Williamson played prominent roles in the Lake Mohonk Conference into the early twentieth century. Each of these missionaries had learned the importance of political engagement during the years of Grant's Peace Policy. At many of the conferences, the Riggs brothers and Williamson offered lengthy testimony about Indian affairs in South Dakota before various military and government officials.[92] Historian Francis Paul Prucha noted that missionaries like the Riggs brothers and Williamson dominated Indian policy long after the Peace Policy ended by focusing "public opinion behind specific measures of Indian policy and aggressive propagandizing of these measures in the press and in the halls of government."[93]

The prominence of missionaries at the Lake Mohonk Conference was nothing new. Since colonial times, missionaries had supported the government's plan to assimilate native peoples. Grant's Peace Policy expanded on this longstanding partnership between church and state by turning over the daily governance of Indian affairs across the United States to (mainly) Protestant missionaries. Dakota Territory, with its large population of American Indians and multiple reservations, thus serves as an important case study of the unparalleled partnership between church and state that occurred in the post-Civil War period. For several decades, missionaries like the Riggs and Williamson families, Samuel Hinman, and Bishop Henry Whipple controlled (or attempted to control) Indian policy across Dakota Territory.

Grant's extensive partnership with missionary organizations, however, did not work out as planned. President Grant believed that the character of the Indian service would be "distinctly improved by taking the nomination to the office of agent out of the domain of politics" and placing it in the hands of missionary organizations that had no "motives but those of disinterested benevolence."[94] In practice, however, Grant's policy did the exact opposite—it brought religious organizations into the political fray as they competed to gain and retain control of Indian agencies. Indeed, Grant's Peace Policy in Dakota Territory seemed to bring out the worst in both ABCFM and Episcopalian missionaries, as they called each other names, worked to undermine their respective missions, hatched plots behind each other's backs, and, in one extreme case, almost came to blows.[95] Ely Parker, Grant's first commissioner of Indian affairs, summarized the unintended effect of the Peace Policy, writing, "Religious bigotry, intolerance and jealousies by the various Christian bodies at home and between agents sent out, robbed all the efforts made of their benevolent and humane character."[96]

Ironically, while the missionaries argued among themselves over religious and political freedom, they did not support the Indians' right to make their own religious and political choices. Once again, as demonstrated in Dakota Territory, both missionaries and government agents denigrated the intelligence and political capacity of American Indians, who were viewed as unable to make their own political decisions and in need of supervision by those who were supposedly better able to govern. After Grant's Peace Policy ended, the federal government and missionary organizations continued to exert political control over reservations even as South Dakota and North Dakota gained statehood in 1889 and, with it, the ability to write their state constitutions and elect their own officials.

The story of Grant's Peace Policy in Dakota Territory illustrates conflicts between church and state, religion and politics, rival Protestant missionary organizations, and Indians and the United States government. It also illustrates the foibles of human nature. As servants of God, missionaries were expected to stand above the political fray. Grant's Peace Policy, however, ended up dividing missionaries, even though they all had the same ultimate goal—the conversion of American Indians to Christianity. These tensions also illustrate some of the problems inherent in a federal Indian system that dictated Indian policy from afar and relied on far-flung religious agents to develop and carry out a coherent and "enlightened" Indian policy, often without any background or training in Indian affairs or government service in general.

NOTES

1. Thomas Riggs to Alfred Riggs, 3 Jan. 1871, Oahe Mission Collection, Alfred L. Riggs Papers, South Dakota Conference of the United Church of Christ Archives, Center for Western Studies (CWS), Augustana College, Sioux Falls, S. Dak. The ABCFM, headquartered in Boston, was one of the largest and best-funded missionary organizations of the nineteenth century. It was interdenominational and comprised the Presbyterian, Congregational, Dutch Reformed, and Associate Reformed churches. The ABCFM established missions around the world and across the United States in areas populated by American Indians beginning in the early 1800s.

2. During the time frame of this chapter, Congress governed Dakota Territory. On 2 November 1889, Dakota Territory became North Dakota and South Dakota and entered the union as states. Because of the lack of a divide between North Dakota and South Dakota during Grant's presidency, reservations in both states are discussed without geographic distinction; however, more reservations were located in present-day South Dakota than North Dakota.

3. David S. Trask, "Episcopal Missionaries on the Santee and Yankton Reservations: Cross-Cultural Collaboration and President Grant's Peace Policy," *Great Plains Quarterly* 33 (Spring 2013): 89. Trask argues that historians have "focused on conflicts among policymakers" and not among missionaries.

4. Douglas Firth Anderson, "'More Conscience Than Force': U.S. Indian Inspector William Vandever, Grant's Peace Policy, and Protestant Whiteness," *Journal of the Gilded Age and the Progressive Era* 9 (Apr. 2010): 170.

5. Henry E. Fritz, "The Making of Grant's 'Peace Policy'," *Chronicles of Oklahoma* 37, no. 4 (1959): 411.

6. Robert H. Keller, Jr., *American Protestantism and United States Indian Policy, 1869–82* (Lincoln: University of Nebraska Press, 1983), p. 3.

7. R. Pierce Beaver, "The Churches and President Grant's Peace Policy," *Church and State* 174 (1962): 183. *See also* Peter J. Rahill, *The Catholic Indian Missions and Grant's Peace Policy, 1870–1884* (Washington, D.C.: Catholic University, 1953). For a discussion of sectarian conflict between Methodists and Catholics, *see* Robert E. Fricken, "After the Treaties: Administering Pacific Northwest Indian Reservations," *Oregon Historical Quarterly* 106 (Fall 2005): 445–61.

8. Jon K. Lauck, *Prairie Republic: The Political Culture of Dakota Territory, 1879–1889* (Norman: University of Oklahoma Press, 2010), p. 63.

9. Keller, *American Protestantism*, p. 2.

10. Ulysses Grant, *Second Annual Message to Congress*, 5 Dec. 1870, American Presidency Project, presidency.ucsb.edu.

11. Kerry R. Oman, "The Beginning of the End of the Indian Peace Commission of 1867–1868," *Great Plains Quarterly* 22 (Winter 2002): 37. *See also*

Stephen J. Rockwell, *Indian Affairs and the Administrative State in the Nineteenth Century* (Cambridge: Cambridge University Press, 2013), pp. 225–26.

12. Henry Benjamin Whipple, *Lights and Shadows of a Long Episcopate* (New York: Macmillan Co., 1899), p. 511.

13. Beaver, "Churches and President Grant's Peace Policy," p. 178; Candy Moulton, *Valentine T. McGillycuddy: Army Surgeon, Agent to the Sioux* (Norman: University of Oklahoma Press, 2011), p. 232. *See also* George H. Philips, "The Indian Ring in Dakota Territory, 1870–1890," *South Dakota History* (Fall 1972): 345–68.

14. Oman, "Beginning of the End," pp. 35–36; Donald Chaput, "Generals, Indian Agents, Politicians: The Doolittle Survey of 1865," *Western Historical Quarterly* 3 (July 1972): 269–72, 282.

15. For references to corruption and terrible conditions on the Crow Creek reservation from 1863 to 1866, *see* John P. Williamson to Thomas Williamson, 24 Dec.1863, Thomas S. Williamson Papers, Minnesota Historical Society, St. Paul, Minn; and U.S., Congress, Senate, *Condition of the Indian Tribes: Report of the Joint Special Committee Appointed under Joint Resolution of March 3, 1865*, S. Rept. 156, 39th Cong., 2 sess., pp. 365–66, 402, 405. *See also* William E. Lass, "The 'Moscow Expedition,'" *Minnesota History* 39 (Summer 1965): 227–40, and Colette A. Hyman, "Survival at Crow Creek, 1863–1866," *Minnesota History* 61 (Winter 2008–2009): 154.

16. R. Pierce Beaver, "American Missionary Efforts to Influence Government Indian Policy," *Church and State* 77 (1963): 77.

17. Ulysses S. Grant, "First Inaugural Address," (4 Mar. 1869), American President Project.

18. Samuel D. Hinman, *Journal of the Rev. S. D. Hinman: Missionary to the Santee Sioux Indians* (Philadelphia: McCalla & Stavely, 1869), p. 83; Richard R. Levine, "Indian Fighters and Indian Reformers: Grant's Indian Peace Policy and the Conservative Consensus," *Civil War History* 31 (Dec. 1985): 329. For more on Quaker agents, *see* Joseph E. Illick, "'Some of Our Best Indians are Friends . . .': Quaker Attitudes and Actions Regarding the Western Indians during the Grant Administration," *Western Historical Quarterly* 2 (July 1971): 283–94; and Lawrie Tatum, *Our Red Brothers and the Peace Policy of President Ulysses S. Grant* (Lincoln: University of Nebraska Press, 1970).

19. U.S. Department of the Interior, Office of Indian Affairs, *Annual Report of the Commissioner of Indian Affairs to the Secretary of the Interior*, 1870 (Washington, D.C.: Government Printing Office, 1870), p. 10. *See also* Fritz, "Making of Grant's 'Peace Policy'," p. 428.

20. *Annual Report of the Commissioner of Indian Affairs* (1872), p. 73.

21. Ibid. (1870), p. 10; Beaver, "Churches and President Grants 'Peace Policy',"

p. 178; Paul Stuart, "Administrative Reform in Indian Affairs," *Western Historical Quarterly* 16 (Apr. 1985): 141.

22. Grant, "Second Annual Message to Congress," 1872.

23. Beaver, "Churches and President Grant's Peace Policy," p. 179; Robert W. Galler, Jr., "A Triad of Alliances: The Roots of the Holy Rosary Indian Mission," *South Dakota History* 28 (Fall 1998): 154; Francis P. Prucha, *American Indian Policy in Crisis: Christian Reformers and the Indian, 1865–1900* (Norman: University of Oklahoma Press, 1976), p. 53.

24. *Annual Report of the Commissioner of Indian Affairs* (1872), pp. 73–74.

25. David Sim, "The Peace Policy of Ulysses S. Grant," *American Nineteenth Century History* 9 (Sept. 2008): 244; Martha L. Edwards, "A Problem of Church and State in the 1870s," *Mississippi Valley Historical Review* 11 (June 1924): 49.

26. Hinman, *Journal*, p. 83.

27. Beaver, "American Missionary Efforts," p. 80.

28. Sim, "Peace Policy of Ulysses S. Grant," p. 247; William E. Unrau, "The Civilian as Indian Agent: Villain or Victim?" *Western Historical Quarterly* 3 (Oct. 1972): 418.

29. Anderson, "'More Conscience than Force,'" p. 174.

30. Levine, "Indian Fighters and Indian Reformers," p. 329.

31. Sim, "Peace Policy of Ulysses S. Grant," p. 243.

32. Stephen R. Riggs, *Tah-Koo Wah-Ka : or, The Gospel among the Dakotas* (Boston: Congregational Sabbath-School & Publishing Soc., 1869), p. 359.

33. Hinman, *Journal*, p. xviii.

34. Martha Riggs Morris to Alfred Riggs, 23 Aug. 1871, Alfred L. Riggs Papers.

35. Samuel D. Hinman to Joseph Cook, 4 Feb. 1870, Joseph Cook Papers, Episcopal Diocese of South Dakota, CWS.

36. Treat to Stephen R. Riggs, 25 Dec. 1869, Stephen R. Riggs Papers, Oahe Mission Collection, CWS.

37. Riggs, *Tah-Koo Wah-Ka* , p. 359.

38. Whipple, *Lights and Shadows of a Long Episcopate*, p. 61.

39. Fritz, "Making of Grant's 'Peace Policy'," p. 414; Beaver, "American Missionary Efforts," p. 80.

40. Hinman, *Journal*, p. 73.

41. Beaver, "American Missionary Efforts," p. 80.

42. Rufus Anderson, *History of the Missions of the American Board of Commissioners for Foreign Missions, to the Oriental Churches*, Vol. 1 (Boston: Congregational Publishing Soc., 1872), pp. 152, 209.

43. Paul William Harris, *Nothing But Christ: Rufus Anderson and the Ideology of Protestant Foreign Missions* (New York: Oxford University Press, 1999), pp. 22–23; Ronald N. Satz, *American Indian Policy in the Jacksonian Era* (Norman: University of Oklahoma Press, 1974), p. 252. *See also* William G. McLoughlin, *Champions of*

the Cherokees: Evan and John B. Jones (Princeton, N.J.: Princeton University Press, 1990).

44. Stephen Riggs to Alfred Riggs, 11 Mar. 1867, and Thomas Riggs to Alfred Riggs, 3 Jan. 1871, Alfred L. Riggs Papers.

45. John Williamson to Thomas Williamson, 6 April 1863, Thomas S. Williamson Papers. After their removal from Minnesota following the Dakota War of 1862, over two hundred Dakota men were incarcerated at a prison in Davenport, Iowa; Dakota women, children, and the elderly were removed to Crow Creek Indian Reservation in Dakota Territory. In spring 1866, the prisoners and their families were reunited in Niobrara, Nebraska, at what would become the Santee reservation.

46. Stephen Riggs to Alfred Riggs, 28 July 1866, Alfred L. Riggs Papers.

47. John Williamson to Thomas Williamson, 6 Apr. 1863, Thomas S. Williamson Papers.

48. Robert Galler, "Tribal Decision-Making and Intercultural Relations: Crow Creek Agency, 1863–1885," *Indigenous Nations Studies Journal* 3 (Spring 2002): 106.

49. Stephen Riggs to Alfred Riggs, 31 Oct. 1873, Alfred L. Riggs Papers.

50. *Iapi Oaye* 2 (Oct. 1873): 40.

51. Stephen Riggs to "Home," 10 Aug. 1867, Stephen R. Riggs Papers.

52. William Hobart Hare, *Addresses Relating to the Growth of the Church in the Missionary Jurisdiction of South Dakota* ([Sioux Falls, S.Dak.]: Episcopal Diocese, 1898), p. 46.

53. Samuel D. Hinman, "Extracts from Letters of Rev. Samuel Hinman—January 25, 1868," Samuel Hinman Papers, Episcopal Diocese of South Dakota, CWS.

54. Quoted in Grant K. Anderson, "Samuel D. Hinman and the Opening of the Black Hills," *Nebraska History* 60 (Winter 1979): 537.

55. Stephen Riggs to "Home Notes," 10 Aug. 1867, Stephen R. Riggs Papers.

56. Stephen Riggs to Thomas Williamson, 21 Nov. 1874, ibid.

57. Thomas Williamson to Joseph Cook, 27 Nov. 1876, Thomas S. Williamson Papers.

58. *Missionary Herald* 65 (Jan. 1869): 33 and ibid. 67 (Jan. 1871): 11.

59. Stephen Riggs to Alfred Riggs, 5 Aug.1870, Alfred L. Riggs Papers.

60. Hinman, "The Dakota Mission," E. N. Biddle Papers, Episcopal Diocese of South Dakota, CWS.

61. Jacob Dolson Cox to Selah Treat, 19 July 1870, Thomas S. Williamson Papers.

62. Stephen Riggs to Alfred Riggs, 26 Sept. 1870, Alfred L. Riggs Papers.

63. Thomas Riggs to Alfred Riggs, 3 Jan. 1871, Stephen Riggs to Alfred Riggs, 22 Apr. 1874, Stephen Riggs to Alfred Riggs, 23 Feb. 1871, Stephen Riggs to Alfred

Riggs, 31 Oct. 1873, Thomas Riggs to Alfred Riggs, 18 Dec. 1870, and Thomas Riggs to Alfred Riggs, 3 Jan. 1871, all Alfred L. Riggs Papers.

64. Stephen Riggs to Thomas Williamson, 12 Feb. 1867, Stephen R. Riggs Papers.

65. Stephen Riggs to Alfred Riggs, 12 Oct. 1871, Alfred L. Riggs Papers.

66. Quoted in Keller, *American Protestantism and United States Indian Policy*, p. 45.

67. Thomas Riggs to Mary Riggs, 8 June 1872, Alfred L. Riggs Papers.

68. Stephen Riggs to Alfred Riggs, 12 May 1871, ibid.

69. Stephen Riggs, "Shall it be Exclusion?" *Missionary Herald* 76 (Sept. 1880): 345.

70. Stephen Riggs to Alfred Riggs, 11 Mar. 1867, Alfred L. Riggs Papers.

71. Thomas Riggs to Alfred Riggs, 18 Dec. 1870, ibid.

72. Stephen Riggs to Alfred Riggs, 21 Jan. 1871, and 7 Nov. 1871, ibid.

73. Riggs, "Shall it be Exclusion?", pp. 345-46.

74. Stephen Riggs to Alfred Riggs, 18 Jan. 1872, Alfred L. Riggs Papers.

75. Thomas Riggs to Alfred Riggs, 18 Dec. 1870, ibid. *See also* Riggs to Alfred Riggs, 13 Apr. 1872, ibid.

76. Selah Treat to Columbus Delano, 16 Dec. 1870, Thomas S. Williamson Papers.

77. *Iapi Oaye* 3 (June 1874): 24.

78. Stephen Riggs to Alfred Riggs, 22 Apr. 1874, Alfred L. Riggs Papers.

79. Thomas Riggs to Alfred Riggs, 3 Jan. 1871, ibid.

80. *Iapi Oaye* 6 (Jan. 1877): 4.

81. Riggs, "Shall it be Exclusion?", p. 344

82. Hinman, *Journal*, p. 27.

83. John Williamson to Thomas Williamson, 20 June 1865, Thomas S. Williamson Papers.

84. Stephen Riggs to Mary Riggs, 13 Aug. 1866, Stephen R. Riggs Papers; Keller, *American Protestantism and United States Indian Policy*, p. 52.

85. Robert Galler, "Making Common Cause: Yanktonais and Catholic Missionaries on the Northern Plains," *Ethnohistory* 55 (Summer 2008): 441, 445.

86. Eugene F. Provenzo, Jr., and Gary N. McCloskey, "Catholic and Federal Indian Education in the Late Nineteenth Century: Opposed Colonial Models," *Journal of American Indian Education* 21 (Oct. 1981): 11.

87. Quoted in Mary Claudia Duratschek, *Crusading along Sioux Trails: A History of the Catholic Indian Missions of South Dakota* (n.p., Grail Publication, 1947), p. 165.

88. Beaver, "The Churches and President Grant's 'Peace Policy'," pp. 184-85.

89. Edwards, "Problem of Church and State," p. 52.

90. Ruth Ann Alexander, "Gentle Evangelists: Women in Dakota Episcopal Missions, 1867–1900," *South Dakota History* 24 (Winter 1994): 190–91.

91. Beaver, "Churches and President Grant's 'Peace Policy'," p. 177; Robert M. Utley, "Peace on Paper: War on the Plains," *Wild West* 21 (Oct. 2008): 35.

92. For an example of Thomas Riggs's testimony, *see Proceedings of the Sixth Annual Meeting of the Lake Mohonk Conference of the Friends of the Indian* (1888): 30–33.

93. Prucha, *American Indian Policy in Crisis*, p. 144. *See also*, Francis P. Prucha, *The Great Father: The United States Government and the American Indians*, 2 vols. (Lincoln: University of Nebraska Press, 1984), 1: 153.

94. *Annual Report of the Commissioner of Indian Affairs* (1872), p. 73.

95. Episcopalian William Welsh visited Thomas Riggs at his new station to the Lakotas, but it did not go well. According to Riggs, Welsh insulted him, his brother Alfred, his father, and Dr. Williamson, calling them "scandalous" and "contemptible." In turn, Riggs called Welsh "rascally" and an "old idiot." As tensions rose, Thomas Riggs reported that he remained "cool," although he "would have given a good $100 if I could have knocked [Welsh] down as he deserved" (Riggs to Mary Riggs, 8 June 1872, Alfred L. Riggs Papers.)

96. "General Parker's Autobiography," in *Publications of the Buffalo Historical Society*, 8 (1905): 535.

JEFF WELLS

3 | POPULIST POLITICS
AND THE SOUTH DAKOTA REFORM
PRESS ASSOCIATION

. . .

The Populist revolt of the 1890s marked a brief moment when an insurgent political movement challenged the Republican Party's almost continual domination of South Dakota politics from statehood to the present. Journalists played a key role in the organization, promotion, and rise of the Farmers' Alliance, an early expression of the Populist movement, and the People's (or Populist) Party. The reform press of the Populist movement sought to circumvent the established press, loyal to the entrenched economic interests and old political parties, and speak directly to the people. The work of the reform press represented an expression of civic traditions but, more importantly, demonstrated the Populists' embrace of modern practices such as collective political action.

As Howard Lamar observed in *Dakota Territory*, the press on the Northern Great Plains exercised collective political action as early as 1882. Lamar, however, viewed this collaboration as a sign of the weak influence of the participating editors rather than an expression of collective strength or innovation. Therefore, it is not surprising that Lamar found no leaders of exceptional ability among the Dakota Territorial Farmers' Alliance. An organization formed to promote the interests of farmers and laborers, the Alliance used modern organizational tactics to connect its supporters, including sympathetic newspaper editors.[1]

Throughout the period of Populist journalism in South Dakota, the movement's editors remained committed to organized action, viewing collaboration as a reinforcement of their individual strength. Their organization even served as a model for competitors loyal to the old parties. An examination of the Populist press and the South Dakota Reform Press Association (SDRPA) reveals that South Dakota Populists were not merely backward-looking agrarians, as presented

58

by R. Alton Lee, or practitioners of civic republicanism, as described by Jon Lauck. Instead, as Charles Postel argues, the Populists were modern, forward-looking, and sought to use the technology and innovations already employed by contemporary businesses and, indeed, by their foes from the old parties.[2]

Foremost among the works that address the Populist movement in South Dakota is Lee's *Principle over Party: The Farmers' Alliance and Populism in South Dakota, 1880–1900*. Lee demonstrates that South Dakota was on the cutting edge of the movement, "supplying both proponents of and significant leadership for reform."[3] He emphasizes the cooperative experience of the Dakota Farmers' Alliance and, thus, links his study with Lawrence Goodwyn's *Democratic Promise: The Populist Movement in America*. Goodwyn observes that the southern Farmers' Alliance's cooperative efforts and Charles W. Macune's Subtreasury Plan spawned a movement culture that sought solutions to the economic problems facing farmers and other Americans in the late nineteenth century. The Farmers' Alliance then transferred that movement culture to its political successor, the People's Party, which became the most significant third-party movement since the Civil War. Robert C. McMath, Jr., in *Populist Vanguard: A History of the Southern Farmers' Alliance*, stressed the Alliance's importance in forming the Populist movement.[4] Although the People's Party formed after the era that constitutes the primary focus of his study, Jon Lauck's *Prairie Republic* situates South Dakota Populism within a republican tradition. Lauck, therefore, joins those scholars—including McMath, Gene Clanton, and Worth Robert Miller—who emphasize the Populist inheritance of the republicanism that animated the American Revolution. Charles Postel, in contrast, breaks the Populists free of inherited traditions—including republicanism—and presents them as modernists trying to shape and adapt innovations for the benefit of farmers and laborers.[5]

The influential role of journalists in South Dakota Populism provides a brief and vivid example of the importance of the partisan press during the state's early decades. The vast expanses between towns and cities increased the importance of newspapers to civic discourse in the American West, including the Northern Great Plains. The sort of political discussion found in the town halls and barrooms of the East took place on the pages of newspapers in the West because distance made it difficult for citizens to assemble. Newspapering in the West, as in the East, remained a town- and city-centered business. Western newspapers, however, reached beyond the immediate community and served distant farms, ranches, mines and lumber camps, thus elevating the political influence of the region's editors.[6] In South Dakota, an engaged and highly literate citizenry supported a thriving newspaper culture. Editors voiced their opinions on major issues, vocally identified with particular political parties, endorsed candidates, and often sought elected or appointed office. In 1890, South Dakota journalists published more than 234 newspapers. The number held steady throughout the decade, with more than 245 newspapers published in 1896.[7]

In examining the actions of the reform press as a group, the influence of some key individuals—particularly Henry Langford Loucks— cannot be ignored. Populist journalism in South Dakota passed through three phases. Loucks's influence over the Dakota Territory and South Dakota reform press was at its greatest from the mid-1880s until 1892 as he encouraged collective action among those newspapers that supported the Farmers' Alliance and the Knights of Labor. During this era, he supported the 1891 formation of the SDRPA. From 1893 until 1896, Loucks devoted more of his time to the Populist movement at the national level. His main contribution to South Dakota Populism during these years was his fight to keep the People's Party from cooperating with the Democratic Party through a political tactic known as fusion. In Loucks's absence, the SDRPA assumed the responsibility for coordinating the state's Populist press. The acceptance of fusion in 1896 and Loucks's subsequent exit from the People's Party characterized the third and final phase of Populist journalism in South Dakota. During the People's Party's final years, the SDRPA floundered as Populist journalists owed their allegiance to fusion and the administration of Populist Governor Andrew E. Lee.

Loucks, the central figure in the early years of the reform press in Dakota Territory and South Dakota, was born 24 May 1846 near Ottawa, Canada. He moved his family to Springfield, Missouri, in 1879 and to Dakota Territory in 1884. He settled on a farm near Clear Lake, Deuel County, in what would become South Dakota. The same year, he organized a county suballiance, a local chapter of the northern Farmers' Alliance. In January 1886, Loucks garnered unanimous election as president of the Dakota Territorial Farmers' Alliance. In this role, he promoted the Alliance's education and cooperative efforts. The Dakota Alliance's early success with cooperative efforts led to an invitation for Loucks to serve as business agent for the Minnesota Alliance and president of the cooperative Scandinavian Elevator Company.[8]

Loucks viewed a network of trusted journalists as critical to the success of the agrarian and labor movement, but by 1889, the *Dakota Farmer*, an early supporter of Loucks and the Alliance, turned against the order and criticized its businesses and leadership. Meanwhile, the *Dakota Ruralist*, founded by J. C. McManima in 1886, won Loucks's support and the Alliance's official endorsement in 1889.[9] In the 20 July 1889 issue of the *Ruralist*, Loucks defended an Alliance boycott of newspapers that opposed the movement and quoted a bankers' circular that advised: "It is advisable to do all in your power to sustain such daily and prominent weekly newspapers, especially the agricultural and religious press, as will oppose the issuing of greenback paper money [a position favored by some Farmers' Alliance members], and that you also withhold patronage or favor from all who will not oppose the Government issue of money."[10] Loucks himself assumed the editorship of the *Dakota Ruralist* in 1891.

When the territorial Farmers' Alliance first considered political solutions to the problems that farmers and laborers faced, it did so as a faction within the dominant Republican Party (GOP). Dakota farmers consistently voted Republican during the territorial period, but a tradition of factional squabbles characterized the party's history. The recipients of patronage appointments and lawyers, particularly those who lived at the capital of Yankton, controlled the GOP in the territory's early years. In the late 1870s, Sioux Falls Republicans, led by Richard F. Pettigrew, challenged the dominance of Yankton residents within the party. A bitter battle with a territorial governor who favored moving the capital to Bismarck in the northern part of the territory forced Pettigrew and his Sioux Falls supporters to align with the Yankton Republicans, including editor George W. Kingsbury, during the 1880s. As the territory prepared for statehood in 1889, supporters promoted Loucks for the United States Senate from South Dakota. The Republican press swiftly denounced the idea, noted Loucks's Canadian birth, and questioned his eligibility. Meanwhile, an Alliance-backed faction fought a powerful group led by Pettigrew, known as

the Combine, for the control of the Republican Party. With the support of a favorable press, Pettigrew prevailed and won election to the
Senate.[11] Concerned with other seemingly more threatening rivals
within the state Republican Party, Pettigrew dismissed Loucks and
the Alliance as "unholy, unRepublican cranks."[12]

North Dakota and South Dakota received statehood on 2 November
1889. The Dakota Territorial Farmers' Alliance held its last convention
on 26 November 1889 at Aberdeen, where the organization adjourned
and divided along state lines. Loucks won election as president of the
South Dakota Farmers' Alliance. In this role, he encouraged coopera-
tion with the more radical southern Farmers' Alliance and the Knights
of Labor. He won the presidency of the northern Alliance during a December 1889 joint meeting with the southern Alliance at Saint Louis.
Although the sectional Alliances failed to merge, Loucks led the South
Dakota Alliance into closer affiliation with the southern Alliance, but
he remained president of the northern Alliance in an ongoing effort to
encourage unity between the two sectional orders.[13]

On 4 June 1890, during the state Alliance convention, Loucks urged
the creation of an independent political party in South Dakota. Delegates formed the party the next day and named it the Independent
Party on 6 June. This forerunner of South Dakota's People's Party
nominated Loucks for governor during its July 1890 convention. Pettigrew soon urged Republicans to attack the character of Independent
leaders. He called Loucks and Alonzo Wardall, an Alliance leader and
close associate of Loucks, scoundrels not worthy of the votes of intelligent farmers. The Republicans then adopted a platform that incorporated many farmer-favored issues, such as the secret ballot, prohibition, and currency inflation by allowing the coinage of silver. In the
November election, the Republican gubernatorial candidate won with
a plurality. Loucks finished second and would have won if Democrats
had backed the Independent ticket. The Republicans won a one-vote
majority over the combined Independent and Democratic caucuses
in the state senate. In the state house, the Independents and Democrats held a combined one-vote majority over the Republicans.[14]

When the 1891 legislature convened, divisions within the three
parties kept any candidate for the United States Senate from receiving the necessary votes until the Independents nominated Congregational minister James H. Kyle of Aberdeen and brokered a deal to get

Democratic support for his candidacy. Kyle had been a Republican until the previous summer when he left the party because it favored high tariffs. Kyle's election thrilled Loucks. Although Kyle defeated Pettigrew's favored candidates, the senior senator offered to serve as a mentor and invited Kyle to caucus with the Republicans. Kyle declined, joined the Democratic side, and inaugurated a bitter rivalry with Pettigrew. Throughout the remainder of the decade, the actions of Kyle and Pettigrew caused repercussions within the reform press.[15]

Loucks directly experienced the hostility of the mainstream press during the southern Farmers' Alliance's December 1890 national convention at Ocala, Florida. An article distributed to papers across the nation (likely by the Associated Press or another wire service and dated-lined Jacksonville, Florida, 13 December 1890) promised that Jacksonville's *Florida Times-Union* planned to publish a lengthy article on the Ocala convention with "incontestable proof" of "the existence of a gigantic plot to use the national organization as a means of promoting the third party scheme." The article called the third party a "pet scheme" of the "mostly Republican" northwestern Alliancemen and identified delegates from Plains states, including Loucks, as the leaders of the third-party movement. The author of the article sensed a Republican conspiracy and maintained that the northwestern Farmers' Alliance delegates actually opposed the Subtreasury Plan and supported it and other actions of the Ocala convention because of their belief that the proposals would divide the Democratic Party in the South.[16]

The creation of the National Reform Press Association (NRPA), perhaps the most significant development of the Ocala gathering, occurred outside of the convention's official business. A wire-service article attributed the origin of the NRPA to a meeting of third-party advocates aboard a steamship on an excursion to Titusville, Florida. Those assembled agreed to limit membership to those papers that supported Charles W. Macune's subtreasury proposal. The group would organize a legislative board to designate the specific measures the reform press supported. The NRPA excluded conservative alliancemen —those who opposed the subtreasury—because, according to the article, "the Reform Press combination is only one of many means by which the third party issue is to be forced upon the Alliance, with a hope of dividing the Democratic party of the South."[17] Whereas earlier efforts to organize the reform press had sought editorial conformity through central control, the NRPA tried to ensure that its papers delivered a consistent message by restricting membership to like-minded editors. Over the next few years, NRPA members shared content and held regular meetings that included discussions of both politics and business practices. The formation of the NRPA inspired the creation of state affiliates—including the SDRPA.

The northern Farmers' Alliance met in January 1891 at Omaha, Nebraska. Delegates endorsed the Ocala plan and called for a February 1892 meeting to establish a third party. Leaders of the southern Farmers' Alliance and allied groups planned to meet for the same purpose in May 1891 at Cincinnati. Loucks, however, suffered injuries in a farm accident that caused doctors to amputate his left leg below the hip in April 1891, keeping him from attending the Cincinnati meeting. He wrote extensively for the *Dakota Ruralist* during his convalescence, as the central committee of the South Dakota Independent Party selected J. M. Pease of the *Mitchell Union Labor Gazette* and E. B. Cummings of the *Ruralist* as delegates to the NRPA meeting to be held in conjunction with the Cincinnati conference. The third-party advocates at the convention reached a compromise with those who wanted to delay the creation of a new party. The convention established a party executive committee that would meet at Saint Louis in February 1892 and declare a third party if differences with the old parties had not been resolved before then.[18]

Loucks soon returned to action and chaired a meeting of state Farmers' Alliance and Independent Party men held in July 1891 at Huron. Alliance leaders urged chapters to patronize the state, county, and local reform press. During the gathering on 9 July 1891, the state's Independent editors formed the SDRPA, a state affiliate of the NRPA. Isaac Landers of the *Clark Honest Dollar* won election as president, and William E. Kidd of the *Aberdeen Star* garnered the secretary and treasurer position. Loucks and another editor joined Landers and Kidd on the executive committee. The association appointed Frank Wilder of the *Aberdeen Appeal*, Landers, Kidd, Pease, and Father Robert Haire of the *Aberdeen Dakota Knights of Labor* to a committee on plate matter and patent insides. Editors used patent insides, or preprinted pages, to reduce labor needs. The preprints often provided the first and fourth or second and third pages of four-page newspapers. The companies that supplied preprints often customized pages to match the appearance of the locally printed pages. The preprint companies, located in cities, received exchanges from the East faster than the far-flung editors, so the patent insides provided the latest national news.[19]

Born in Freedom, Michigan, in 1845, Robert Haire converted to Catholicism while a student at the University of Michigan. He studied theology at Louvain, Belgium, and was ordained a priest in 1874. He served parishes in Michigan before he answered Bishop Martin Marty's call to lead a group of settlers to Dakota Territory in 1880. He homesteaded and traveled around northeastern South Dakota establishing parishes. He promoted woman suffrage, prohibition, and labor reform. He edited the *Dakota Catholic American* and Knights of Labor publications. In 1889, Marty forced him to leave the priesthood, but Haire remained active in the labor movement and helped found the state's Independent Party.[20]

Loucks continued to rise in prominence in both the state reform press and the national Farmers' Alliance organizations. In July 1891, Loucks's close friend, E. B. Cummings, the editor of the *Dakota Ruralist*, moved to Indiana to edit an alliance newspaper there. Loucks assumed the chief editorship of the *Ruralist*. A few months later, in December 1891, the National Farmers Alliance and Industrial Union, a product of the merger between the two sectional alliances and other agrarian groups, elected Loucks vice president. He assumed the presidency after Leonidas Polk's sudden death on 11 June 1892. Loucks, a committed third-party man despite the false accusations in the mainstream press, presided over the national People's Party's first nominating convention in July 1892 at Omaha. Loucks maintained both the presidency of the South Dakota Farmers' Alliance and the editorship of the *Dakota Ruralist* even after he temporarily moved to Washington, D.C., to oversee the national alliance. He won reelection as national alliance president in late November 1892, an endorsement that signaled the organization's commitment to the new third party.[21]

Back in South Dakota, Arthur Linn, publisher of the *Canton Farmers' Leader* tried to arouse the reform press for the 1892 campaign:

Wake up you youthful giants of the Reform Press. Devote every energy to the importance of educating the unconverted to the necessity of the great reforms demanded by the people. Your cause is as just as that for which Washington and his noble patriots fought. All that is necessary is for the people to realize their present danger from being Carnegized with Pinkertons, and how they have been robbed and plundered by unjust class legislation. Tell the people the truth and they will rally to our standard as the boys did in 61.[22]

Both the South Dakota People's and Democratic parties rejected fusion in 1892. Loucks strongly denounced the tactic. "We cannot afford to sacrifice our principles for the sake of office nor yet can we afford to do it for the sake of temporary success," he wrote in September.[23] Meanwhile, the Republicans viciously attacked Loucks and cruelly mocked his inability to attend his own son's funeral when the ten-year-old died of heart failure while Loucks was attending to Farmers' Alliance business in Washington, D.C. Yet, Republicans again tried to appeal to farmers with support for issues such as the direct election of railroad commissioners, postal savings banks, rural free delivery, and the coinage of silver.[24]

South Dakota's electoral votes went to Republican nominee Benjamin Harrison, and the GOP regained undisputed control of the legislature; yet, the election results failed to dissuade the stalwarts of the reform press. "There is no backing down since the election by the reform press," wrote the *Canton Dakota Farmers' Leader*. "All of our exchanges, thus far received, renew their fealty to people's party principles, and declare their determination to stand by them and continue the fight until victory perch upon our banner."[25]

The Republican-controlled 1893 legislature enacted laws intended to weaken the People's Party and discourage its fusion with the Democrats. Under the new laws, a candidate's name could not appear more than once on the ballot for the same office and candidates were prohibited from withdrawing just before the election. Fused parties received only one party's allotment of election judges, and the state's ballot was redesigned to encourage straight-ticket voting. Meanwhile, Pettigrew worked to ensure the loyalty of various ethnic groups. The Republicans swept all but one of eleven state judicial seats during the 1893 election. The Populists and Democrats tried to fuse in some of the races; consequently, Loucks blamed fusion for the electoral failure. In turn, the chairman of the state Populist committee blamed Loucks.[26]

The Panic of 1893, however, provided an opportunity for the Populists to appeal for votes from suffering farmers. Undoubtedly facing the realization that the Populists or fusionists might control the next legislature and block his reelection, Pettigrew reevaluated his opposition to the coinage of silver. In 1893, he expressed support for the coinage of silver at sixteen to one and urged the Republican Party to abandon its support for the gold standard. He also organized bimetallic leagues—presented as nonpartisan to attract Populists and Democrats—to promote the GOP. In 1894, the South Dakota Republican Party accepted Pettigrew's new position on silver. The senator then worked to ensure the election of a legislature willing to return him to Washington, D.C.[27]

South Dakota Populists gathered for their state convention in July 1894 at Mitchell. Loucks continued to fight fusion, an arrangement gaining favor with more Populists. Loucks's unwillingness to cooperate, as well as and the anti-fusion election laws, benefitted South Dakota Republicans. The GOP again controlled the legislature, and Pettigrew won reelection to the Senate by a unanimous vote. Editors Freeman Knowles of the *Deadwood Independent* and John E. Kelley of the *Flandreau Herald* garnered nominations for Congress. E. B. Reed of the *Rapid City Black Hills Union* won the nomination for state auditor in a bitter contest with fellow Populist editors J. H. Kipp of the *Mound City Campbell County Courier* and G. W. Everts of the *Onida Journal.*[28]

In Brown County, a People's Party stronghold, some Populists objected to the socialist views promoted by William E. Kidd, the editor of the *Aberdeen Star* and, beginning in December 1894, the coeditor of the *Dakota Ruralist*. Born in Kiddville, Michigan, in 1849, Kidd and his wife moved to Brown County in 1882, farming for seven years before entering the newspaper business. Kidd used his newspapers to advocate socialism; however, Senator Kyle owned a stake in Kidd's *Aberdeen Star*, and at a stockholders' meeting in the spring of 1895, the senator expressed his concern over the socialist direction of the People's Party and voiced opposition to the government ownership of means of transportation, such as railroads, and the Subtreasury Plan. The other stockholders rejected Kyle's positions, and Kidd soon denounced Populists such as Kyle who sought to modify the party's Omaha platform.[29]

Kyle made amends for his comments and joined Loucks and Kidd at a September 1895 meeting of the SDRPA at Woonsocket. The association planned to meet again in October at the state fair at Sioux Falls and again in November at Aberdeen. The gathering at Aberdeen included a celebration of the release of labor leader Eugene V. Debs from jail at Woodstock, Illinois. South Dakota's Populist press had a good reason for frequent meetings, as a scandal involving a Republican elected official promised to prompt outrage among voters in 1896. Republican State Treasurer William Walter Taylor's poor investments of the state's money resulted in massive financial losses following the Panic of 1893. On the day he was supposed to turn the state's funds over to his successor, he was in New York City trying to arrange a loan to cover what he owed. Taylor fled to Central America, leaving South Dakota officials scrambling to find funds to keep the state government running. Although the state eventually recovered all but $98,000 of the $367,000 Taylor owed, the scandal hurt the Republican Party's standing.[30]

The Populists hoped to capture control of the state legislature after the Taylor scandal and mismanagement of the state fair by Republican and Democratic board members. The SDRPA editors met in secret during the state fair, but the *St. Paul Pioneer Press* claimed the session dealt with candidates for 1896. Editors Loucks, Kidd, Freeman Knowles, John E. Kelley, and Robert E. Dowdell all earned consideration as delegates to the People's Party national convention or as candidates for state office. According to reports, Loucks wanted to serve in the United States Senate but would not challenge Kyle.[31] The Republican *Deadwood Black Hills Daily Times* delighted at the scramble for positions. "For state auditor there are about an even dozen candidates, and they are all editors of pop papers," the *Times* wrote. "What an elegant scramble, to be sure, they will have."[32] Despite the attacks, the editors of the SDRPA continued to prepare for the 1896 campaign and met again on 21 and 22 November 1895 at Aberdeen.[33]

The frequent meetings continued in the new year as the editors faced resistance from both outside and inside the reform movement. The SDRPA gathered for a three-day meeting in January 1896 at Yankton. Loucks addressed the twenty-two editors who attended from among the association's forty-one member newspapers.[34] The *Kimball Graphic* predicted the "success or failure of the [Populist] party depends largely upon this organization, its deliberations and proceedings will be read with interest by politicians of all political creeds."[35] However, the *Hurley Turner County Herald*, a Republican paper, questioned the SDRPA's membership claims: "A Yankton correspondent to the Sioux City Tribune giving a 'vouched for' list of the 'Reform (populist) Press association' newspapers in the state includes the name of Record, Hurley. The populist movement is in about the same condition as the Hurley Record—a has been."[36] Clate Tinan, the Democratic editor of the *Kimball Graphic*, also wondered whether the SDRPA inflated its membership numbers. "In glancing through the list of papers sent out as belonging to the association there we found 'GRAPHIC, Kimball' sticking out like a sore thumb into space," Tinan wrote. "Whether the Graphic was added to the list to give tone and respectability . . . is for somebody to find out."[37] The Democratic *Deadwood Daily Pioneer* dismissed the editors as mere office seekers. "A curious fact about these reform papers is that they show the most signs of activity in the opening of a campaign in which there is a prospect of securing a little patronage," the editor wrote.[38] The chairman of the state People's Party also sought to diminish the SDRPA's influence and predicted that the delegates to the party's state convention, planned for July at Huron, would reject the slate of candidates proposed by the reform press at its Yankton meeting.[39]

In Brown County, a March 1896 victory in a local election by a fusion ticket led by Kidd renewed Populist interest in cooperating with allies from other parties. Although fusion on the northern plains usually meant aligning with Democrats, the South Dakota Populists gained an unlikely partner. As the 1896 election approached, Pettigrew, secure in the United States Senate for four years, continued to advocate for silver and announced his support for the government regulation of railroads. He even started to correspond with Loucks. In June 1896, Pettigrew joined other Silver Republicans in walking out of the Republican National Convention at Saint Louis after the party adopted a platform favoring the gold standard. "This entire section favors your action and nine-tenths of the people favor free coinage even though the machine denies it," wrote Freeman Knowles, the Populist editor of the *Deadwood Independent*.[40] Pettigrew and the Silver Republicans attended the Populists' July 1896 convention at Huron and announced support for the party's candidates.[41]

The reform press continued to organize for the campaign into the summer. During a meeting at Redfield, the SDRPA appointed S. A. Cochrane and Dowdell to plan a series of summer camp meetings. J. H. Kipp, the chairman of the SDRPA's campaign committee, predicted before the state's People's Party convention that the party would gain four thousand Democratic votes and six thousand to eight thousand Republican votes regardless of what happened at the Democratic National Convention at Chicago. The Democrats, however, nominated former Nebraska congressman William Jennings Bryan, an advocate of the free coinage of silver, for president. Loucks lost his battle against fusion at both the state and national levels and the People's Party also nominated Bryan. At the state Populist convention, Pettigrew's endorsement of Andrew E. Lee, a businessman and former mayor of Vermillion, resolved a fight over who would receive the Populist gubernatorial nomination. With the support of the Silver Republicans already in place, the People's Party nomination of Bryan for president prompted South Dakota Democrats to fuse with the Populists for both the state and presidential tickets.[42]

As Kidd organized the Populist campaign in South Dakota, Republican editors tried to convince farmers that no connection existed between the demonetization of silver in 1873 and the persistent low prices on wheat. The GOP scribes also claimed that the high tariff, instead of raising the prices farmers paid for manufactured items, provided urban workers with plenty of money to spend on farm products. The Republican editors attacked the Norwegian-born Lee not only for his success in business and his extensive land ownership but also for his poor pronunciation. In spite of these attacks, fusion, the tactic long opposed by Loucks, resulted in the greatest electoral victory for South Dakota Populists. Bryan carried the state by less than two hundred votes. Lee also won a narrow victory. Freeman Knowles and John E. Kelley garnered election to the United States House of Representatives. The silver fusion ticket, under the People's Party name, gained control of the state legislature.[43]

Nevertheless, the Populist victory proved fleeting. As the state legislative session opened in 1897, Pettigrew, Lee, and other fusionists opposed Kyle's reelection amid reports that the Populist senator was negotiating with Republicans. The Populists, however, failed to agree upon a replacement candidate. Five Populists—including Loucks and Kyle—received nominations. On 18 February 1897, ten Populists and three Democrats in the legislature defected, backed Kyle's reelection, and pledged to support the Republicans. Kyle won reelection, and Lee appeared to lose control of the legislature.[44]

Despite the senatorial election disrupting the fusion coalition, the Populists won some legislative victories. The 1897 legislature passed a law regulating railroads and empowering the state railroad commission with the authority to establish maximum rates. The legislature also passed election reform laws intended to counteract the 1893 anti-fusion legislation, reduce corruption, and increase transparency. Lee and the Populist legislators also tried to provide relief to the cash-strapped editors of the reform press, creating the office of insurance commissioner in a blatant effort to direct business toward loyal newspapers. The insurance commissioner was empowered to designate the newspapers with which insurance companies were required to publish legal notices. Lee appointed J. H. Kipp as the insurance commissioner over the objections of Kidd and Loucks. Kipp soon fell under the influence of the Republican state auditor and awarded the insurance notice to Republican newspapers.[45]

The Reform Press Bureau, formed to provide legislative news from the Populist perspective, complained in March 1897 that the Republican press distorted accounts of the recently adjourned session:

> To presume that the people at large know anything but the most meagre [sic] fragments of the facts concerning the history of the legislature which has just adjourned is to presume that the daily press reports during the winter have been fair, truthful and complete—a presumption which nobody can or will make when informed that nearly all the news sent to the dailies during the winter was the work of Ole Tomlinson of the Argus-Leader, who never tells the truth except by accident, and L. E. Cavalier, who got all his news from Tomlinson, and who is mentally incapable of telling the truth if he started with the design to do so.[46]

Although a few of the rural Populist weeklies sent representatives to the capital, the reform press claimed most papers received a "perfect flood of falsehood, direct and implied" over the wires. "A broadside of dirt, filth, and scandal," directed against Populist politicians, "poured forth continually from journalistic pirates" and resulted in the public adopting false conclusions. The Reform Press Bureau planned to answer false information during the next session with weekly letters to the state's silver papers.[47]

The invective exchanged between the Populist and Republican press in 1897 exceeded that of an election year. "Never in the history of any state has the press of any party showed such bitterness towards any executive as has the Republican papers of this state showed towards Gov. Lee," wrote Arthur Linn in the *Canton Dakota Farmers' Leader*. "The Leader defies every Republican paper in the state to name one individual act wherein Gov. Lee is not doing his plain duty to protect the taxpayers and expose thieves."[48] Republican John Baldwin of Saint Lawrence responded to a dispatch from Pierre published in the *Sioux Falls Press* regarding his conduct as state engineer of irrigation, "John smiled and said, 'Well, that is about as near the truth as the Reform Press Bureau at Pierre gets.'"[49]

Thomas Ayres, Governor Lee's private secretary, found himself the target of frequent Republican attacks because of his service as the chief contributor to the Reform Press Bureau. Ayres and his father started the *Vermillion Plain Talk* in 1884 and criticized both Republicans and Democrats.[50] Ayres continued to write after joining Lee, a fellow Vermillion resident, at Pierre. Despite Populist claims that he only spent "perhaps two hours a week skinning Republican politicians and newspapers," Ayres's critics accused him of writing for the reform press while drawing a public salary.[51] "If this charge is true what of it," wrote the *Brookings Individual*. "The private secretary is bound to have some leisure. While it is necessary for him to reside at Pierre he isn't employed all the time unless there is something for him to do."[52] Much of the Republican criticism of Ayres emanated from Pierre, so the Populists responded by threating to move the capital. "If the Pierre boomers think they have a 'cinch' on the capital they are mistaken," wrote the *Canton Dakota Farmers' Leader*. "They are welcome to pound Gov. Lee, Tom Ayres and the Populists generally, and keep it up, for it will make Huron all the happier."[53]

The South Dakota Reform Press Association flourished when it challenged Republican rule, but maintaining unity while defending the fusion administration proved more difficult. The South Dakota agrarian and labor movement had fought to control the state's government since its inception, but acrimony characterized the first few months of fusion administration. The actions at the SDRPA's 5 June 1897 meeting at Huron showed the group was at a crossroads—reflective of its past, divided at present and cautious about the future. The association, as usual, closed its meetings to outsiders; however, leaks fed information to both Populist and Republican papers. Only eight members attended, including S. A. Cochrane, who had replaced Republican John Baldwin as the state engineer of irrigation. The group approved two new members and extended an honorary membership to Father Haire. The SDRPA accepted H. S. Volkmar's resignation as secretary after he sided with Kyle, much to the delight of the Republican press, but took no action regarding his membership. The SDRPA sought to establish a publishing house to provide preprinted pages or ready-to-print plates to the approximately seventy Populist, Democratic, and Silver Republican newspapers that supported the fusion coalition. In addition to a weekly column from Pierre, the SDRPA wanted to provide clippings from allied papers around the state to show readers the strength of the reform press beyond their local newspapers. The inclusion of the Democratic and Silver Republican papers, however, meant moderating the Reform Press Bureau's content. Among the new members was Pettigrew's longtime ally George W. Kingsbury.[54]

The Populist administration, like its Republican predecessors, took full advantage of the patronage system and filled appointed positions and state jobs with loyalists. The Republican press viewed each new fusion editor appointed or hired to a job at Pierre as a potential contributor to the Reform Press Bureau. "The editorial staff of the reform press bureau at Pierre has been enforced by the arrival of Editor [Frank G.] King of the Gettysburg Herald," the *Daily Huronite* quipped after King accepted at job in the office of the insurance commissioner.[55] "The head knockers of the 'reform press' bureau, which seeks to cast a halo about the administration of his excellency, the governor, met in the eastern part of the state recently to outline the policy of the pop press of the state," wrote the *Hot Springs Weekly Star* following a fall 1897 SDRPA meeting. "According to reports it was thoroughly representative—so far as the pop state officers go."[56] The *Star*'s commentary, however, was not unfounded. In addition to Ayres, the "governor defacto" by the *Star*'s estimation, other Populist editors included Kipp, the insurance commissioner, and William T. La Follette, a railroad commissioner.[57]

The Populist central committee gathered in March 1898 at Huron to plan its strategy for the upcoming election. Lee and Pettigrew advocated for fusion. Loucks once again voiced his opposition, but the party's leaders overwhelmingly supported cooperating with the Democrats. Loucks believed that Lee appointed too many Democrats to offices at the expense of long-time Populists. Lee and Pettigrew tried to reason with Loucks and even considered appointing him as state oil inspector. Lee, however, realized Loucks would view the offer as a bribe and decided not to act.[58]

The 1898 election marked another transition for South Dakota Populism. The Populists, Silver Republicans, and Democrats held conventions in July 1898 in which the three parties agreed to support a single ticket and nominate Lee for reelection. Loucks believed the Democrats controlled the People's Party and announced his return to the Republican Party. Knowles and Kelley lost reelection bids, but Lee narrowly retained his position. The other fusionist candidates for state offices lost. The Republicans gained significant majorities in both legislative chambers. Regardless, Loucks, Haire, and other veteran reformers rejoiced as voters approved a constitutional amendment to allow the initiative and referendum.[59]

The SDRPA gathered on 28 December 1898 at Huron and appointed a committee to remain in Pierre during the 1899 legislative session. A cynical dispatch said the committee guaranteed "that publishers of populist papers are not ignored in matters that will contribute to their bank accounts." The association opposed the abolition of the office of insurance commissioner. The repeal of the law, passed by the Populist legislature two years earlier, would end "all hope of their receiving for publication any insurance statements."[60] Although only a few members attended the session, the editors loyal to the fusionist governor continued to consolidate power and elected Robert E. Dowdell as president and Ayres as secretary and treasurer. Occupied with matters related to the Spanish American War, Lee accomplished little on the domestic front during his second term. Among his few legislative accomplishments was a veto of Republican efforts to reenact the anti-fusion legislation repealed two years before.[61]

The SDRPA and the central committee of the South Dakota People's Party, increasingly indistinguishable organizations, met in December 1899 at Huron. The party committee asked Volkmar, the editor of the *Milbank Review*, to resign from the Populist national committee.[62] According to reports in Republican papers, the committee also discussed candidates for the 1900 election. William T. La Follette was named as a possible candidate for governor. "This is what the reform editors do," the *Mitchell Capital* wrote. "The populists may object to their way of doing. La Follette would be an easy mark for governor."[63] The editors reportedly speculated that Ayres would campaign for secretary of state or state auditor. "The habit of office-seeking is so strong with republicans that it is impossible for a gathering of fusionists to meet anywhere in the state without at once arousing the suspicion of the correspondent of republican newspapers that some pie is going to be cut," the *Pierre Populist* protested, claiming: "No man's political aspirations were cultivated or even discussed. The Association is not and will not be in the business of promoting candidates; that is not its mission."[64]

The *Pierre Populist* protested too much. Reports of SDRPA meetings almost exclusively spoke of politics and potential candidates. The association no longer viewed educating the masses as its primary mission. Fusion even stretched its loyalty to the People's Party as it had elsewhere on the northern plains. The newly reorganized Reform Press Association of Minnesota openly boosted the Democratic Party. George S. Canfield, secretary of the association, invited members to Jackson Day festivities in Saint Paul, where Bryan addressed the group. H. W. Sawyer, of the SDRPA, undoubtedly aware of the organization's politics, met with the Minnesota group in an effort to interest the editors in ready prints furnished by the reform press of South Dakota. About a week later, former members of the SDRPA—including Volkmar—organized a Democratic press association during the state press association's annual meeting in January 1900 at Sioux Falls. A Republican press association formed at the same time and within months started its own press bureau to rival the Populist operation. Meanwhile, reform editors in the Black Hills organized the Reform Press Association of the Black Hills in February 1900 at Deadwood. The group considered itself aligned with the SDRPA but a separate and distinct organization.[65]

The Republicans won big in the 1900 election. The 1901 legislature enacted strict anti-fusion laws that forced the Populists to join the Democratic Party. The SDRPA, however, persisted in some form for at least another year. In January 1901, Ayres, acting as SDRPA president, summoned a group of reformers to Huron. The meeting resulted in the creation of the Direct Legislation League with Kidd as president and Ayres as secretary. The group prepared to invoke the initiative and referendum if the incoming legislature passed laws inconsistent with the group's goals. The SDRPA gathered again in March 1901 at Huron to consider a series of articles that criticized the legislature. During the session, the association met with the State Referendum League. The conferees planned to present petitions calling for a referendum on bills to create a dairy commissioner, to provide for the election of at-large county commissioners, and to allow the governor to remove appointees.[66]

The fate of the SDRPA after 1901 remains unclear; however, the number of Populist newspapers in South Dakota swiftly declined after the turn of the century. The number of newspapers affiliated with the People's Party dropped to less than a dozen by 1905. Only two papers remained loyal to the vanquished party in 1910.[67]

South Dakota's Populist editors went in a variety of political directions following the demise of the People's Party. Former governor Lee, former senator Pettigrew, and former congressman Kelley joined the Democratic Party. After the Lee administration ended in 1901, Tom Ayres helped settlers locate homesteads and get their farms platted and filed. In 1911, a drought drove farmers from their land, and Ayres's business failed. Owing eight thousand dollars to a Pierre banker, Ayres tried to start a real-estate business in Nebraska. Five years later, the bank offered Ayres a Perkins County farm at ten dollars an acre. Ayres worked as a writer and political organizer for the Nonpartisan League during the early 1920s. In 1924, he unsuccessfully sought the Democratic nomination for the United States Senate. He then ran as the Farmer-Labor candidate. He was serving as editor of the *Aberdeen Dakota Free Press* when he died in 1932. Other editors, including Loucks, returned to the Republican Party. Kidd joined the Socialist Party and edited the *Dakota Ruralist* until his death in 1902. Haire also joined the Socialist Party. Together they made Brown County, formerly a Populist stronghold, into a hotbed of socialism. Freeman Knowles also

76

turned to the Socialist Party and launched the *Deadwood Lantern*, a Socialist newspaper, in 1905, and often stood as the party's candidate for offices. In 1908, a federal court at Deadwood convicted Knowles of printing obscene material in the *Lantern*. He died in 1910.[68]

Loucks continued to write. He authored several books, including *Farm Problems and State Development* (1914) and *Common Sense Rural Credits* (1915). Despite his announced return to the Republican Party, Loucks never actively participated in his old party. Instead, he campaigned as an independent for the United States Senate during the first national election of senators by popular vote in 1914. Loucks, who relied on astrology to shape his campaign, finished fifth among five candidates. As he continued to write, he authored works conspiratorial in nature, including *The Conspiracy of the House of Morgan Exposed and How to Defeat It* (1916), *Our Daily Bread: Must Be Freed from the Greed of Private Monopoly* (1919), and *How to Restore and Maintain Our Government Bonds At Par* (1921). He died on 29 December 1928.[69]

This examination of the SDRPA reveals that South Dakota Populism, like the state itself, was young and forward-looking. It embraced modern organizational practices and tried to use the press to coordinate advocacy on behalf of farmers and laborers. The diverse factions within the People's Party and the fusion coalition prevented the reform press from achieving the unity it sought. Loyal Populists struggled with the politics of fusion and whether to place principle over party. The efforts of the reform press to impose a common voice through the Reform Press Bureau drove some editors from its ranks and made it an easy target for Republican criticism. After the People's Party's failure, South Dakota's Populist journalists, like those elsewhere, scattered in many political directions and complicated historians' search for a true successor.

In the end, the Populist revolt marked a brief challenge to the Republican Party's almost continual domination of South Dakota politics. To maintain this almost constant supremacy, the GOP occasionally adopted the policy positions or tactics of its rivals. The history of South Dakota Populism and the South Dakota Reform Press Association provides at least one example of both. In 1892 and 1894, the Republican Party adopted reform positions and prevailed at the polls. The Republicans' 1896 commitment to the gold standard hurt the GOP and contributed to the election of Lee, a Populist, as governor.

The SDRPA inspired the state's Republican press to organize its own organization and news bureau. Fusion with the Democrats and Silver Republicans weakened the South Dakota People's Party, however, and the state Republican Party's continued willingness to adapt limited Populism's appeal.

NOTES

1. Howard Roberts Lamar, *Dakota Territory, 1861–1889: A Study of Frontier Politics* (New Haven: Yale University Press, 1956), pp. 217, 276.

2. R. Alton Lee, *Principle over Party: The Farmers' Alliance and Populism in South Dakota, 1880–1900* (Pierre: South Dakota Historical Society Press, 2011), p. 2; Jon Lauck, *Prairie Republic: The Political Culture of Dakota Territory, 1870–1889* (Norman: University of Oklahoma Press, 2010), pp. 134, 245; Charles Postel, *The Populist Vision* (New York: Oxford University Press, 2007), p. 27. In speaking of the farmers, Lee writes, for example, "[Farmers'] vision of society derived from the pre-Civil War agrarian era, a time when the worker received a greater portion of the fruits of his or her labor" (p. 2). Postel, on the other hand, describes Alliance farmers in the Cross Timbers district of north central Texas as agents in "developing the commercial structures of a modern agricultural society" through "boosting real estate values" and "strengthening links with the market" (p. 27). Postel's statement equally applies to the agrarians of southeast Dakota Territory.

3. Lee, *Principle over Party*, p. 6. Although Lee explores the South Dakota Alliance and its cooperative experiences in depth, he does not examine the history of the SDRPA.

4. Ibid., p. 20; Lawrence Goodwyn, *Democratic Promise: The Populist Moment in America* (New York: Oxford University Press, 1976); Robert C. McMath, Jr., *Populist Vanguard: A History of the Southern Farmers' Alliance* (Chapel Hill: University of North Carolina Press, 1975). For an overview of other works on South Dakota Populism published prior to the early 1990s, *see* William C. Pratt, "South Dakota Populism and its Historians," *South Dakota History* 22 (Winter 1992): 309–29. Macune, an Alliance leader from Texas, wanted the federal government to build warehouses in every county that produced more than five-hundred thousand dollars a year in agricultural produce. Farmers, who stored their harvested crops at the subtreasury warehouses and waited for market prices to increase before they sold, would also be able to borrow up to 80 percent of the value of the crops that they deposited at the subtreasury, with the loans payable in greenbacks, effectively taking the nation off the gold standard. Farmers found the plan attractive because they lacked the cash necessary to make large-scale cooperatives functional. Unlike cooperatives, the Subtreasury Plan required legislation and

meant that farmers would have to rely on politicians to support the proposal. Goodwyn, *Democratic Promise*, pp. 166–167, 169.

5. Jon Lauck, *Prairie Republic*, p. 134; Robert C. McMath, Jr., *American Populism: A Social History, 1877–1898* (New York: Hill & Wang, 1993); O. Gene Clanton, *Populism: The Humane Preference in America* (Boston: Twayne, 1991); Worth Robert Miller, *Oklahoma Populism: A History of the People's Party in the Oklahoma Territory* (Norman: University of Oklahoma Press, 1987).

6. Barbara Cloud, *The Coming of the Frontier Press: How the West Was Really Won* (Evanston, Ill.: Northwestern University Press, 2008), pp. xiv, 31, 39. Cloud, p. 39, observes that special interests, such as utopian colonies, relied on newspapers to build community over considerable distance. The same is true of insurgent political movements.

7. Lauck, *Prairie Republic*, pp. 48–50; *N. W. Ayer & Son's American Newspaper Annual* (1890): 661–72, and (1896): 716–27. The Ayer's directory reports 267 newspapers published in the state in 1890 and 272 in 1896; however, the directory lists daily and weekly editions of the same newspaper as two distinct titles. Lauck views the Dakota Farmers' Alliance public sphere activities—including newspaper and pamphlet circulation—as consistent with the republicanism that infused the territory's political culture. The identification of Populists with republicanism, however, should not be construed as an acknowledgement that they looked solely to the past for a solution to the problems that confronted farmers and laborers in late-nineteenth-century America. In organizing the reform press, South Dakota Populists embraced modern solutions while they remained committed to republicanism. Lauck, *Prairie Republic*, p. 245; Worth Robert Miller, ed. "The Populist Vision: A Roundtable Discussion," Kansas History 32 (Spring 2009): 18–45. Worth Robert Miller questions the helpfulness of the backward-looking versus forward-looking dichotomy and asks "Can a late nineteenth-century farmer, laborer, or middle-class urban reformer be committed to values derived from the republicanism of the American Revolution and still be a modernizer?" The history of the SDRPA suggests the answer is yes.

8. Lee, *Principle over Party*, pp. 15, 18, 20, 24, 28. Jeffrey A. Johnson provides an overview of Loucks's personal life and political career. Jeffrey A. Johnson, "'Equal Opportunity For All, That's All': South Dakota's Henry L. Loucks and the Fight for Reform," *South Dakota History* 46 (Spring 2016): 1–28. The National Farmers' Alliance, also known as the northern or northwestern Farmers' Alliance, grew out of a New York state farmers' group and organized at Chicago in 1880. Milton George, the publisher of the Chicago-based *Western Rural*, promoted the northern alliance. The southern National Farmers' Alliance and Industrial Union began in Texas and spread throughout the South during the 1880s. The state alliances of the Dakotas, first organized as part of the northern alliance, changed affiliation to the southern alliance in 1889. Loucks vacated the

Minnesota position after only a few months. McMath, *Populist Vanguard*, p. xii; Lee, *Principle over Party*, p. 28.

9. Lee, *Principle over Party*, pp. 32–33, 49.

10. *Washington (D.C.) National Economist*, 3 Aug. 1889. Dakota Territory was admitted to the Union as two states on November 2, 1889.

11. Lee, *Principle over Party*, pp. 42–46, 57–60.

12. Quoted ibid., p. 60.

13. Ibid., pp. 60–64. State legislatures elected United States senators prior to the ratification of the Seventeenth Amendment in 1913.

14. Ibid., pp. 68–74.

15. Ibid., pp. 75–76; Lawrence Goodwyn, *Democratic Promise,* pp. 156–57.

16. "East of the Rockies," *Sacramento (Calif.) Daily Record-Union*, 14 Dec. 1890.

17. Ibid.

18. Lee, *Principle over Party*, pp. 81, 83–84; "Going to Cincinnati," *St. Paul (Minn.) Daily Globe*, 10 May 1891; "Delegates to Cincinnati," *Huron Daily Huronite*, 11 May 1891.

19. "Alliance-Independent Conference," and "Reform Press Association," *Huron Daily Huronite*, 10 July 1891; Cloud, *The Coming of the Frontier Press*, p. 60. Those present at the founding meeting of the SDPRA included Henry Neill, *Madison Independent*; Loucks; Haire; L. D. Sutherland, *Miller Gazette*; Wilder; Cochrane, *Ipswich Gazette*; Kidd; R.S. Whitaker, *Aberdeen Star*; J. M. Pease, *Mitchell Gazette*; and Landers. The *Huron Daily Huronite* listed Frank Kelly as the other journalist on the executive committee; however, because a Frank Kelly does not appear on the list of those attending the meeting, Frank Wilder was probably the other member. Newspaper articles from throughout the period refer to the organization as both the South Dakota Reform Press Association and the Reform Press Association of South Dakota.

20. "Haire, Robert Father," Biographical File Index, State Archives Collection, South Dakota State Historical Society, Pierre; Anna Marie Weinreis, "Dakota Images," *South Dakota History* 18 (Spring/Summer 1988): 117. Haire later promoted the initiative and referendum. Populist Governor Andrew Lee appointed him to the state Board of Charities and Corrections and the Board of Regents. Bishop Thomas O'Gorman restored Haire to the priesthood in 1901. He died in 1916.

21. Lee, *Principle over Party*, pp. 87–91.

22. Editorial, *Canton Dakota Farmers' Leader*, 15 July 1892.

23. "That Fusion," *Dakota Ruralist*, 14 July 1892, quoted in Lee, *Principle over Party*, p. 94.

24. Lee, *Principle over Party*, pp. 92–94.

25. Editorial, *Canton Dakota Farmers' Leader*, 25 Nov. 1892.

26. Lee, *Principle over Party*, pp. 109–10.

27. Ibid., pp. 119–21.

28. Ibid., pp. 120–23; "A Day of Business," *Mitchell Capital*, 15 June 1894.

29. Robert W. Edelen, "Dakota Images," *South Dakota History* 22 (Winter 1992): 440; Lee, *Principle over Party*, pp. 122, 128, 217.

30. Editorial, *Huron Daily Huronite*, 13 Sept. 1895; "A Great Show," *Hurley Turner County Herald*, 19 Sept. 1895; editorial, *Sioux Falls Argus-Leader*, 3 Oct. 1895; "Pop Editors Will Meet," *Sioux Falls Argus-Leader*, 14 Nov. 1895; "People's Disciples Hobnob," *Sioux Falls Argus-Leader*, 23 Nov. 1895; Lee, *Principle over Party*, pp. 123–25; C. Perry Armin, "A State Treasurer Defaults: The Taylor Case of 1895," *South Dakota History* 15 (Fall 1985): 177–99.

31. "Populist Politics," *Deadwood Weekly Pioneer*, 24 Oct. 1895; *N. W. Ayer & Son's American Newspaper Annual* (1895): 830; editorial, *Deadwood Black Hills Daily Times*, 26 Oct. 1895. SDRPA officers elected at the Woonsocket meeting included: Stacey Cochrane, *Brookings Individual*, president; S. H. Bronson, *Howard Advance*, vice-president; G. W. Lattim, *DeSmet Kingsbury County Independent*, secretary and treasurer; and Karl Gerner, *Madison Independent*, Robert E. Dowdell, *Artesian Advocate*, and Frank Kelly, *Woonsocket News*, executive committee. "Reform Press Officers," *Sioux Falls Argus-Leader*, 14 Sept. 1895.

32. Editorial, *Deadwood Black Hills Daily Times*, 26 Oct. 1895.

33. Ibid., *Hurley Turner County Herald*, 21 Nov. 1895.

34. "Pop Editors in Town," *St. Paul (Minn.) Daily Globe*, 15 Jan. 1896.

35. "Reform Press," *Kimball Graphic*, 18 Jan. 1896.

36. Ibid., *Hurley Turner County Herald*, 16 Jan. 1896.

37. Ibid., *Kimball Graphic*, 25 Jan. 1896.

38. Ibid., *Deadwood Daily Pioneer*, 21 Jan. 1896.

39. Ibid., *Hurley Turner County Herald*, 5 Mar. 1896. The *Herald* endorsed the 1896 Republican ticket on 6 August 1896.

40. Quoted in Lee, *Principle over Party*, p. 129.

41. Ibid., pp. 128–31.

42. "Reform Press Association," *Canton Dakota Farmers' Leader*, 29 May 1896; news item, *Belleville (Kans.) Telescope*, 25 June 1896; Lee, *Principle over Party*, pp. 131–35; "Lee For Governor," *Canton Dakota Farmers' Leader*, 24 July 1896. Historians often view the endorsement of Bryan as the death knell of the People's Party. Lawrence Goodwyn derided free silver as a "shadow movement." Robert Durden, however, explains that many committed Populists supported fusion and free silver in 1896. More recently, James L. Hunt explains that loyal Populists such as Marion Butler and Tom Watson saw silver as an issue to attract Democratic voters to Populism's broader reform agenda. Postel, *The Populist Vision*, pp. 344–45; Goodwyn, *Democratic Promise*, pp. 387–423; Robert F. Durden, *The Climax of Populism: The Election of 1896* (Lexington: University of Kentucky Press, 1965), pp. ix, 6, 14–15; James L. Hunt, *Marion Butler and American Populism* (Chapel Hill: University of North Carolina Press, 2003), pp. 84–85.

43. Lee, *Principle over Party*, pp. 135, 137–38.

44. Ibid., pp. 140–43. Kyle claimed that he remained a Populist but supported Republican leadership in the United States Senate. He joined the GOP in 1898.

45. Ibid., pp. 144–45, 148–49. The Chicago, Milwaukee & Saint Paul Railroad immediately challenged the railroad commission rate authority law in court. In 1901, the United States Supreme Court declared the legislature's delegation of the power to set rates to the railroad commission as unconstitutional.

46. "Reform Press Bureau," *Canton Dakota Farmers' Leader*, 26 Mar. 1897. C. W. Lukes, the editor of the *Pierre Journal*, supplied news to the *Sioux Falls Press*, the *Omaha (Neb.) World-Herald*, and the *St. Paul Pioneer Press*. Lukes remained, by the bureau's estimation, truthful.

47. "Reform Press Bureau," *Canton Dakota Farmers' Leader*, 26 Mar. 1897.

48. *Canton Dakota Farmers' Leader*, 14 May 1897.

49. "Baldwin Talks," *Huron Daily Huronite*, 22 Apr. 1897.

50. Bernie Hunhoff, "Homer Ayres Cowboy Activist," *South Dakota Magazine* 6 (Jan./Feb. 1990):17–20.

51. "Pierre or the Penitentiary," *Canton Dakota Farmers' Leader*, 14 May 1897.

52. Quoted in *Canton Dakota Farmers' Leader*, 21 May 1897.

53. Quoted in "Pierre or the Penitentiary," *Canton Dakota Farmers' Leader*, 14 May 1897.

54. News item, *Huron Daily Huronite*, 5 June 1897; "South Dakota Reform Press," *Omaha (Neb.) Daily Bee*, 7 June 1897. The new members were Kingsbury of the *Yankton Press & Dakotan* and C. J. Maynard of the *Kimball Brule Index*. Federal postal laws allowed editors to mail copies to each other without paying postage. Editors copied much of their news from these exchanges and expected distant editors to use their locally written content. An editor thus wrote for both a local and a distant audience. The *Rapid City Black Hills Union* used preprinted pages from the Nebraska Reform Press Business Association. Cloud, *The Coming of the Frontier Press*, pp. 70–71; "To Reform Publishers," *Rapid City Black Hills Union*, 24 June 1898.

55. *Huron Daily Huronite*, 7 July 1897.

56. *Hot Springs Weekly Star*, 17 Dec. 1897.

57. La Follette was the older brother of Robert M. La Follette, a progressive Republican who had won election as Wisconsin governor in 1900 and served in the United States Senate from 1906 to 1925.

58. Lee, *Principle over Party*, 151–53.

59. Ibid., pp. 153–54, 159–60. *See* Brad Tennant, "People's Democracy: The Origins of the Initiated Measure in South Dakota," in *The Plains Political Tradition: Essays on South Dakota Political Culture*, vol. 2, ed. Jon K. Lauck, John E. Miller, and Donald C. Simmons, Jr. (Pierre: South Dakota Historical Society Press, 2014), pp. 8–29.

60. "Looking After Patronage," *Omaha Daily Bee*, 31 Dec. 1898.

61. Ibid.; Lee, *Principle over Party*, p. 162. Those present at the meeting included Democrat Glenn M. Farley, *Madison Outlook*; Ora Williams, *Sioux Falls Press*; F. F. Hanford, *Davis Globe*; Dowdell, *Artesian Courier*; Kidd, *Dakota Ruralist*; and J. W. Peckham, *Alexandria Journal*.

62. "Volkmar is Asked to Quit," *Omaha Daily Bee*, 4 Dec. 1899. The SDRPA selected A. Sherrin, *Watertown Times*, as president; Fred Wright, *DeSmet Independent* as vice-president; and Ayres, *Vermillion Plain Talk*, as secretary.

63. *Mitchell Capital*, 8 Dec. 1899.

64. Quoted in "Making for Candidates," *Canton Dakota Farmers' Leader*, 15 Dec. 1899

65. "Jackson Day," *Willmar (Minn.) Tribune*, 3 Jan. 1900; "Busy Day for Bryan," *Princeton (Minn.) Union*, 11 Jan. 1900; news item, *St. Paul Globe*, 13 Jan. 1900; "Press Association Meets," *St. Paul Globe*, 21 Jan. 1900; "Press Association Meets," *St. Paul (Minn.) Globe*, 21 Jan. 1900; "Two Newspaper Organizations Formed," *Sioux Falls Argus-Leader*, 19 Jan. 1900; news item, *Sioux Falls Argus-Leader*, 18 July 1900; "Reform Press Association," *Daily Deadwood Pioneer*, 4 Feb. 1900. Those attending the Reform Press Association of the Black Hills meeting included Arthur W. Gird, *Rapid City Black Hills Union*; C. Von Wohrman, *Hill City Harney Peak News*; A. S. Shockley, *Belle Fourche Times*; A. C. Potter, *Lead Call*; W. L. Elswick, *Spearfish Register*; and W. S. Monkman, *Terry Peak Record*. Gird won election as president. Other officers included: Monkman, vice president; Potter, secretary; and Wohrman, treasurer.

66. Lee, *Principle over Party*, p. 162; "Reformers Meet," *Minneapolis Journal*, 1 Jan. 1901; "Pops to Move on Huron," *Minneapolis Journal*, 21 Mar. 1901; "Wants The Referendum," *Saint Paul Globe*, 23 Mar. 1901.

67. *American Newspaper Directory* (New York, Geo. P. Rowell & Co., 1901, 1902, 1903, 1905, 1906, 1909); *N. W. Ayer & Son's American Newspaper Annual* (1910). The 1910 *American Newspaper Annual*, pp. 828, 834, listed the *Hill City Harney Peak Mining News* and the *Sioux Falls Fremad*, a Norwegian- and Danish-language newspaper, as Populist.

68. Lee, *Principle over Party*, p. 173; "Kelley, John Edward," *Biographical Directory of the United States Congress*, bioguide.congress.gov.; "Ayres, Homer," Biographical File Index, State Archives Collection; Hunhoff, "Homer Ayres Cowboy Activist," pp. 17–20; "Principles—Not Parties Tom Ayres' Concern," *Aberdeen Dakota Free Press*, 10 June 1932; William C. Pratt, "Another South Dakota; or, The Road Not Taken: The Left and the Shaping of South Dakota Political Culture," in *Plains Political Tradition: Essays on South Dakota Political Culture*, vol. 1, ed. Jon K. Lauck, John E. Miller, and Donald C. Simmons, Jr. (Pierre: South Dakota Historical Society Press, 2011), pp. 113–15; "Knowles, Freeman," Biographical File Index, State Archives Collection; "Freeman Knowles Released," *Rapid City*

Daily Journal, 23 June 1908. Pratt views South Dakota Populism as part of a persistent left-of-center political tradition in the state.

69. Thom Guarnieri, "H. L. Loucks and the *Dakota Ruralist*: Voices of Reform" (master's thesis, South Dakota State University, 1981), pp. 111–15.

KENNETH L. SMITH

4 | PRESBYTERIANISM, PROGRESSIVISM, AND CULTURAL INFLUENCE

WILLIAM M. BLACKBURN, COE I. CRAWFORD, AND THE MAKING OF CIVIC DAKOTA

. . .

When newly elected senator Coe I. Crawford departed South Dakota for Washington, D.C., in 1909, he could boast of many significant achievements. As governor since 1907, he had fanned a wave of intense progressive sentiment and overseen impressive political reforms. Railroad regulation had been extended and strengthened. Laws had been enacted to eliminate corporate funding of campaigns, require public disclosure of political contributions, and institute direct election of United States senators. A food and drug commission and a telephone commission had been established, and a state fund to provide public schools with free textbooks was in operation. "He accomplished in two years," wrote a biographer, "what governors LaFollette (of Wisconsin) and Cummins (of Iowa) did in their respective states in six."[1] In the United States Senate, Crawford deliberated on national and international issues alongside such progressives as Joseph Bristow of Kansas, Elihu Root of New York (President Roosevelt's former secretary of state), and Robert ("Fighting Bob") LaFollette of Wisconsin. He participated in numerous domestic and foreign policy debates and was instrumental in moving the Seventeenth Amendment to the states for ratification. Crawford's boast as a twelve-year-old rural Iowa boy had come to pass: "Someday," the youthful admirer of Daniel Webster had declared, stabbing a husking knife into a pumpkin for emphasis, "I'm going to the United States Senate."[2]

When Rev. William M. Blackburn, the newly elected president of what is now the University of North Dakota, stood before the organizers of the Dakota Education Association in Fargo in June 1884 to deliver his first speech in the territory, he chose as his theme "individuality." Blackburn criticized "the prudent man" who "has not the courage to work out opinions of his own" and whose convictions inevitably "bow to the social ideas of propriety, and bend to fashion and break down before the social gods." In contrast, he lauded the man of "superior excellence" who refuses to surrender his individuality, maintains his "high moral energy," and goes forth as an exemplar of "powers—muscular power, mental power, mental and spiritual power."[3] Attendees regarded the talk as "the intellectual treat" of the gathering.[4] They were also doubtless impressed with the speaker's resume. Blackburn had been a successful pastor, seminary professor, and noted church historian. He had authored more than forty books, published countless sermons, and helped guide his Presbyterian denomination through a traumatic and far-reaching doctrinal conflict. He would, in the next fifteen years, contribute a noteworthy influence on the fast-developing Dakota frontier society.

As it happened, Blackburn served only one year as the president of the university. The summer of 1885 found him in Pierre, South Dakota, where as president of an infant Presbyterian college known as Pierre University he would work for fourteen years alongside Crawford, who served the school as treasurer and senior board member. The two became close friends and confidantes. They often conferred on business and personal matters, visited in each other's homes, participated together in reading circles and church activities, and worshiped together at the church where Blackburn preached most Sundays. The relationship imparted, during a crucial period in the life of the young attorney, a substantial body of thought and perspective distilled through decades of experience. Crawford later wrote:

> [Blackburn] gave me more than any man I have ever known— and I have known, very happily, some of the choicest men of my time. But that old philosopher came into my life when I needed him and I became his debtor a thousand fold. He was the real coin. No sham. No veneer. The real thing. . . . His heart went out to the whole world. I remember how he always asked the Lord to "bless the stranger within these gates;" and in a thousand ways his voice comes back to me across the intervening years.[5]

As his biographers have noted, Crawford's political success stemmed largely from his remarkable power as a public speaker, and his ability to communicate is on display in this tribute to his mentor.[6] Connections between individuals—father and son or mentor and student—are subjective and difficult to trace accurately even where information is abundant. There is reason to believe, however, that Crawford's recollections were more than sentimental. The voice that resounded "in a thousand ways" in Crawford's mind was a key source of the "mental and spiritual power" that lay behind one of the region's most significant political careers.

As Jon K. Lauck noted in the seminal book *Prairie Republic* (2007), "The settlers who peopled Dakota did not arrive with intellectual blank slates, nor did the social order they created emerge out of a formless state of nature."[7] The values that guided Crawford the reformer and helped shape the region's political and cultural tradition were deeply rooted in history and memory. To a great extent, they were passed along through the medium of the religious faith he shared with William Blackburn. Neither man was a "blank slate" upon arriving in Dakota Territory. Both were molded by a rich Protestant denominational tradition, one that was, in turn, being shaped by diverse internal elements and stretched, sometimes to the breaking point, amid the tensions of a growing America. As a highly influential Presbyterian educator, Blackburn significantly influenced his denomination's response to those tensions and became a substantial role model himself.

Protestant denominations, and Presbyterians in particular, wielded enormous influence during the era of Midwest settlement. From 1800 to the 1830s, notes Bradley Longfield, the Presbyterian church "had grown from fewer than 20,000 to almost 250,000 members who represented the demographic center of the American population. Presbyterians, perceived to be preeminent in 'wealth and intelligence' among the evangelical churches, were an elite, national, educated, and influential body that reflected the social, religious, and economic forces coursing throughout the nation."[8] Indeed, C. C. Goen has asserted that by the mid-1830s the Presbyterian General Assembly "rival[ed] the federal government for popular influence and esteem."[9] This influence would reverberate strongly all the way into the mid-twentieth century.

Crucial to Presbyterian prestige and influence was a deep commitment to educational work. The founding of Pierre University and its sister school, Jamestown College, in 1883 mirrored the long Presbyterian pattern of establishing schools in newly settled areas in hopes of definitively shaping the culture of the young frontier states. William Blackburn, who would inherit the leadership of the institution at Pierre, was profoundly shaped by his experiences at Hanover College, a frontier institution founded in 1827 on the banks of the Ohio River in eastern Indiana. Blackburn studied there from 1846 to 1850, absorbing the ideals and education that were believed to magnify cultural influence. President Sylvester Scovel, one of Blackburn's key mentors, dramatized the urgency of this mission in an 1847 college address, calling on his listeners (which included Blackburn) to offer their "mite of influence to the institutions of your own native West," which he deemed "a broad land that will soon sway the destinies of the Union." These schools would send forth "the leaders of the host, to dissipate ignorance, to conquer error, to subdue and homologate the masses of society."[10] Recalling his years under Scovel, Blackburn would later assert that the measure of a college and its leadership "may be tested by two questions." First, "has this college been, and is yet to be, a power for good in the world? Second, did [its leaders] contribute any force to make it capable of a powerful influence?"[11]

Blackburn's powers of influence were further deepened and broadened by four years at Princeton Seminary, where he studied with the renowned theologian Charles Hodge, under whom his writing talents flourished and his ardor for history grew. For Blackburn, as for his teachers, knowledge was powerful, and power was understood as consisting first in quiet, profound thought and second in written and verbal expression. He was fascinated by orators such as Daniel Webster, whose brain he imagined as a "bright furnace" in which "thunderbolts" were being slowly manufactured. Webster had "moved the world through that greatest of engines called a quill," providing a prime example of the power of thought and words.[12] Blackburn's prolific writing and speaking career was grounded in this fascination.

Immediately following his 1854 ordination by the Lake Presbytery of the Old School Presbyterian denomination, Blackburn began to write steadily.[13] While serving pastorates in Erie, Pennsylvania, and Trenton, New Jersey, from 1854 to 1868, he published ten full-length books, including biographies of Reformation leaders and several novels for adolescents. Scores of his sermons and essays were circulated, laying the groundwork for a seven-hundred-page work on church history, which, when completed in 1879, would become a standard text for a generation of Protestant leaders. Blackburn was becoming an influential voice both in church circles and beyond.[14]

In 1868, Blackburn received a calling from an educational institution positioned strategically to influence the future of the midwestern frontier—the Theological Seminary of the Northwest in Chicago. Twenty years earlier, Cyrus McCormick had moved from Virginia to Chicago, guided by a vision of a thriving agricultural heartland made possible by his advanced harvesting machines. McCormick became wealthy in pursuit of that vision, but his life's aim went well beyond profits. As the primary benefactor of the seminary (established in 1859), McCormick—a devout Calvinist—was exercising what biographer William T. Hutchinson called a consuming interest of the last twenty-five years of his life, "the maintenance of 'good old' Presbyterianism against assaults by heretic or unbeliever."[15] For the next thirteen years, Blackburn would negotiate an uneasy relationship with a powerful philanthropist whose vision for influencing the culture would deviate significantly from his own.

Postwar Chicago gave a much heartier welcome to McCormick's industrial innovations than to his "good old" Calvinist traditions. The burgeoning metropolis was, as popular preacher David Swing noted, a city of "large and liberal air," one that welcomed new ideas as eagerly as new industries.[16] Presbyterianism was flourishing in Chicago, but some of its ministers, the conservative industrialist believed, were seriously compromising its message. McCormick, a southerner by heritage and close friend of fellow Illinois Democrat Stephen A. Douglas, had lost considerable standing with his denominational brethren during the war years. Moreover, he had seen the seminary fall under the control of a board whose politics and theological leanings ran counter to his own. In 1866, the seminary board defied McCormick, appointing former Hanover College president and longtime anti-slavery activist Erasmus D. MacMaster as chair of theology. When the elderly MacMaster died later the same year, the board replaced him with an even more radical professor, Willis Lord. Deeply affronted, McCormick threatened to withhold the remaining twenty-five thousand dollars of the one hundred thousand dollar pledge he had earlier made to the seminary. The board was unmoved. Turning a deaf ear to McCormick, they selected William Blackburn, a friend and ally of Lord, to fill the endowed chair of Biblical and Ecclesiastical History in 1868.[17]

Four years later, after the Chicago fire of 1871 impoverished the seminary's other main supporters, McCormick found and seized a chance to redirect the focus of the seminary and, by extension, promote his own conservative influence. He brought to Chicago one of the nation's most brilliant defenders of rigid Old School Calvinism, the young Princeton Seminary alumnus and precocious writer Francis L. Patton, a philosophically astute archconservative. The installation of twenty-nine-year-old Patton in the Cyrus H. McCormick Chair of Didactic and Polemic Theology in the Seminary of the Northwest was a major strategic success for the industrialist.[18] With renewed influence over the seminary, McCormick restored his earlier endowment, plus an extra twenty thousand dollars. He also guaranteed the new professor—who relinquished a lucrative pastorate in Brooklyn to relocate in Chicago—a salary of five thousand dollars per year, twice that of the other three professors. In a related move, McCormick in 1873 purchased the *Interior,* the region's most important periodical, and installed Patton as editor.[19] Conservative forces seemed to be on the rebound. Yet, in an arena where sacred and secular affairs still greatly overlapped, McCormick's actions drew harsh criticism. In March 1874, the *Chicago Tribune* denounced the appointment of Patton:

It is sad that such a narrow-minded bigot [as Dr. Patton] is where he can palsy the influence of two such eminent divines as Dr. Patterson and the Rev. Dr. Blackburn. But it were better that able men should lecture to empty benches for the rest of their lives than to have our entire race of clergymen poisoned with the antiquated dogmatism of their associate."[20]

Tribune readers might soon have looked upon this editorial as prophetic. David Swing, the city's best-known, most dynamic Presbyterian preacher, had long been an object of suspicion for McCormick's conservative faction. Whereas the collegial Blackburn maintained cordial friendships with both Swing and Patton, the young professor was determined to expose the alleged errors of the popular cleric. In April 1874, Patton went before the Chicago Presbytery with formal charges. "Swing," Patton alleged, "has not been zealous and faithful in maintaining the truths of the gospel; and has not been faithful and diligent in the exercise of the public duties of his office as a minister. . . . [Swing] does not sincerely receive and adopt the confession of faith of this church containing the system of doctrine taught in the Holy Scriptures." Patton backed these core charges with twenty-eight specifics, including claims that Swing's preaching "is substantially Unitarian," that he "omits to preach or teach" the scriptural doctrines regarding Christ's sacrifice for the sins of man, justification by faith in Christ, the equality of Jesus with God, the inspiration of "all Scripture," and the "everlasting punishment" of the wicked. The most colorful of the charges against Swing concerned his estimation of certain historical characters. Patton accused him of "unworthy and extravagant laudation" of John Stuart Mill, "who was known not to have believed in the Christian religion," and faulted him for suggesting that Socrates would have been welcomed at the gates of heaven. Also galling to Patton was Swing's judgment that the battles fought by the Israelites, by the command of Jehovah, "surpassed in cruelty those of Julius Caesar."[21]

To the chagrin of the Presbytery, the Swing/Patton heresy trial received blow-by-blow coverage on the front pages of the Chicago press. The views of each of the dozens of Presbytery members who testified were immediately aired in public.[22] As a highly-esteemed member and respected scholar, Blackburn's testimony was crucial. When his turn at last arrived to take the stand, he acknowledged his "honor and love" for both Patton and Swing. He denied holding any animosity toward his seminary colleague, with "whom my relations are peculiarly personal and fraternal." After these niceties, Blackburn painted Patton's case, which appeared strong, as actually quite weak. While admitting the presence of statements in Swing's writings that could be construed as heretical, Blackburn insisted that these portions be interpreted in the light of other passages—"a wonderful number of them—that are evangelical." The method used to interpret Scripture, in which obscure or potentially objectionable passages are explained in the light of clear and acceptable passages, should also apply to Swing's writings. Blackburn asserted, "I do not apply a rule of interpretation to any man's sermons that I am not willing to have applied to every apostle or prophet who ever spoke." Blackburn also reminded his colleagues that both Scripture and church history were filled with difficulties. "There are doubtful passages in almost every writing I have had laid before me," he admitted. "I may say that I examined one passage of Scripture in which I counted eighty-two different interpretations of it;—the doubtful passages require charity, and the plain passages, simple justice."

Blackburn's plea for breadth and tolerance was strongly abetted by his deep study of church history, which contained countless "unpleasant facts, historical or moral." Calling attention to them might be unpleasant, but it certainly was "not criminal or heretical." To castigate Swing, for example, for discussing the blood shed in arguments over the Trinity, was unfair and ahistorical. Such topics "may not be proper to announce . . . in sermons, but they may simply be an enunciation of facts." Blackburn confessed that the same interpretive principle that allowed him to make sense of the Bible also played a role in his view of history. "I am sometimes very glad," he said, "that the people of this world, and in the church, do not know all the facts in church history."

Responding to the second charge, that Swing did not accept the Presbyterian Confession of Faith, Blackburn made one of the most provocative statements of the entire trial: "I am astonished to hear that while we would not receive into our church a thoroughly Bible Preacher, we would only ask him to be a Presbyterian. We thus unchurch thousands of men; and sir, our Divine Master would not be received into the Presbytery of Chicago today, I am afraid, if he stood upon the position upon which he stood when he came into the world, for I do not understand Him to have ever said one single word about Presbyterianism, strict and formulated." Blackburn followed this statement, which forcefully relativized the specific formulations of Presbyterian dogma, with a plea for the recognition of the Presbterian tradition of liberty. In a sharp rebuke to Patton's pretensions, Blackburn declared, "There is no man in this Presbytery authorized to interpret the Confession of Faith," and further, "no man can interpret the Confession of Faith where it is doubtful. The standards must be taken just as they are, and if there be a difference in interpretation, the benefit of the doubt goes to the accused."[23] Blackburn's arguments proved persuasive and, perhaps, decisive. At the end of the five-week spectacle, Presbytery members voted forty-six to thirteen for acquittal. David Swing—widely regarded as Chicago's finest religious orator—had earned the right to continue as a Presbyterian minister.[24] Liberty—grounded in respect for the individuality of a fellow minister—had trumped conformity.

For those directly involved, the trial's fallout was mixed. Swing resigned his affiliation with the Presbyterian church, as the affair had removed "the feeling of brotherhood" he had previously enjoyed within the denomination. Newly independent and more famous than ever, he organized a new congregation. Fifty of Chicago's leading men each subscribed one thousand dollars toward the erection of a vast hall known as Central Church, which soon housed, in the words of Joseph Newton, "one of the great Protestant congregations of the world," with an array of ministries including a Sunday school of four thousand children, a sewing school, a kindergarten, and an industrial school for boys.[25]

While Swing enjoyed the continued and enhanced esteem of the press, Patton fared less well. The *Chicago Tribune* said he suffered from "a hypercritical intellect" and dubbed him "the Don Quixote" of Chicago Presbyterianism. "If the progress of the world had not abolished the forms and customs of Calvin's time," opined the *Tribune*, "Prof. Patton might have a lively week's business in the fagot and torch business."[26] Chicago and its "large liberal air" had little respect for Patton's narrow thinking. His future would not lie in the wide frontier, but he did gain favor with Presbyterian conservatives in the East. In 1880, offers of competitive pay and specialized career advancement lured him back to Princeton College, where he was soon elevated to the presidency. Patton's term from 1888 to 1902 fell between the presidencies of two famous Presbyterian educators—the noted Scottish philosopher James McCosh and the southern political scientist Woodrow Wilson. Wilson's subsequent career as New Jersey governor and United States president would testify to the immense potential that lay in the Presbyterian formula for cultivating cultural influence.[27]

The Swing trial brought Blackburn both gains and losses. He gained the inspiration for a renewed, in-depth study of issues relating to individual freedom and religious authority. He would later express strong disapproval of the sort of coercion a heresy court represented. "The age of strong human authority and force in the church," he wrote, "has in a great degree passed away," and "to Protestantism belongs the credit or blame." Blackburn recognized that his Protestant forebears had "insisted upon the right of private judgment," and now that this principle was established in society, faith must be upheld by reason, not force. "In matters of controversy and discipline the church will see her authority resisted and her creed doubted," wrote Blackburn, "if she employ terms and means which appear coercive, rather than just and reasonable."[28] Here, as elsewhere in Blackburn's writings, individuality was a primary value.

Cyrus McCormick and his allies, however, were unpersuaded of these sympathies. Five years after the Swing trial, they gained control of the seminary board, which promptly fired Blackburn. The insult was clear. The firing, one of Blackburn's correspondents wrote, was borne of "spite, prejudice, jealousy and envy." But in the end, the friend thought, Blackburn would be "more appreciated and in a larger field than before."[29] Indeed, doors quickly opened for him. The board of Western University in Pittsburgh unanimously elected him as president. He declined the offer, accepting instead the pastorate at Cincinatti's Central Presbyterian Church, with a comfortable salary of thirty-five hundred dollars per year.[30]

Three years after his termination at Northwest Seminary, Blackburn received an envelope from an old college friend, postmarked Grand Forks, Dakota Territory. F. W. Iddings, secretary of the board of regents for the new territorial university, wanted to know whether Blackburn would be interested in the position of president and "what salary would command your services." On the reverse side of the regent's stationary, Iddings penned a personal note to his friend and religious colleague: "How are you? Some time since we met in classroom—I am personally very anxious that this important position should be filled by a strong man in our church. Can't you help me out if you cannot look favorably on it yourself. Dr. B., any answer to this must be separate from the others. Fraternally, F. W. I."[31]

Blackburn's decision to accept the presidency of the territorial university was encouraged by another friend, George C. Noyes, who, a decade earlier, had served as counsel for the defendant in the Swing trial. Noyes advised Blackburn that the Red River Valley "is a magnificent country—as flat as the poorest sermon ever preached, but vastly richer and more productive. Blizzards in winter and mosquitoes in summer are the only drawbacks, for I do not regard the cold as formidable. It is a dry atmosphere."[32] Blackburn consented to the uncertainties and thirty-percent salary reduction of the new position and became the university's president and professor of Mental and Moral Philosophy."[33]

As it happened, mosquitoes, lack of scenery, and cold weather would be the least of Blackburn's problems. Most students were unprepared for college work. Facilities were primitive. Curriculum and operating procedures were rudimentary. Disciplinary standards were ill-defined. By midyear, strife over these and related issues had arisen on both the faculty and board. Iddings told Blackburn that he had "won the hearts of the boys and girls," but the embattled president fared less well with other constituents.[34] By April, the controversies were public. In May, after two of the regents were replaced upon expiration of their terms, the board voted three to two for Blackburn's dismissal.

The firing aroused a storm of controversy in the Grand Forks community. Former regent Dr. W. T. Collins spearheaded a well-attended public indignation meeting where a torrent of grievances was unleashed against the former president's treatment. Many leading citizens of Grand Forks sided with Blackburn. *Grand Forks Herald* editor George Winship blasted the firing as evidence of political chicanery. Others stepped forward to quash rumors that the Presbyterian president had a sectarian bias. The town's Baptist and Methodist ministers both spoke up for Blackburn. A. J. O'Keefe assured the crowd that Catholic community of Grand Forks, of which he was a prominent member, had no complaints against Blackburn. City attorney C. R. Pratt likewise dismissed charges of sectarianism, remarking, "Religion never hurt me and I didn't know there was enough in North Dakota to hurt anybody."[35] But the indignation meeting and the subsequent airing of charges and counter charges between the city's two competing newspapers did not alter the verdict. Blackburn would move on, and the controversy over his firing would soon be forgotten.[36]

Of the university presidency, a friend and colleague wrote that Blackburn "had accepted the position with many doubts, and was entirely satisfied to continue the connection but for one year." Thomas L. Riggs opined, "There was too much of politics in a position in a state institution to suit the doctor's make-up."[37] Another nearby opportunity, though, came almost immediately. In June 1885, Blackburn was elected president of Pierre University and professor of Mental, Moral and Political Science and moved his household and his vast trove of books to his final frontier destination.[38] The title "Pierre University"— and the rhetoric Blackburn used to promote it—reflected the surging optimism prevalent during the Dakota boom of the mid-1880s. "Its field," he declared of the college, "is as large as all New York; its place is an empire of mind; and its work is for the United Nation and for the one Kingdom of Heaven." The *Pierre Collegian*, the school's four-page monthly in which this statement and other eloquent reports and pleas for support were issued, featured a cover illustration of the school's stately three-story hilltop building, McCormick Hall.[39] It had been built with monies from the hand of the same philanthropist that a few years earlier had dealt a harsh blow to its current presiding official.

At Pierre, Blackburn became fast friends with Coe I. Crawford, the university treasurer and young lawyer who shared much in common with his elder. Blackburn and Crawford were both of Scottish ancestry and had been raised in devout Presbyterian homes. Both had been inspired since childhood by the speeches of Daniel Webster, possessed a voracious appetite for learning, entertained visions of moving people and institutions by the power of oratory, and were interested in politics broadly defined. For the next thirteen years, the lives of the young attorney and the man he called the "old philosopher" would be intertwined.

Crawford, an Iowa native, had secured a good education and become a schoolteacher by age seventeen. By age twenty-four, he had graduated from the University of Iowa Law School, passed the bar exam, and become a junior law partner. A year later, he moved to Pierre and established an office in a small shack with a sign out front reading "law, land, and loans."[40] The young attorney nurtured big dreams. Pierre was a bustling town of about three thousand, and residents often boasted that it would soon rival the great cities of the Midwest. Crawford shared the common expectation, "In a few years Pierre will be a Sioux City, then an Omaha, then a Kansas City."[41]

Crawford seized civic opportunities as they arose. In 1886, he was elected the state's attorney for Hughes County. In 1888, he gained a seat on the legislative council of Dakota Territory. When South Dakota became a state in 1889, Crawford served as a state senator and chair of the Committee on Revenue.[42] This prestigious position allowed him to draft some of the most important bills introduced in the infant legislature. Here he gained a reputation for "doing most of the speaking," and his oratorical gifts were noted by fellow politicians and the public at large. In 1891, Crawford became attorney general under Governor Charles Sheldon while continuing his law practice on the side.[43]

Crawford's religious background encouraged his political pursuits. The Calvinist tradition to which he and Blackburn were heirs stressed the human tendency toward corruption and self-interest, but it also placed a high value on civic engagement. Crawford's mentor expressed the paradox in an 1887 article entitled "Christianity and Citizenship." Observing that "the fine old word 'politics' has lost much of its true force, and come to mean devotion to self rather than to the state," Blackburn lamented that the word "too often implies the management of public affairs by all arts of dishonesty and for personal advantage. In many minds the politician is not the statesman, the patriot, the expert in the science of government, but the cunning tactician, the wily demagogue, the schemer for an office." But this, Blackburn argued, was unjust and contrary to Scripture. The Apostle Paul, he declared, "recognized the honor and force given it [the word] by Demosthenes, Plato and Xenophon." Properly understood, politics "brings the highest type of civil life almost into identity with Christian life. It is rightly the name for the science of civil affairs, both private and public." Pierre's respected professor of Mental, Moral and Political Science endorsed vigorous participation in the arena of public affairs.[44]

Corruption was more than a theoretical matter in early South Dakota government. Individuals such as Crawford reaped modest benefits by using political connections to arrange favorable business deals. Others behaved worse. William Walter Taylor, South Dakota's first state treasurer, nonchalantly deposited three hundred sixty seven thousand dollars of state funds in his personal bank account, and lent money to land speculators, confident that the western boom would continue as it had in the 1880s. It did not. Land values collapsed after the Panic of 1893, and the money Taylor had "invested" was tied up in lands now worth much less than their purchase price and held largely by seedy speculators. When Taylor retired in January 1895, the truth was revealed. The money had disappeared and so had the state treasurer. Rumor had it that he was hiding out in South America. Enraged South Dakotans called for justice, and the duty fell on the shoulders of Attorney General Crawford.

Chasing down Taylor was the most harrowing task Crawford had ever faced. For over a year, he worked with United States and Latin American authorities, followed leads, and traveled. When he managed to contact Taylor, he found the mildly repentant former treasurer willing to surrender in exchange for one hundred thousand dollars. Crawford refused. Eventually, the two men reached an agreement in which Taylor promised to turn himself over to authorities in exchange for a reduced prison term. When the details of this "deal" became known, a popular outcry arose against Crawford. The *Sioux Falls Argus Leader* complained that a common citizen convicted of stealing a far smaller amount would receive a much harsher sentence and called the day of Taylor's sentencing "the blackest day which South Dakota has known." Crawford responded bitterly, protesting that he had apprehended the embezzler in the only way possible. Harassed and exhausted from this effort to salvage public good from individual selfishness, Crawford denounced the editor of the *Argus Leader* as a "cold-blooded, shameless, and unscrupulous liar."[45]

Unjust though it was, criticism of Crawford for his "corrupt bargain" with Taylor dampened his chances for further political climbing. He gained the Republican nomination for United States representative for South Dakota in 1896, but he lost the election badly, due partly to the Taylor affair but also to the surge of Populist sentiment that swept the Midwest, peaking in 1896 with William Jennings Bryan's presidential candidacy. Crawford's anti-Populist, anti-silver stance—adopted largely to please his party—was bucking the tide of public feeling just when that tide was highest. Crawford showed his mid-1890s attitude toward Populism through a story he often recited on the campaign trail, describing "a certain Irishman who heard a tree toad for the first time and went out to see what it was. Finding nothing, he returned to his house and remarked to his wife, 'Biddie, 'tis nothin' but a dommed noise.'"[46] Crawford's views on Populism paralleled those of Blackburn, who penned a series of satirical newspaper columns in 1892 for the *Pierre Weekly Free Press* entitled "The Ocolic Demands." Written under the pseudonym "A Honist Reformur," the columns were caricatured expressions of Populist positions, filled with deliberate misspellings and grammatical irregularities. The columns presented Populists as ignorant cranks, more worthy of ridicule than fear. For Blackburn, as well as for Crawford, Populism was a manifestation of the uneducated thinking of a crowd, not the informed individuality so often extolled from the college president's lectern.[47]

As Crawford's 1896 defeat showed, however, South Dakotans could be quite intolerant of candidates who stood in the way of reform. Moreover, Populists had a significant positive impact on Dakota politics. In 1892, they implemented the Australian ballot. In 1898, they made South Dakota the first state to adopt the recall and referendum.[48] Populist agitation, which Blackburn and Crawford had made light of, was, in fact, laying the foundation for Crawford's later political success. Paradoxically, the Populist party faded after 1898. The "dommed noise" Crawford had joked about diminished quickly, leaving the field open for another wave of reform.[49]

The year 1898 was a pivotal time in the educational enterprise that had absorbed the efforts of Blackburn and Crawford. Finally acknowledging that Pierre would not be the great city early boomers predicted, Pierre University trustees voted to restart the financially struggling school at Huron, where they rechristened it Huron College. Crawford continued as treasurer and Blackburn became president emeritus, professor of Moral Science, Economics and Geology, as well as librarian and museum curator. These titles reflected interests he had tirelessly pursued during his tenure at Pierre. With an increasing interest in regional matters, he had become an avid amateur student of earth sciences and turned his historian's pen to chronicling Dakota's past. Blackburn had served as secretary of the South Dakota State Historical Society since its founding in 1891. As the society's librarian, he had gathered materials that would form the core of its archives. He had also composed "A History of Dakota," a chronicle featured in the inaugural edition of the society's biennial publication, *South Dakota Historical Collections*.[50] On 28 December 1898, Blackburn's earthly term reached its end. The "old philosopher" whom Crawford knew as an "intimate friend" died in his study, one day short of his seventieth birthday. Crawford and a large throng "followed the casket out to the cemetery in the bluffs, east of the old college buildings, overlooking the Missouri" and laid their friend to rest. "His physical strength was inadequate," Crawford noted, but "his courage was sublime" and "his spirit unconquerable."[51]

Crawford would need similar courage and determination for the political mission he would soon undertake. Shortly before Blackburn's death, Crawford had accepted the position of general counsel for the Chicago & North Western Railroad. Upon his hiring, Blackburn had penned a note to his friend, telling him he was "fortunate to be out of politics."[52] As a railroad attorney, however, Crawford began to realize that he was not actually done with politics: corporate power was severely entangled with government. The abuse of free rail passes was the biggest red flag. Crawford had accepted passes since at least 1892 and given them little thought. But when hundreds of requests for free transportation began to flood his office, he saw what a powerful tool the railroads possessed. Politicians of every stripe, attorneys, real estate agents, businessmen, judges, sheriffs, and even federal employees received passes, and the effects were becoming apparent to Crawford. The granting of free passes, he concluded, was "the most seductive and dangerous influence at work in the field of politics and official life . . . because it benumbs sensibility and acts like an opiate in dulling the edge of conscience."[53]

As his observations turned into convictions and then into determination, Crawford began to contemplate the increasing need and acceptability of reform to mainstream American life. Moreover, his senatorial aspirations remained. In 1902, he began building support to become the Republican nominee for the United States Senate. His party spurned him in favor of another candidate. This rejection helped draw his sympathies away from the old Republican machine and closer to the burgeoning progressive movement.

Crawford's memories of the Taylor scandal and his inside knowledge of the railroad convinced him that politics and business were equally infested with the depravity spoken of in his Calvinist tradition. This revulsion, and what biographer Calvin Perry Armin described as his "naturally independent and stubborn temperament," led to Crawford's 1904 resignation from the Chicago & North Western and spurred his planning for a United States Senate run.[54] Crawford knew now that he could not reach the Senate by relying on nomination by the machine-run state legislature. The only way to achieve his dream would be through a direct primary law. Enacting this law would require a strong progressive governor and a persuadable legislature. Believing he could provide the necessary leadership, Crawford campaigned for governor on a progressive Republican platform. He lost in 1904, but he immediately launched a new effort and won in 1906.

Crawford's fortunes had changed dramatically. He entered the governorship with a solid majority of progressive legislators in both houses and declared in his inaugural speech that each element of his campaign platform would be fulfilled. Subsequent legislative sessions did just that: railroad passes were banned; strict regulations were placed on lobbyists; a "comprehensive and practical" direct primary law was enacted, corporate campaign contributions were prohibited; and public disclosure of campaign funds was required. The legislature also passed ten laws relating to railroads. "Never," wrote Armin, "were a governor's recommendations taken so seriously in a South Dakota legislature and never before or afterward did that body enact so much progressive legislation."[55]

Crawford's success as governor put him in great demand as a conference speaker, and he often held forth on what he saw as his core beliefs. By 1907, his rhetoric was in step with the "social gospel" being propounded nationally by leaders such as Walter Rauschenbusch. Speaking to a Presbyterian group in Missouri, Crawford declared:

> Everywhere about us, alongside of wealth and luxury and plenty, dwell squalor, poverty, and wretchedness. Shouts of joy are mingled with the cries of despair. The human life in the world is the thing that appeals to me. You cannot fill churches nowadays to hear discussions of nice questions of theology and points of doctrine. You cannot reach the great masses by talking to them about the rewards and punishments in the next world. They can be reached upon the warm human side by sympathetic and practical help.[56]

Such speeches emphasized religion as *action*, and insisted—as had his mentor—that real faith cannot stay within the walls of a church. The specific words went beyond what Blackburn might have preached, but they align well with Crawford's recollection that Blackburn's "heart went out to the whole world."[57]

Crawford's United States Senate career from 1909 to 1915 was less spectacular than his governorship. Arriving in Washington, he was immediately confronted by the Payne-Aldrich tariff reduction bill, ostensibly offered to reduce the burden of taxes on a variety of imported goods. On closer examination, Crawford found that the complex bill was deceptive and that it would actually increase tariffs on most items. Yet, in a last-minute decision under pressure from President William Howard Taft, Crawford voted for the bill. Only later would he fully grasp his error. By voting with the Republican "old guard," he was seen to be supporting, early in his freshman term, what the midwestern progressives had been working hard to defeat.[58] Crawford did win plaudits for his key role in the struggle to enact the Seventeenth Amendment—enacting direct election of senators—but it was not enough. In 1914, the actual voters of every state chose their senators, and South Dakotans rejected Crawford.

His political career ended, Crawford came home to a state where the reforms he had spearheaded were taken for granted. As new figures such as Peter Norbeck, the powerful progressive governor and three-time United States senator, took the spotlight, the memory of Crawford largely faded from public view. Back in Huron, Crawford maintained his law practice, served on the board of the college, and tended to the needs of his clients. Perhaps as a reflection of Blackburn's admonition to "bless the stranger," and perhaps in atonement for his earlier questionable land dealings, Crawford served, with sporadic pay, as legal counsel for several groups of Hutterites—pacifists—who, in the wake of the Great War, were constrained to abandon their South Dakota lands for Canada. Crawford filed multiple briefs defending the much-reviled group's claim to legitimate status as a religious corporation with full rights to hold and sell their lands. In a few short years, he had gone from riding an immense wave of popularity to defending a deeply unpopular immigrant group.[59]

When Crawford died in 1944, his biographer noted, most of the state's citizens had forgotten him and his past achievements. But a week after his memorial service in the Huron Presbyterian church—presided over by his son, the Rev. Robert Dean Crawford—those citizens unconsciously honored him in another way. They flocked to local polls to vote in South Dakota's primary election.[60] Having been instantiated in law and accepted as normative, the origins of the primary law had become largely invisible. The same was true of other important elements that had shaped the state.

In a chronicle composed several years after statehood, Crawford's mentor had observed that the creation "of civic Dakota has been the work of statesmen," including "the farmer, the merchant, the lawyer, the physician, the editor and the college president."[61] As a historian, Blackburn believed that, absent such chronicles as he had written, these men and their work would be quickly forgotten. The Swing heresy trial was seen, if noticed at all, as a mere footnote in history. In his memorial of Blackburn's life, Thomas L. Riggs mentioned the affair, but saw little meaning in it. "No one now remembers this trial," he wrote; "we do not know what it was about and [we] wonder what was gained by it." Riggs explained, "Dr. Blackburn did not hold to Professor Swing's views, but defended the man in his right to hold these without being branded a heretic."[62] The trial had indeed faded from public memory. Yet its successful resolution—thanks in part to Blackburn— signaled a degree of tolerance and breadth that would later be taken for granted, in much the same way that the progressive reforms of the first decade would soon be assumed to be normative. The religious energies that had driven Patton and his partisans to heresy-hunting in Chicago had been channeled—again, partly through Blackburn— toward public service and political reform in South Dakota.

The situation might have turned out differently. The growth of genuine respect for conscience and toleration of disagreement was no more inevitable in the western prairies than it was elsewhere. Had McCormick's partisans won the 1874 heresy trial, their vision of a narrower, more dogmatic Presbyterianism might have made greater headway in the Midwest, imparting a different sort of influence to the Presbyterian denomination and perhaps to the broader society.[63] The career paths of Blackburn and his former colleague at Northwest Seminary, the arch-conservative Francis Patton, hint also at divergent possibilities. Whereas Blackburn cast his fortunes to the frontier with its boisterous energies and uncertainties, Patton returned to the heart of elite Presbyterianism, serving as president of Princeton College from 1888 to 1902 until a singularly influential Old School Presbyterian by the name of Woodrow Wilson succeeded him. Patton's leadership at Princeton saw numerical growth but reflected the same conservatism —both in doctrinal and practical matters—that characterized his earlier career. According to Wilson biographer William Maynard, Patton had become a "lazy president" who increasingly "seemed hopeless behind his muttonchops" and was caricatured as "sitting for hours in his

study 'grasping a cologne scented handkerchief in his thin hands.'"
Confronted with concerns that Princeton was becoming a domain of
the privileged classes, Patton had replied with a shrug, "Princeton is a
rich man's college."[64] It is hard to envision such a man transplanting
himself to a western frontier town to expose himself to the rigors of
a pioneer academic life. It is even harder to conceive of a complacent
Brahmin such as Patton providing serious inspiration for an ambitious western politician such as Coe Crawford.

As for the specific progressive legislation for which Crawford would
be noted, there is little evidence to suggest that Blackburn directly
inspired any of it. Indeed, both men had resisted the populism of the
early 1890s that presaged the intense stream of progressive reform
over which Crawford would later preside. But Blackburn's support of
the iconoclastic preacher David Swing, his resistance to the stultifying
conservatism of McCormick, the sensitivity he gained from his unfair treatment in Chicago and North Dakota, and the value he placed
on individual initiative, all suggest that he would have cheered the
success of Crawford and of his political agenda had he lived to see
it. Moreover, the intense, lively political persona Crawford exhibited
in his campaigns are certainly in line with the qualities Blackburn
often praised in speeches and sermons. Crawford's bold career as a
progressive—his break with the railroad, his revolt against the established South Dakota political machine, and his efforts to shift power
away from entrenched interests—all fit well within the framework of
values Blackburn often extolled. This framework, while emanating
from within a denominational tradition so conservative that it officially titled itself "Old School," served to nurture a genuine respect for
individuality, liberty, and public service. Its net effect was to impart a
broadening influence that eased Crawford's transition into bold progressive leadership. These values are among the key ingredients in a
Dakota civic tradition wide enough to nurture both steadfastly conservative and audaciously liberal tendencies. Expressed through the
life of a highly respected educator, clergyman, and historian, these
virtues would add a measure of benevolent seasoning to the civic life
of a broadening West. They are what Coe I. Crawford had in mind
when he described his mentor as "the real coin. No sham. No veneer.
The real thing. . . . I remember how he always asked the Lord to 'bless

the stranger within these gates;' and in a thousand ways his voice comes back to me across the intervening years."[65]

NOTES

1. Calvin Perry Armin, "Coe I. Crawford and the Progressive Movement in South Dakota," *South Dakota Historical Collections* 32 (1964): 131.

2. Quoted ibid., p. 28.

3. William M. Blackburn, "Individuality," H74.10, Folder #50, Blackburn Manuscripts, State Archives Collection, South Dakota State Historical Society (SDSHS), Pierre.

4. Louis Geiger, *University on the Northern Plains: A History of the University of North Dakota, 1883–1958* (Grand Forks: University of North Dakota Press, 1958), p. 32.

5. Coe I. Crawford, "William Blackburn," *Huron College Quarterly* 1 (Oct. 1923): 11.

6. Armin's substantial biography of Crawford is complemented by Edward LeRoy Meyer's Ph.D. dissertation on Crawford's rhetorical career, "Coe I. Crawford and the Persuasion of the Progressive Movement in South Dakota" (PhD diss., University of Minnesota, 1975). A contemporary observer said Crawford was "by far the most spirited, logical and convincing campaign orator the state has ever produced" ("Coe I. Crawford," in *Who's Who in South Dakota*, ed. O. W. Coursey [Mitchell, S.Dak.: Educator School Supply, 1913], p. 27).

7. Jon K. Lauck, *Prairie Republic: The Political Culture of Dakota Territory, 1879–1889* (Norman: University of Oklahoma Press, 2007), p. 55.

8. Bradley J. Longfield, *Presbyterians and American Culture: A History* (Louisville, Ky.: Westminster John Knox Press, 2013), pp. 95–96.

9. C. C. Goen, *Broken Churches Broken Nation: Denominational Schisms and the Coming of the American Civil War* (Macon, Ga.: Mercer University Press, 1985), pp. 12–13.

10. Sylvester Scovel, "Inaugural Address: The West and Western Institutions," in James Wood, *Memoir of Sylvester Scovel, D. D., Late President of Hanover College* (New Albany, Ind.: John B. Anderson, 1851), pp. 129–30.

11. Blackburn, "The Presidents of Hanover College," B#14, Scrapbook, Blackburn Manuscripts, SDSHS. Scovel made a strong impression on Blackburn for his "deep interest in our spiritual welfare" and his leadership of the school during a plague of cholera, to which Scovel finally succumbed on 4 July 1849.

12. Blackburn, untitled manuscript, n.d., Folder #35, William Maxwell Blackburn Collection, Chester Fritz Library Special Collections, University of North Dakota (UND). This manuscript, which dwells repeatedly on the thought of "power" and "the sublime," is one of Blackburn's most fascinating pieces of

writing. The approximate date of the manuscript is evident from its reference to famous orator Edward Everett, whom Blackburn had recently heard giving his famous speech on George Washington. Everett delivered this speech more than one hundred times during an 1856–1857 tour, and Blackburn's manuscript suggests that it had quite an impact on him. *See National Cyclopedia of American Biography* (1904), s.v. "Everett, Edward."

13. "Old School" Presbyterianism, as distinct from "New School" Presbyterianism, refers to a formal denominational schism that lasted from 1837 to 1870. Theological differences relating to the interpretation of Calvinism had caused the split, but broader ideas about society were also involved. Historian Lefferts Loetscher explains: "Old Schoolers were more accustomed to a hierarchical view of society and of church government. New Schoolers, prominent in the North, laid more stress on individual liberty and allowed a greater role for human feelings and will" (Loetscher, *The Broadening Church: A Study of Theological Issues in the Presbyterian Church since 1869* [Philadelphia: University of Pennsylvania Press, 1954], pp. 5–6). Blackburn's emphasis on individuality ran counter to this formula, which would tend to place him closer to New School thinking, though he was a minister in good standing in the Old School wing.

14. Blackburn published over forty full-length books in his lifetime. For a complete list of his publications and extant sermons, *see* Ken Smith, *American Educator: The Life of William Maxwell Blackburn* (M.A. thesis, University of North Dakota, 1998), app. Blackburn's history of the church was aimed at all audiences, not just Presbyterians. His preface reflects an irenic approach consistent with his belief in individuality. "Decided as are my convictions in theology and polity," he wrote, "due heed has been given to the following maxim of Lord Bacon: 'It is the office of history to represent the events themselves, together with the counsels, and to leave the observations and conclusions thereupon to the liberty and faculty of every man's judgment'" (Blackburn, *History of the Christian Church, From its Origin to the Present Time* [Cincinnati, Ohio: Cranston & Stowe, 1879], p. 4).

15. Hutchinson, *Cyrus Hall McCormick: Harvest, 1856–1884* (New York: D. Appleton-Century Co., 1935), p. 7. Hutchinson added that McCormick "was often willing to defer decision upon important business matters during this period if the needs of his denomination seemed to require his whole attention."

16. Quoted in Joseph Fort Newton, *David Swing, Poet Preacher* (Chicago, Ill.: Unity Publishing Co., 1909), p. 59.

17. Hutchinson, *Cyrus Hall McCormick*, pp. 232–34.

18. Patton's first book, *The Inspiration of the Scriptures* (1869) marked him as a rising star amid conservative Old School Presbyterians. His early life and his time in Chicago are discussed in James H. Moorhead, *Princeton Seminary in American Religion and Culture* (Grand Rapids, Mich.: Wm. B. Eerdmans, 2012),

pp. 228–32. The appeal of Patton to the McCormick wing of Chicago Presbyterianism is readily apparent in the speeches that marked his induction into the professorship. *See The Presbyterian Theological Seminary of the North-West* (Chicago, Ill.: Inter-Ocean, 1873), pp. 8–9.

19. It is not clear what effect this inequity in pay had on the other professors, but it must have stimulated some resentment against Patton and McCormick. After 1882, an equal pay policy was adopted at the seminary, "as it was known that the new professors would not accept positions in an institution where such inequalities prevailed" (Le Roy J. Halsey, *A History of the McCormick Theological Seminary of the Presbyterian Church* [Chicago: By the Seminary, 1893], pp. 276–77). Prior to 1873, Arthur Swazey had served as editor of the *Interior*, and William Blackburn had contributed numerous articles. For example, Blackburn contributed the first article in the first issue of the *Interior*, 17 Mar. 1871.

20. *Chicago Tribune*, 1 Mar. 1874.

21. David Johnson et al., eds., *The Trial of the Rev. David Swing* (Chicago, Ill.: Jansen, McClurg, & Co., 1874), pp. 8, 10, 13–14.

22. Not only was the trial open to reporters, it also followed, in accordance with the Presbyterian tradition, strict formal procedures that were catalogued and published, along with complete transcripts of all testimonies. The official record of the proceedings, made available by the Chicago Presbytery as Johnson, *Trial of the Rev. David Swing,* contains 286 pages. The quotations from the trial come from this source.

23. Johnson, *Trial of Rev. David Swing,* p. 232.

24. Ibid., p. 281–82.

25. Newton, *David Swing*, p. 243.

26. *Chicago Tribune*, 21 May, p. 4., 10 May, p. 11, 1874

27. Hutchinson, *Cyrus Hall McCormick*, pp. 264–66. McCormick warned Patton that his departure would bring "almost entire temporary ruin" to Presbyterian efforts in the Northwest. Patton's decision to leave seems related more to career ambition than pay, as McCormick promised him a salary that would equal any he could obtain elsewhere. Wilson's career at Princeton and his succession of Patton is detailed in William B. Maynard, *Woodrow Wilson: Princeton to the Presidency* (New Haven, Conn.: Yale University Press, 2008).

28. Blackburn, "How Far is the Church Responsible for Modern Skepticism in Regard to Christianity?" F#50, Blackburn Manuscripts, SDSHS.

29. Quoted ibid.

30. Blackburn's salary at Central Church was announced in a clipping from a Chicago newspaper that he kept in his personal scrapbook. B#12, Scrapbook, Blackburn Manuscripts, SDSHS.

31. Iddings to Blackburn, 1 Mar. 1884, F#39, Blackburn Collection, UND. The Iddings letter is strong testimony to the importance of networking among

friends within a religious denomination for gaining access to secular institutions. Subsequent controversies at UND suggest that this private networking was a source of antipathy for those outside such circles.

32. Noyes to Blackburn, 18 Mar. 1884, ibid. Noyes, a longtime friend of Blackburn, had served as counsel for the defense in the 1874 heresy trial. Johnson, *Trial of the Rev. David Swing*, p. 8.

33. A detailed account of the university's first year, including the hiring and role of President Blackburn, and subsequent controversies can be found in Geiger, *University on the Northern Plains*.

34. Iddings to Blackburn, 1 Mar. 1884. *See also* Iddings to Blackburn, 26 Dec. 1884, F#39, Blackburn Collection, UND.

35. *Grand Forks Daily Herald*, 15 May 1885.

36. The preponderance of evidence points to disagreements about curriculum and institutional purpose as the main root of the controversies. Various personal and political conflicts were intertwined in this bigger question. For a detailed discussion, *see* Ken Smith, "The Struggle to Define Higher Education at the University of North Dakota, 1883–1892," *North Dakota History* 3 (Summer/Fall 1999): 17–29.

37. Riggs, "William Maxwell Blackburn," p. 31.

38. Blackburn, clipping with explanatory notes, B#12, Scrapbook, Blackburn Manuscripts, SDSHS. Pierre University was one of two Dakota colleges that Presbyterians planted in the early 1880s. Jamestown College faced similar circumstances in the 1890s. It closed in 1893 in the wake of regional economic crisis and was revived again in 1909 under the leadership of Barends Kroeze. *See* Kroeze, *A Prairie Saga* (St. Paul, Minn.: North Central Publishing Co., 1952).

39. *Pierre Collegian*, Oct. 1887, p. 3.

40. Armin, "Coe I. Crawford," p. 34.

41. Crawford, "William M. Blackburn," p. 8.

42. George F. McDougall, *Over a Century of Leadership: South Dakota Territorial and State Governorships* (Sioux Falls, S.Dak.: Center for Western Studies, 1987), p. 82.

43. Armin, "Coe I. Crawford," pp. 42–43

44. Blackburn, "Citizenship and Christianity," *Presbyterian Chronicler* 6 (15 Jan. 1887). Such rhetoric, it should be noted, seems to approach the blurring of church and state, a phenomenon with which Blackburn was familiar, although he was not entirely consistent in his response to it.

45. *Sioux Falls Argus Leader,* 12, 29 Oct. 1895.

46. Armin, "Coe I. Crawford," p. 50.

47. "Ocolic Demands," *Pierre Weekly Free Press*, 1892, B#11, Blackburn Manuscripts, SDSHS. Blackburn clipped each column and kept them in a scrapbook

with his own annotations. "Ocolic Demands" is a play on the Ocala Platform, a declaration adopted at a large Populist gathering at Ocala, Florida, in 1890. Central to this platform was the Subtreasury System, a scheme widely viewed as socialistic. For details on the Ocala convention and its implications, *see* Lawrence Goodwyn, *Democratic Promise: The Populist Moment in America* (New York: Oxford University Press, 1976), pp. 223–32.

48. Alice Joyce notes, "For thirteen years, the initiative and referendum question was kept before the people of the state by the Farmer's Alliance, the Knights of Labor, the Initiative and Referendum League, and the Populist Party" (Joyce, "South Dakota Progressivism," 1889–1926 [Master's thesis, Catholic University of America, 1959], p. 6).

49. By 1900, the wind seemed to have gone out of the Populist party. The organization held its national convention in Sioux Falls, but attendance was sparse. Governor Andrew Lee gave the opening address in a tent designed to hold twelve thousand, but only fifteen hundred showed up. The Populists adopted an unpopular anti-imperialist plank in their 1900 platform, which hurt them in the wake of the patriotic fervor of the Spanish-American War. Furthermore, economic conditions had improved. These factors, plus the powerful campaigning of Theodore Roosevelt and Mark Hanna, spelled overwhelming defeat for the Populists in 1900. For more on the Populist Party in South Dakota, *see* R. Alton Lee, *Principle over Party: The Farmers' Alliance and Populism in South Dakota, 1880–1900* (Pierre: South Dakota Historical Society Press, 2011).

50. *Announcement of Huron College, Huron, South Dakota, for 1898–1899, With Courses of Study* (Huron, S.Dak.: Huronite Print, 1898), pp. 4–5; Blackburn, "A History of Dakota," *South Dakota Historical Collections* 1 (1902):43–80.

51. Crawford, "William M. Blackburn," p. 11.

52. Quoted in Armin, "Coe I. Crawford," p. 57.

53. Ibid., p. 121. Crawford's papers contain dozens of letters regarding passes. Some ask for year-long passes, others for sight-seeing trips, trips for mothers-in-law, trips for a young schoolteacher who wanted to see the Black Hills, trips to political conventions, and so forth. Some writers reminded Crawford that others had received passes, implying that fairness required the granting of all requests. Immediately after the 1898 election, Marvin G. Hughitt, president of the Chicago & North Western, wrote to Crawford recommending that since the campaign was closed, "We must now return as far as possible to the practice of declining to grant free interstate transportation." Hughitt said nothing, however, of intrastate passes and added, "in cases where it may seem necessary to give favors of this nature, it should be done in some form that will not disclose the fact that it is free transportation" (Hughitt to Crawford, 7 Nov. 1898, Coe I. Crawford Papers, H74.186, State Archives Collection, SDSHS).

54. Armin, "Coe I. Crawford," p. 79.

55. Ibid., p. 124.

56. "Gov. Crawford Speaks," *Cincinnati Tribune*, 15 Nov. 1907. Walter Rauschenbusch's influential *Christianity and the Social Crisis* (New York: Macmillan Company, 1907), which laid a framework for what became known as the Social Gospel, had been in print for nearly a year before this particular speech. It seems likely that Crawford had read the book. Decades later, reading Rauchenbusch would have a profound impact on another prominent South Dakota progressive politician, George McGovern. Biographer Thomas J. Knock notes, "Of all the books McGovern would ever read, none surpassed the impact of *Christianity and the Social Crisis*" (Knock, *The Rise of a Prairie Statesman: The Life and Times of George McGovern* [Princeton, N.J.: Princeton University Press, 2016], p. 83).

57. Crawford, "William Blackburn," p. 11.

58. Armin, "Coe I. Crawford," p. 151.

59. Joanita Kant, *Hutterites of South Dakota: The Schmiedeleut* (Coral Springs, Fla.: Llumina Press, 2011), pp. 20–24, summarizes the abuse the colonies endured for their refusal to purchase Liberty Bonds or enlist their young men for service. Newspapers encouraged persecution of Hutterites through inflammatory editorials. Acts of theft and violence against the colonies ensued. A patriotic citizens council sued Bon Homme Colony in an attempt to expel it from the state. Two Hutterite men, imprisoned for resisting the draft, died under severe abuse. "Daily life," explains Kant, "became intolerable for Hutterites on the home front," and ultimately "seventeen of eighteen Hutterite colonies in South Dakota, and one of two colonies in Montana, moved to Canada. As a result, only two Hutterite colonies, including Bon Homme in South Dakota, remained in the United States" (p. 24). The Crawford Papers, H74.186, SDSHS, contain legal briefs and responses relating to multiple South Dakota Hutterische Gemeindes, including Rockport, Elm Spring, Wolf Creek, Lake Byron, and Yale colonies. These groups were all under various legal challenges relating to their efforts to sell their property without being defrauded by unscrupulous land grabbers. Tracing the specifics is beyond the scope of this essay, but Crawford's dealings with the Hutterites offer a potentially revealing look into his social attitudes after the end of his political career.

60. Armin, "Coe I. Crawford," pp. 217–18.

61. Blackburn, "History of Dakota," p. 79. Blackburn had in mind a particular generation of leaders—"most of whom are still alive"—who had framed the state constitution.

62. Riggs, "William Maxwell Blackburn," p. 29.

63. The importance of the Swing trial has been duly noted by William R. Hutchison, who argues that it was one of several nationally publicized ecclesiastical controversies that foreshadowed the eventual fundamentalist/modernist

schism nearly fifty years later. "Self-consciousness as a modernist movement lay some years in the future," noted Hutchison, "but the foundations had been laid for the definition . . . of a New Theology in which the modernist impulse would be a major force" (Hutchison, *The Modernist Impulse in American Protestantism* [Cambridge, Mass.: Harvard University Press, 1976], p. 75).

64. Maynard, *Woodrow Wilson*, p. 56. Woodrow Wilson, in contrast, was an activist president who initiated Princeton's transformation into a genuine modern university.

65. Crawford, "William Blackburn" p. 11.

ERIC STEVEN ZIMMER, ART MARMORSTEIN,

AND MATTHEW REMMICH

5 | "FEWER RABBIS THAN U. S. SENATORS"

JEWISH POLITICAL ACTIVISM IN

SOUTH DAKOTA

. . .

Sometime in the late 1960s, a telephone rang on the Rosebud
Indian Reservation. "Hello?" answered William J. ("Bill")
Janklow, an ambitious young attorney who had spent the
last few years working legal aid there.

Skipping any salutation, a voice on the line from Rapid
City probed: "What's a Jewish kid [like you] doing down on the
reservation?"

"Well, I'm not Jewish," Janklow replied. "My father was."

"Mr. Janklow," the man parried, "your name is 'Janklow,' right?"

"Yes," the lawyer said, confused and curious.

"'Janklow' is 'Jankelov [in Yiddish],'" the man asserted. "'Jankelov'
means 'son of Jankel,'" which was itself Yiddish for Jack or Jacob. The
man quipped, "Nobody who's a Jankelov isn't Jewish somewhere."[1]

This exchange launched a long friendship between Stanford M.
("Stan") Adelstein and Bill Janklow. Nearing forty years old, Adelstein
was a wealthy Jewish businessman in Rapid City who had been involved in state and national Republican Party politics, as well as local
affairs, for decades. Janklow would become the South Dakota attorney
general a few years later, then serve four terms as governor and briefly
represent the state in the United States House of Representatives in
the first years of the twenty-first century. Interested in American Indian issues, Adelstein had heard about the work Janklow was doing
on the reservation and called for a friendly introduction, using his
joke about the lawyer's heritage as an ice breaker.

Their shared heritage offered entrée into a relationship emblematic of Jewish political organizing in South Dakota, as well as of the
nature of the state's political culture. A few years after their introduction, Adelstein would write Attorney General Janklow, asking whether
non-ordained lay leaders could marry Jewish couples in South Dakota.

With no rabbi for several hundred miles, the Synagogue of the Hills in Rapid City struggled to officiate celebrations—such as weddings —that extended over spiritual and legal boundaries. A practicing Lutheran who did not identify closely with his Jewish ancestry, Janklow nonetheless empathized with Adelstein's concerns. He carefully affirmed an earlier legal opinion that allowed certain synagogue officials to solemnize marriages. To avoid further confusion about this issue, however, Janklow encouraged the synagogue to draft a set of bylaws that would distinguish it "from just a group of individuals practicing Judaism," which, Janklow clarified, "probably would not constitute a church recognized under the marriage statutes."[2] Using his heritage to make personal connections and advocate for minority groups, as he often did, Adelstein had secured in Janklow a political ally whose position helped a small group of Jews sort out a legal difficulty in a very Christian state.

In his book *God is Not One,* Steven Prothero points out that with only around fourteen million followers, Judaism is much smaller than other major world religions. But in terms of historical significance, he contends, Judaism is arguably the most important of all. Indeed, despite their small share of the world population, Jews have had a disproportionately large impact on many communities around the world. Another writer, historian Max I. Dimont, has chronicled the remarkable survival of the Jewish community over the millennia, as well as the effects Diaspora Jews have had on many civilizations. Treating Jewish influence with a lighter touch, comedian Adam Sandler's "The Hanukkah Song" provides a list of famous American Jews, including virologist Jonas Salk, who developed the first polio vaccine, "Ben and Jerry" of ice cream fame, and actress Scarlett Johansson, but the list merely scratches the surface.[3] Jewish influence also permeates American politics. Three members of the current United States Supreme Court, eight United States senators, and twenty-one members of Congress are Jewish, along with several of President Donald J. Trump's cabinet secretaries and senior advisors. Around twenty percent of Nobel Prize winners are Jewish, including the 2016 recipient of the Nobel Prize in Literature, Bob Dylan.

How big does a Jewish congregation have to be before it begins to play a prominent role in its community? And at what point does a Jewish presence begin to affect politics in a major way? The legacies of Jewish activism in South Dakota suggest that even tiny Jewish communities have measurable political influence, even when it is indirect and—as has been the case for most of South Dakota's history—overlooked. A few prominent members of the Sioux Falls, Aberdeen, and Rapid City Jewish communities have leveraged their relationships and political influence within the state. The three synagogues in South Dakota have also been enclaves of political action but rarely for a single party or cause. Instead, they have been home to people who, bonded by their faith, knit themselves into the tapestries of small communities.[4] Simply put, South Dakota Jews inscribed themselves on the state's political landscape in small but significant ways.

There have never been many Jewish people in South Dakota. In 1899, there were nearly eighteen hundred; by 2016, the number had diminished to only two hundred fifty, the fewest in the nation.[5] During his many decades living and working in South Dakota, Stan Adelstein grew fond of jesting that his state had "fewer rabbis than U.S. Senators."[6] South Dakota's Jewish immigrants arrived in three waves. First, in the late nineteenth century, Jewish families came to the United States from Europe, settled in midwestern states such as Iowa, Illinois, and Minnesota, then pressed westward.[7] Seeking religious and ethnic camaraderie, they established small enclaves. By the 1890s, the eastern half of South Dakota was home to "a good many Jewish families," predominantly "merchants, businessmen, and even some farmers," the latter of whom were encouraged to move to the Dakotas by the New York-based Jewish Agricultural Aid Society.[8] For example, Ashley, North Dakota, about sixty miles northwest of Aberdeen, had a sizeable number of Jewish homesteaders.[9] Owning one's own farm was a particular source of pride to a people who, for much of their history, had lived in places where Jews were not permitted to own land.

East-central South Dakota was also home to a group of Jewish settlers who came to the state as part of the Am Olam movement. Throughout the late-nineteenth and early-twentieth centuries, anti-Semitic violence in Russia pushed Jewish emigrants to the United States. It also contributed to the development of several intellectual movements, including Zionism. Am Olam, which meant "eternal people," argued that by establishing agricultural communes in new countries, Jews could maintain a sense of cohesion while improving themselves and their communities through manual farm labor.

Emphasizing ethnic Jewishness over religious orthodoxy, Am Olam communities first appeared in the United States in the 1880s in such states as Montana, Kansas, Nebraska, and the Dakotas.[10]

The first Am Olam Jews in South Dakota established two communes about twenty-five miles southwest of Mitchell just a few months apart in 1882. With more than forty Jewish families between them, the communities struggled along, eventually disbanding by the end of the decade. They failed because their "emphasis on community and social equality did not mesh with the intense individualism and fierce competitiveness" of American society. Some Am Olam families went to Sioux Falls; others left the state entirely.[11]

While some Jewish immigrants to the Dakotas tried to establish themselves as farmers, most took more traditional Jewish occupations. In Aberdeen, for instance, Jews were heavily involved in retail. David and Anna Strauss, a German-Jewish couple opened a shop in Aberdeen as early as 1887, while Isaac Pred started a clothing store in the city with his sons Abe and Dan in 1916.[12] The Feinstein brothers ran a similar business under the slogan, "If it came from Feinstein's, it must be right."[13] There were Jewish-owned grocery stores, scrap yards, and other businesses as well, and more Jews trickled into the area over the next few decades.[14]

Although they had no rabbi and often lacked enough worshippers for a *minyan*—a quorum of ten people (usually men) above age thirteen—Aberdeen-area Jews celebrated the High Holidays of Rosh Hashanah and Yom Kippur together. Before 1915, Jewish families held religious services in a rented building in downtown Aberdeen. In 1916, the group purchased a former Wesleyan church and, in March 1917, officially incorporated the Congregation B'nai Isaac. By the 1930s, some fifty families worshipped there, and the Aberdeen Jewish community thrived. In 1951, they remodeled the building, exchanging its steeple for four angular peaks and lifted the building from its foundation so that a full basement—replete with a recreation hall/meeting room and kosher kitchen—could be added.[15]

In the late nineteenth century, two congregations developed in and around Sioux Falls. Orthodox Jews from a variety of Eastern European countries and Reformed Jews from Germany, similar to Jewish immigrants from other areas, came as homesteaders and entrepreneurs, settling in the southeastern corner of what became South

Dakota. During this time, the Jews met as an informal congregation in various venues throughout the city, but by the turn of the century, both denominations had established congregations in Sioux Falls. In 1903, the Reform Jews organized the Mount Zion Cemetery Society to manage funerals for Sioux Falls Jews at a site near the Mount Pleasant Cemetery on Twelfth Street. By 1916, the number of Jews residing in Sioux Falls justified the founding of a synagogue, and both congregations came together to purchase the United Evangelical Church at 320 North Minnesota Avenue. After some minor remodeling, the facility was converted from church to synagogue, and the congregation went forth as the Sons of Israel.[16]

This period of Jewish unity in Sioux Falls, however, proved short-lived. Reflecting broader denominational disagreements, local Reform Jews took umbrage with the Orthodox-leaning services orchestrated by the Sons of Israel. Feeling alienated in their own congregation, the Reformers began meeting separately and secured formal recognition as a separate group by the Union of American Hebrew Congregations in 1919. By 1924, the Reformers outnumbered their orthodox counterparts and purchased the Grace Lutheran Church at 523 West Fourteenth Street, redesigning the building to fit their needs. They named the new facility Mount Zion Synagogue after a temple of the same name in Saint Paul, Minnesota. In 1973, the Jewish population faded in and around Sioux Falls, forcing the remaining members of the Sons of Israel, the Orthodox-leaning congregation, to sell their synagogue and disband in 1975, and the new owner demolished the building. Similar to Jewish congregations across South Dakota, Mount Zion continues to offer services today but has struggled as young Jewish families have moved away.[17]

Far away on South Dakota's western edge in Lawrence County, another Jewish hub developed in Deadwood in the late 1870s. Several prominent Jews helped write Deadwood's early story. Sol Bloom established a clothing and shoe store on Main Street, while Jacob Goldberg ran a grocery. Nathan Colman served as a postmaster and, later, as an electoral judge in Deadwood and a delegate at several Republican state conventions. He was not a rabbi, but he nonetheless led celebrations, including weddings, that were conducted in the Jewish-owned Franklin Hotel. The Deadwood Jewish community used a Torah that had been shipped over from Germany in 1888, celebrating weddings and bar and bat mitzvahs for decades.[18]

By 1930, the core of the Black Hills population had shifted from Lawrence County to Pennington County. The number of Deadwood Jews had dwindled when the gold rush cooled off and Jewish parents "encouraged their children to seek their livelihood in the professions, which required education in distant cities."[19] In the 1940s, so few Jews resided in Deadwood that a man delivered the Torah to Stan Adelstein's childhood home. The move made sense: with no synagogue West River, Adelstein's parents—Morris and Bertha Adelstein, who owned a successful heavy construction company—could best care for the sacred scroll. It resided there for years, although its whereabouts were unknown in the 1940s and 1950s when the Adelsteins moved to Denver. Not until Stan Adelstein returned to Rapid in the late 1950s was the document again used in regular celebrations.[20]

Smaller pockets of Jewish people dotted the plains. In 1905, twenty young couples and eighteen single men all homesteaded in a rural area some forty miles north of Quinn, which came to be known as "Jew Flats." Otherwise, small Jewish communities comprised of only a few families—and occasionally, even just a single individual—offered a place to speak Yiddish, take in a kosher meal, or observe Shabbat on the unforgiving Dakota plains. Adelstein's grandmother, Bertha Martinsky, for example, homesteaded early in the twentieth century, then opened a mercantile store in Kadoka. A devout adherent of Jewish traditions, she refused to work on Shabbat or during the High Holidays, and she received kosher meats by rail from Des Moines, Iowa, making hers one of only a few kosher kitchens in many miles. Her home thus became a common stopover for Jews passing through West River, keeping Jewish traditions alive after Deadwood's Jews dissipated.[21]

As this brief history indicates, the continued presence of Jewish communities was never a given on South Dakota prairies. Yet many Jews were able to thrive and leave a mark on their local communities and sometimes the state as a whole. Early in the twentieth century, the Mount Zion congregation produced David Mendel, who served as a state legislator from 1910 to 1912, and the better-known Benjamin Strool, a Russian Jewish immigrant who founded Strool Township on a homestead tract in northwestern Perkins County in 1905.

A merchant by trade, he supplied the township's residents, as well as bypassers and those living on outlying ranchland. Strool Township boomed briefly, boasting a bank, hardware store, barber shop, and local newspaper. Yet Strool himself struggled to attend Jewish services and follow religious dictum: his non-Jewish wife made small culinary adjustments where she could, cooking pie crusts, for instance, with butter rather than pork lard. As drought wiped out area homesteads, most township residents left during the second decade of the twentieth century. Strool opened a shop in Sioux Falls, but by 1920, he had returned to Perkins County, where he helped organize the Democratic Party Central Committee. In 1932, Strool won the office of the commissioner of school and public lands in the Democratic wave that brought Franklin Delano Roosevelt to the White House, Tom Berry to the governor's mansion, and former Rapid City mayor Theodore Werner to Congress. Strool later worked for the Office of Price Administration based out of Sioux Falls, and in 1948, he was South Dakota's alternate delegate to the Democratic National Convention that nominated Harry S Truman.[22]

Among the best examples of the disproportionate influence that members of southeastern South Dakota's tiny Jewish community wielded are Mort and Sylvia Henkin, who built a media empire in Sioux Falls. After his father Joe's death, Mort became president of both KSOO Radio and KFSY-TV. In 1964, he was elected president of the South Dakota Broadcasters Association.[23] Sportscaster, television personality, and Sioux Falls native Pat O'Brien recalled that Henkin was only the second Jew he had ever met and that he seemed an outsized character whose personality and talents belonged somewhere else—he "seemed big time," according to O'Brien, and "a New York kind of guy." Lucky for O'Brien, Henkin planted himself firmly in Sioux Falls, where he gave the future sportscaster his first opportunities in media.[24]

The Henkin family both fit into the Sioux Falls community and helped shape it. After serving in the Civil Air Patrol during World War II, a role for which she was later awarded the Congressional Gold Medal, Sylvia became an integral part of the family business. She was a notable on-air personality, and in the 1960s and 1970s, she pioneered a local daytime talk show called "Party Line." After Mort's death in

1974, Sylvia took over her husband's responsibilities as president and general manager of KSFY. In 1989, she was selected to the South Dakota Broadcaster's Hall of Fame. During her careers, Sylvia embodied the fact that civic engagement was one of the distinguishing features of Jewish influence on the political culture of South Dakota. She was the first woman to serve both as president of the Sioux Falls Chamber of Commerce and on the board of FirstBank South Dakota. She became a Sioux Falls city commissioner and served on the board of the local Young Men's Christian Association. Over many years of community activism, she earned the moniker "Grand Ol' Dame of Sioux Falls," while others just called her "Sioux Falls' biggest cheerleader." Who would have guessed that the person most responsible for starting the Sioux Falls Saint Patrick's Day parade was Jewish?[25]

Civic and political engagement and community service were also important to a handful of other prominent Sioux Falls Jews. Orrin Melton, for example, was president of the Sioux Falls Kiwanis Club, the Greater Sioux Falls Safety Council, and the Minnehaha County Mental Health Center. He was an active member of the Elks, Rotary International, and the Sioux Falls Chamber of Commerce, among other civic activities over a long career of public service that covered the latter half of the twentieth century. Another Jewish businessman from Sioux Falls, Joel Rosenthal, was a longtime Janklow ally and served as chairman of the state Republican Party for the last half of the 1980s and from 1995 to 2003.[26] Both are striking examples of how successfully Jews in South Dakota have been able to fit into and contribute to communities in the region. Sylvia Henkin said it best, telling one journalist that, over her long life, Sioux Falls has given her "a wonderful sense of belonging" and the distinct feeling that "I just don't know any place in the world I would be more comfortable in and feel more welcome."[27]

An exceptionally high commitment to civic engagement and a striking ability to fit into the larger community have likewise been hallmarks of the Aberdeen Jewish community. Many Congregation B'Nai Isaac members have influenced the political culture of the community through service, with some finding opportunities for more direct political involvement. One example was Moses Lindau. Born in 1910, he opened a law practice in Aberdeen just after World War II.

In 1950, Governor George T. Mickelson appointed him Brown County judge. Voters re-elected Lindau, a talented legal mind, to that position every other year until 1972.[28]

Early in his judicial career, Lindau focused on reducing juvenile delinquency, which he considered a major problem in the United States. He strongly believed in rehabilitation and critiqued a penal system that seemed more intent on punishment than helping troubled youths turn their lives around. Judge Lindau once observed that perhaps only ten percent of the juvenile cases that came before his bench involved true delinquents. The remainder were misguided children, often the victims of broken homes. Too many parents, Lindau thought, prioritized their own convenience over the needs of their children. Many were unwilling to maintain decent homes or refused to work through marital problems and provide the stability their children needed. For example, Lindau, sensing that a twelve-year-old defendant was acting out because of an unstable home life, declared the boy delinquent and ordered him to the Bethesda Children's Home in Beresford at his parents' expense. Within months, the boy's grades and behavior had improved. This experience also forced his parents to evaluate their relationship, and they divorced. Once the boy's father remarried and showed that his new relationship created a healthy environment for the boy, Lindau released him from Beresford. During his re-election campaign in 1956, Lindau touted his record on juvenile issues, noting that during his five years on the bench, he had helped reduced delinquency cases by eighty percent.[29]

Leaders of other faiths supported Lindau's actions. In 1966, his opponent penned a harsh newspaper advertisement questioning Lindau's judgment based on his heritage. Five local clergymen assembled a rebuttal, pointing out Lindau's work with the Catholic Charities, the Lutheran Welfare Society, and the Sunshine Bible Academy in his attempts to assist troubled youths. "From our observations and our dealings with Judge Lindau," the clergymen noted, "we are convinced that he conducts the Juvenile and County Court of Brown County and his own personal life in accordance with the teaching of our Lord and Savior, Jesus Christ."[30]

Lindau also considered mental health a paramount problem. In his spare time, he served as a member of both the Brown County Mental Health Association and the Northeastern Mental Health Center. Behind the bench, he recognized that alcoholism often exacerbated mental health issues. Committing alcoholics to a state hospital might help them sober up for a few weeks, but as he saw defendant after defendant relapse, Lindau preferred to lean on private community groups. He often required alcoholic perpetrators to report to Alcoholics Anonymous, where they had a better chance at long-term recovery.[31]

Other members of the B'Nai Isaac community took forays into the political arena. In 1953, Manley Feinstein left Feinstein Brothers, Inc., in Mitchell to help run Feinstein's Ready-to-Wear in Aberdeen. He became an integral part of several civic organizations, including the Aberdeen Chamber of Commerce and the Aberdeen Jaycees. For a time, he became the president of the Dakota Council of B'nai B'rith, an international Jewish civic group with a chapter in Bismark, North Dakota. Feinstein was elected to the Aberdeen School Board in 1962 and again in 1965, serving as board president for part of that time. Throughout the 1970s, he also served on the State Highway Commission following an appointment from Governor Richard Kneip.[32]

Perhaps Feinstein's most significant impact on state politics came via his ardent support of fellow Mitchell resident, George McGovern. Feinstein had supported McGovern since the Democrat's first congressional run in 1956, giving McGovern a new pair of size 12AA black slip-on shoes with a silver buckle at the beginning of each campaign. "Wear these shoes, and you won't lose," Feinstein promised.[33] Feinstein was one of seventeen South Dakota delegates to the 1972 Democratic convention, where he described a deep sense of satisfaction after helping McGovern win the party's nomination. He was excited to see the Democratic Party—long a bastion of racial discrimination, especially in the South—evolve. At the convention that year, Feinstein, a Jew from South Dakota, cast ballots alongside men and women, old and young, rich and poor, and from a variety of racial and ethnic backgrounds.[34] That year too, for only the second time in more than two decades (McGovern had lost his first senate bid in 1960), Feinstein's lucky shoes failed to deliver. The senator lost in a landslide to Richard Nixon in 1972, and Feinstein returned to the highway commission. Whether he would have served the McGovern administration, we will never know.

Electoral politics, however, was only a small part of the Aberdeen

Jewish community's influence. In 1965, the *Aberdeen American News* ran a story on Abe Pred, a third-generation member of the Pred clothing family. Although Pred had served as a state senator, his profiler focused on the major portion of Pred's community work: baseball. Pred himself possessed a rare athletic prowess, but throughout his life, he sponsored many local community teams. Over the years, those teams won seven state championships and became two-time runners-up at the national level.[35]

Although rabbis came and went from B'nai Isaac, many played significant roles in local affairs while they were there. The congregation was particularly robust in the early 1950s, and Rabbi Selig Auerbach led the congregation from 1950 to 1953. He held regular Sabbath services and led Hebrew school and a "Tallis and Teffilin Breakfast Club"—referring to the ceremonial cloth and wrap worn by the faithful—on Sunday mornings. Rabbi Auerbach's commitment to community extended beyond the synagogue's walls. He was part of the local ministerial association, serving as head of their public relations committee. He was involved in the Rotary Club and the Boys' Club and spoke at a meeting of the American Association of University Women on religious training in the home. He was also a guest speaker at what was then Northern State Teachers College and even gave the benediction at a special event honoring the Salvation Army captain and his wife. The rabbi's wife, Hilda Auerbach, was equally committed to the Aberdeen community, serving on the boards of the Howard Hedger Elementary School and the Young Women's Christian Association, despite that organization's clear religious affiliation. Hilda also played a leadership role in the local Girl Scouts.[36]

In March 1953, a few months after Rabbi Auerbach and his family moved to Wisconsin, Rabbi Abraham A. Kertes took over at B'nai Isaac. Born in Hungary, Kertes left Austria right before the Nazi annexation in 1938. Assigned to minister to Jewish refugees and Holocaust survivors after the war, he had lived for a time in Israel. But Aberdeen was his "eureka"—the place where Kertes found something special. The community offered more than tolerance—they offered love. Kertes and his wife spent more than ten years in Aberdeen, moving only when the rabbi's health declined. Kertes then bid farewell: "Aberdeen is my real home, not just a residence. The people of Aberdeen are my friends. From the mayor to all my neighbors, I love them all as my brothers who deserve to be loved, without regard to what church they attend."[37]

Although Aberdeen seems to have been a welcoming place for Jews, young people tended to go away to college, find a spouse and a career, and establish themselves elsewhere. Newspapers from the 1950s and 1960s are full of gleeful accounts of big Jewish weddings in Aberdeen —almost always followed by the note that bride and groom were going to make their home in cities such as New York. Fewer young couples meant fewer children, and B'nai Isaac dwindled to a point where it no longer received a permanent rabbi. Judaism is not a proselytizing religion, and if young Jewish couples choose not to remain in the community, their congregation can only survive if others move in. Such immigration was rare in Aberdeen through the middle and later decades of the twentieth century. Where earlier waves of Jews had come to the Dakota plains in search of land or opportunity in newly established towns, only jobs at Northern State University or one of the local hospitals now brought Jews to the community. The Jewish retail and grocery niches disappeared, and even Pred's and Feinstein's eventually shut their doors.

Despite the evaporation of most Jewish-owned businesses and the fact that the synagogue has no permanent rabbi, the small Jewish community still plays an outsized role in Aberdeen civic affairs. One couple, Bernice ("Bea") and Herschel Premack, have personified the continued influence of the small Congregation B'nai Isaac. Herschel was born into the third generation of Aberdeen's Premack family, which had long operated a scrap-dealing business. Bea moved to town upon her marriage to Hershel, and as a young couple during the 1950s, they supervised an active youth group at the synagogue. When there was no longer a rabbi to lead services, Herschel took over as lay leader. For nearly forty years, he has led regular Sabbath services at B'nai Isaac. Throughout that time, the Premacks have sought to promote understanding and tolerance among all faiths and ethnic backgrounds. In the 1950s, youths at B'nai Isaac hosted an open-house outreach program to Christian youth groups. Kids from a half-dozen organizations came to the synagogue for an event that one observer promised could educate Christian students about other religions while deepening their reverence for their own faith.[38]

More than a half century later, the tradition of promoting understanding and tolerance continues. Bea Premack and synagogue president Jerry Taylor hold many outreach events that include Methodists, Lutherans, and a Muslim student from Northern State University who participates in an evening study group. They lead students and church youth groups on synagogue tours and educate confirmation classes at Christian churches about the Jewish faith. Over the years, Bea Premack has racked up numerous awards and wide recognition for her community work. She received the Aberdeen Exchange Club's "Golden Deeds" award in 1991 and served on the board of the Northern State University Foundation, the Presentation College Advisory Board, the Aberdeen Area Arts Council, the Resource Center for Women, and the United Way. She was also named the honorary First Lady of Aberdeen and an Outstanding Volunteer in Arts and Culture for South Dakota. In 2009, she was appointed to the South Dakota Advisory Committee to the United States Civil Rights Commission. More recently, she has become a key player in the newly formed Aberdeen Area Diversity Committee.[39]

Another B'nai Isaac congregant, Gail Pickus, has been similarly active in the Aberdeen community. Like Premack, she held the honorary title First Lady of Aberdeen in the mid-1990s and has been recognized for her work with service projects such as Camp Courage, a program that provides a camping experience for young people with developmental challenges. Pickus has made extensive philanthropic contributions to the arts, and she has serviced with many groups, including Foster Grandparents, the Library Foundation Board, and the women's Jewish civic group Hadassah.[40]

What Rabbi Kertes said of Aberdeen in the 1950s is still accurate today: the Hub City has continued to welcome its small Jewish community. While Jews in other cities have long faced barriers to participation in civic affairs, this situation has not been the case in Aberdeen. Herman ("Buddy") Pickus, for instance, served as president of the Aberdeen Country Club—striking when one considers that, as recently as the 1990s, Jews still faced restrictive membership policies around the country. In 1994, the Anti-Defamation League had to fight to get Palm Beach's Shellfish Club opened to Jewish members, while Donald Trump claimed that his decision to open Mar-a-Lago to Jews and African Americans led Palm Beach officials to delay approvals for the nascent club.[41]

Less striking but perhaps more important is the connection between the Jewish community and Aberdeen's Masonic Lodge. In addition to their other civic, commercial, and cultural commitments, the men of B'nai Isaac have been extensively involved with Yelduz Shrine, with many—including Judge Lindau, Manley Feinstein, and Herschel Premack—playing prominent roles over the years. Perhaps this service is no great surprise when one considers the overlap between Masonic and synagogue core values, and their common emphasis on ethics, personal growth, tolerance, education, diversity, philanthropy, family, and community—all elements that have defined Aberdeen's small Jewish community for generations.[42]

Even though a number of Jews left South Dakota for seemingly better opportunities, one who would have a major political influence actually moved back to the state. Stan Adelstein returned to Rapid City in 1957 to work for the Northwestern Engineering Company, which his father had founded with a partner in the 1920s.[43] The younger Adelstein had remained in Colorado to study engineering at Boulder, then spent several years in the United States Army Corps of Engineers. During his service, he met army chaplain Rabbi Joel Messing, who argued that American Jews—especially those of privilege—carried an "obligation to leadership" to stand up in their communities and help those in need.[44] When Adelstein arrived, the Black Hills Jewish community was still fragmented following the dissolution of the Deadwood congregation, and he helped organize the Synagogue of the Hills, a congregation comprised of Jewish residents who lived in the Black Hills and those stationed at nearby Ellsworth Air Force Base. Lacking an ordained rabbi, lay leaders such as Adelstein organized Shabbat meetings in an Air Force chapel or the attic of the Congregational church in Rapid City. When the synagogue could afford it, they brought traveling rabbis to lead High Holidays services—a tradition that continues in different parts of the state even today. During peak attendance, more than two hundred members met at the base chapel. But for decades, the congregation had to suspend services periodically for lack of attendance.[45]

Because they were the best-known Jews in many miles, Adelstein and his wife, Ita, regularly fielded calls from the faithful as well as the curious. Once it was "a distressed widow of three days in Sundance, Wyoming, needing someone to discuss how Jews visualize life after

death." Later, a Christian minister in Spearfish "wanted to know exactly what the breakdown was of the Ten Commandments as the Jews
read them." Another time, a troubled young Jewish couple arrived at
the Adelstein's door "high on drugs but absolutely broke with no food,
a baby, and two dogs." On one occasion, Adelstein's secretary interrupted him with "two young Lubavichers," or members of a Hasidic
sect, who had "arrived at the airport in Rapid City, rented a car and
stopped at Jacobs Motor—because the name was Jewish." They, Adelstein wrote, "were directed promptly to my office." He invited them to
dinner and afterward recalled that he felt that he and Ita had taught
their new Orthodox friends a great deal about what it meant to be Jewish on the Northern Great Plains in the modern world.[46]

South Dakota's political "culture of familiarity and elbow rubbing"
also allowed Adelstein to become deeply involved in politics.[47] It was
useful to be "the Jew from South Dakota," he said, because he and
Ita would otherwise "just be lost" in a sea of Jewish activists if they
lived in a place such as New York. Their reputation, along with their
considerable wealth (Adelstein had taken over his father's company
in the mid-1960s), allowed him to project his voice into the highest
chambers of state and national politics.[48] Adelstein's national political work included an appointment by President Gerald Ford to the National Advisory Council on Economic Opportunity, membership on
the Republican Senate Trust, and leadership positions in a number of
national Jewish advocacy organizations, including the American Jewish Committee and the American Israeli Political Action Committee.
He also lobbied South Dakota's congressional delegation on Jewish
and Israeli causes for decades.[49]

Adelstein came to the Republican Party because of his pro-business
and pro-defense stances, and because his father had been an active
party member. The younger Adelstein became involved around 1960,
just as the party was undergoing an ideological transformation. Four
years later, conservatives would back Arizona senator Barry Goldwater at the Republican National Convention. Although Goldwater lost
the presidency to Lyndon Johnson that year, conservatives rallied and
eventually brought Ronald Reagan to the White House in 1981.[50]

As a businessman, Adelstein believed that government played a
necessary role in the economy, and he did not reject the idea of regulation. He characterized his fiscal conservatism as "enlightened self-

interest" and felt business people should be expected to work to increase their bottom line but were not entitled to do business in an ethical vacuum. "I wasn't really opposed to government rules" he said, as long as they "were fair in general." And with rare exception, he had positive experiences working with regulators, stating, "The people I dealt with in government . . . were doing their job as best they could."[51] For Adelstein, New York Governor Nelson Rockefeller—whom Goldwater had defeated in the 1964 primary—was a "true Republican" who embodied these ideals.[52] The South Dakotan had become acquainted with Rockefeller when he traveled to New York City for political work and Jewish activism. Their relationship continued over the years, and in 1974, Adelstein even brought Rockefeller—who would be sworn in as vice president of the United States only months later—to Rapid City for the South Dakota Republican Party's annual Lincoln Day dinner, using his local connections to have Mount Rushmore light up just as Rockefeller's plane left the Black Hills.[53]

Adelstein's commitment to community and to his construction business dovetailed into a keen interest in local politics. He and other young leaders sought to improve the quality of life in Rapid City and organized door-to-door campaigns to fill the mayor's office and city council with individuals who shared their plans. Adelstein was also involved with many of the municipal projects that reshaped Rapid City from the 1960s to the 1980s. He helped replace the city's fifty-year-old library with the new, twenty-eight thousand-square-foot facility that opened in 1972. He spent years on the board of Saint John's McNamara—a Catholic hospital—and was among the most vocal proponents of an effort to consolidate that facility with Rapid City's other hospital, Bennett-Clarkson. In 1973, the two became Rapid City Regional Hospital, and Adelstein sat on several committees, including one that located, designed, and built a new, nine-floor hospital that opened on Rapid City's south side in 1979. A close friend of longtime mayor Arthur ("Art") LaCroix, Adelsetin also helped with many of the urban development projects that rebuilt Rapid City after a catastrophic flood in 1972. These ranged from the establishment of greenways downtown to the extension of runways at the regional airport and the building of the Rushmore Plaza Civic Center, where Adelstein spent years on the board.[54]

When it came to the Republican Party, Adelstein had proven himself an effective political operative in his early thirties. As an alternate delegate, he attended the 1960 Republican National Convention, where the party nominated Richard Nixon for president. Adelstein also spent many hours in training sessions in Chicago, learning how to support Republican candidates, organize voter turnout drives, and utilize new strategies. When he returned to South Dakota, he suggested that phone banks could give the Republican candidate, a farmer and banker named Archie Gubbrud, an edge over the incumbent governor, Democrat Ralph Herseth, in the 1960 election. Herseth had interrupted a twenty-three-year streak in which six consecutive Republicans held the governor's mansion, and after a sound first term, the Democrat seemed well-positioned for re-election. Gubbrud had served as speaker of the state house, but he was neither well known outside his home county nor an especially energetic orator. He cast himself as a solid centrist who dripped integrity and could reunite a factionalized state party, but many party regulars considered him a heavy underdog.[55]

To support Gubbrud, Adelstein persuaded a group of businessmen to sponsor a phone bank. As the Pennington County precinct coordinator, Adelstein himself managed nearly two-dozen phones and a team of volunteers in what may have been the state's first "get out the vote" initiative. With a similar operation in Lawrence County, the strategy contributed to a strong Republican showing. Richard Nixon lost the presidency, but Republicans captured firm majorities in both houses of the state legislature. Gubbrud trailed Herseth until the ballots started tallying up West River, and he won by just 4,435 votes.[56]

Adelstein's part in this effort made him an overnight star in the Republican Party, which he served in many capacities. In 1968, he began a long stint on the Republican State Central Committee and was elevated to the executive committee five years later. There, Adelstein helped develop long-term strategies, including a cutting-edge effort to put every registered Republican into a computerized database and attempts to attract young voters, veterans, and American Indians to the party. The party also fought hard to win South Dakota's House seat when the state's two congressional districts were consolidated in 1982. Despite that loss, the situation looked good: since 1960, Republicans had won seventy-eight percent of statewide races and seventeen of twenty-two congressional elections.[57]

One perennial candidate was Bill Janklow, perhaps the defining figure of South Dakota politics during the last three decades of the twentieth century. Since their first conversation in the late 1960s, Adelstein and Janklow held frequent, late-night conversations about everything from statewide elections to the fate of Israel. Adelstein fundraised and campaigned vigorously for Janklow throughout his political career and served on several of Janklow's transition teams.[58] Like Adelstein, Janklow had a precarious relationship with the conservative movement. Janklow's actions, as one observer has noted, often did "not represent Republican ideals." During his sixteen years at the helm of state government, Janklow undertook several public initiatives at which small-government conservatives balked.[59] He was, in Adelstein's mind, more comparable to Rockefeller than Goldwater or Reagan. In 1995, Janklow appointed Adelstein to a task force that restructured the South Dakota Department of Transportation, where he helped cut $7 million from the department's annual budget.[60]

A few years later, in 1999, Adelstein and his business partners decided to sell the heavy construction wing of Northwestern Engineering Company. Nearing seventy, Adelstein had never sought public office to avoid conflicts of interest. Now out of the construction business, however, he was free to run, winning his first seat in the state legislature in November 2000. South Dakota went solidly Republican on the coattails of presidential candidate George W. Bush that year, and Republicans, including Adelstein, swept the Black Hills, taking all twenty-one of the region's legislative seats.[61]

Adelstein's first campaign set the tone for his electoral career. For many South Dakota Republicans, their politics cast in the conservatism of the Reagan Revolution, Adelstein was too liberal. In a letter to the *Rapid City Journal* just before the June primary, one Rapid City voter called him "everything from . . . a political chameleon to a socialist."[62] Bill Janklow's brother, Arthur ("Art") Janklow, was also a close friend of Adelstein's and parried with another letter, deploying the kinds of arguments that supporters would lean on in campaigns to come. He called Adelstein "a gentleman who is honest beyond question" before noting his many "leadership positions in our community, state, and national organizations [over] many, many years."[63] This dichotomy returned campaign after campaign. Adelstein's supporters lauded him for his deep commitment to his city and state, as well as his prolific charitable donations. His detractors called him a liberal "RINO" ("Republican in Name Only") and jabbed at Adelstein's wealth and the way he used it. Adelstein, after all, received statewide notoriety after self-funding his primary race in 2000—by far the most expensive of the campaign. An experienced national fundraiser, he barely thought twice about hiring pollsters who deployed sophisticated campaign strategies and poured money into advertisements, and he had to pound the pavement to counter the narrative that he was too wealthy and out of touch to serve average South Dakotans.[64]

Adelstein also had a propensity for supporting candidates on both sides of the aisle through political action committees (PACs). This situation irked other Republicans, as well as those who saw his unlimited giving to PACs as the exploitation of a loophole in the state's campaign finance laws. Over the years, for example, Adelstein had supported Democrat Tom Daschle, partly out of personal reverence but also because, as a moderate Republican, he increasingly found himself more ideologically aligned with Daschle than with staunchly conservative members of his own party. Adelstein's youngest son, Jonathan, even worked for Daschle in Washington, D.C, for several years. On his own side of the aisle, Adelstein was the primary funder of Mike Rounds's dark-horse victories in the 2002 gubernatorial primary and general election.[65]

During his time in the state legislature, Adelstein engaged many issues. He supported a bitterly contested ban on smoking indoors in public. He introduced legislation that sought to close the loop on the old question about which he had written Bill Janklow decades before: expanding the state's definition of "church" to allow officials at mosques, synagogues, and other non-Christian houses of worship to oversee weddings and other ceremonies.[66] He dutifully pushed for and attended menorah-lighting ceremonies at the state capitol. Joined by a small group of South Dakota Jews and surrounded by dozens of Christmas trees, Adelstein described the joy he felt recognizing Hanukkah at the capitol each year. "That's the whole point of America, isn't it?" he said. Jews "may only be six-tenths of one percent of the population, but we have a menorah. One menorah and that many Christmas trees, we probably come out even statistically."[67]

Adelstein moved from the state house to the state senate in 2004, but he lost in 2006 amidst an intense statewide debate over abortion.

A lifelong pro-choice Republican, Adelstein received an award from Planned Parenthood for weathering harsh criticisms after he refused to support abortion bans developed by conservative members of the state legislature in 2004 and 2006. He lost the 2006 Republican primary after his conservative opponent leveraged the abortion issue against him, only to be defeated later after Adelstein supported the Democratic challenger in the general election. After that cycle, Adelstein recaptured his senate seat three times, in 2008, 2010, and 2012. A few months before the start of the 2014 legislative session, however, he contracted a serious infection while undergoing routine hip surgery.[68] The infection hospitalized Adelstein for months, forcing his resignation from the state senate when he realized, as he wrote to Governor Dennis Daugaard, that he did "not wish to see the people of District 32 served by someone who is not able to give 100%."[69]

Through people such as Stan Adelstein, Sylvia Henkin, and Bea Premack, the smattering of Jewish people who have lived and worked in South Dakota and the Jewish congregations of Mount Zion, B'nai Isaac, and the Synagogue of the Hills have left significant impressions upon the communities and political culture of this state for the past one hundred thirty years. Jewish immigrant Max Dimont claimed— perhaps only a bit too extravagantly—that much of the world was "governed by the ideas of Jews—the ideas of Moses, Jesus, Paul, Spinoza, Marx, Freud, [and] Einstein."[70] Dimont looked forward to a peaceful epoch when the morality, justice, and ethics of law and the prophets would unite mankind. In surveying the roles of Jewish people in South Dakota's political history, he might have argued that, by spreading and reinforcing those key values across the Dakota plains, Jewish people have played a vital role in helping provide a solid moral foundation for community action and political activism in South Dakota.

The role and experiences of Jews in the state serves as a reminder that, in geographically large but demographically small and dispersed states such as South Dakota, a small group of committed and active individuals can wield extensive influence. The Jewish experience further reminds us that this clout extends, of course, to electoral politics but also to the civic and community action groups who take on issues of local significance. Those Jews who focused on party politics saw their worldviews shaped by the historical experience of their people, as well as personal interactions in cities like Washington, D.C., and

New York. People such as Adelstein absorbed new ideas and different perspectives and injected them into South Dakota politics, making the state a bit more cosmopolitan while pushing state parties to adopt new platforms and integrate cutting-edge campaign strategies developed in other parts of the nation.

For all that South Dakota Jews have achieved, their participation has continued to be shaped by a determination to cut against their historical dispossession and persecution, fighting instead to exist as Jewish people and contribute to those around them. In a 1978 essay, Stan Adelstein described his reaction when people asked him—as they often did—how he had "managed to stay Jewish for four generations in Rapid City," without either moving away from the state or abandoning his heritage. The answer, he said, was simple: "I remind the questioner that statistically we are a true microcosm of world Jewry. We probably are to Western South Dakota what the world Jewry is to world population. If we cannot survive for four generations in freedom," he asked, "what hope is there for Jewry to survive in a hostile world?"[71]

NOTES

1. Stanford M. Adelstein, interview by Eric John Abrahamson and Eric Steven Zimmer, 29 Feb. 2016, copy in Zimmer's possession. For primers on Jewish and Jewish-American history, *see* Raymond P. Scheindlin, *A Short History of the Jewish People: From Legendary Times to Modern Statehood* (New York: Oxford University Press, 1998); Arthur Hertzberg, *The Jews in America: Four Centuries of an Uneasy Encounter, A History* (New York: Columbia University Press, 1997); Robert A. Rockaway, *Words of the Uprooted: Jewish Immigrants in Early Twentieth-Century America* (Ithaca, N.Y.: Cornell University Press, 1998); Gerald Sorin, *A Time for Building: The Third Migration, 1880–1920* (Baltimore: Johns Hopkins University Press, 1992); Hasia R. Diner, *Roads Taken: The Great Jewish Migrations to the New World and the Peddlers Who Forged the Way* (New Haven, Conn.: Yale University Press, 2015).

2. Janklow to Adelstein, 29 Sept. 1977, Adelstein to Janklow, 16 Sept. 1977, both Folder 150, "Synagogue of the Hills, 1977," Box 2, Northwestern Engineering Company (NWEC) Archive, Rapid City, S.Dak.

3. Steven Prothero, *God is Not One: The Eight Rival Religions That Run the World—And Why Their Differences Matter* (New York: HarperCollins, 2010), p. xxvii; Max I. Dimont, *Jews, God, and History,* 2d ed. (New York: Signet Classic, 2004); Max I. Dimont, *The Indestructible Jews* (New York: Open Road Media,

2014); Katie Levingston, "Adam Sandler Plays a New, Very Funny, Very Jewish Version of 'The Hanukkah Song,' *Vulture,* 25 Nov. 2015, www.vulture.com/2015/11 /adam-sandler-updated-his-hanukkah-song.html.

4. A handful of writers have probed South Dakota's Jewish history; yet few have explored the Jewish role in South Dakota's political process and culture. *See* Howard Shaff and Audrey K. Shaff, *Paving the Way: The Life of Morris E. Adelstein* (Keystone, S.Dak.: Parmelia Publishing, 2005); Violet and Orlando J. Goering, "Jewish Farmers in South Dakota—the Am Olam," *South Dakota History* 12 (Winter 1982): 232–47; Orlando J. Goering and Violet Miller Goering, "Keeping the Faith: Bertha Martinsky in West River South Dakota," *South Dakota History* 25 (Spring 1995): 37–48; Bernice Premack, "A History of the Jewish Community of Aberdeen, South Dakota, 1887–1964," n.d., Records, Synagogue of the Hills, Rapid City, S.Dak.; Janet Dunlap Rathbun, "All Roads Led to Strool: The Rise and Fall of One Man's Town," *South Dakota History* 36 (Winter 2006): 367–84.

5. "Vital Statistics: Jewish Population in the United States, by State, 1899–Present," Jewish Virtual Library, www.jewishvirtuallibrary.org/jewish-population -in-the-united-states-by-state. The Jewish Virtual Library culled its figures from Ira M. Sheskin and Arnold Dashefsky, eds., "Jewish Population in the United States, 2014," *American Jewish Year Book* (Dordrecht, Neth.: Springer, 2014), pp. 143–211; *American Jewish Year Book* (Philadelphia: The Jewish Publication Society of America, 1899), p. 284.

6. Co-author Eric Zimmer has heard Adelstein offer this line—or a derivation of it—many times. Often, it appears as the punchline to an anecdote in which Adelstein tells people how, throughout his life, acquaintances have been surprised to meet a Jewish person from South Dakota, a place "where we have fewer rabbis than U. S. senators!"

7. On Jews in the Midwest, *see* Michael J. Bell, "'True Israelites of America': The Story of the Jews of Iowa," *Annals of Iowa* 53 (Spring 1994): 106; Rachel Calof, *Rachel Calof's Story: Jewish Homesteader on the Northern Plains*, ed. J. Sanford Rikoon (Bloomington: Indiana University Press, 1995); Irving Cutler, *The Jews of Chicago: From Shtetl to Suburb* (Urbana: University of Illinois Press, 1996); Gunther W. Plaut, *The Jews in Minnesota: The First Seventy-Five Years* (New York: American Jewish Historical Society, 1959); Frank Rosenthal, *The Jews of Des Moines: The First Century* (Des Moines, Iowa: Jewish Welfare Federation, 1957); Linda Mack Schloff, *And Prairie Dogs Weren't Kosher: Jewish Women in the Upper Midwest since 1855* (St. Paul: Minnesota Historical Society Press, 1996); Linda Mack Schloff, "Overcoming Geography: Jewish Religious Life in Four Market Towns," *Minnesota History* 51 (Spring 1988): 2–14; Janet E. Schulte, "'Proving Up and Moving Up'": Jewish Homesteading Activity in North Dakota, 1900–1920," *Great Plains Quarterly* 10 (Fall 1990): 228–44; Bernard Shuman, *A History of the Sioux City Jewish Community, 1869–1969* (Sioux City, Iowa: Jewish Federation,

1969); Amy Hill Siewers, "Judaism in the Heartland: The Jewish Community of Marietta, Ohio, 1895–1940," *Great Lakes Review* 5 (Winter 1979): 24–35; Sophia Trupin, *Dakota Diaspora: Memoirs of a Jewish Homesteader* (Lincoln: University of Nebraska Press, 1984); Lee Shai Weissbach, *Jewish Life in Small-Town America: A History* (New Haven, Conn.: Yale University Press, 2005); Jack Seymour Wolfe, *A Century with Iowa Jewry: As Complete a History as Could Be Obtained of Iowa Jewry from 1833 through 1940* (Des Moines: Iowa Printing & Supply Co., 1941); Shari Rabin, *Jews on the Frontier: Religion and Mobility in Nineteenth-Century America* (New York: New York University Press, 2017).

8. Premack, "History of the Jewish Community of Aberdeen," pp. 1–2.

9. "Ashley Jewish Homesteaders Cemetery," Ashley Jewish Cemetery Association, ashleyjewishcemetery.org.

10. Goering and Goering, "Jewish Farmers in South Dakota," pp. 232–35; Scheindlin, *A Short History of the Jewish People*, p. 143. On the rise of Zionism, *see* Walter Laqueur, *A History of Zionism: From the French Revolution to the Establishment of the State of Israel* (New York: Schocken Books, 2003).

11. Goering and Goering, "Jewish Farmers in South Dakota," pp. 238, 244–46 (quotation p. 246).

12. Mary Just Coome, "Pred's Roots: A Peddler Selling Wares," *Aberdeen American News*, 8 Dec. 1985, p. 8C.

13. For example, *see* advertisement, *Aberdeen American News*, 26 Oct. 1924, p. 6.

14. "Ashley Jewish Homesteaders Cemetery."

15. Premack, "History of the Jewish Community of Aberdeen," p. 3; "Synagogue had start in 1915," *Aberdeen American News*, 17 June 1956, p. 10A; Angela Mettler, "Sons of Isaac celebrates 90 years," *Aberdeen American News*, 23 Sept. 2007, p. 1B.

16. "About Our Temple," Mount Zion Congregation, mtzionsf.com/about.php; "Congregation Sons of Israel," Jewish American Society for Historic Preservation, www.jewish-american-society-for-historicpreservation.org/sdakotawyoming /siouxfallssouthdakota.html; Richard Melton, "Bringing the Torah to the Prairie: A Few Notes on Jewish Community Life in Sioux Falls," paper for Dakota Conference, 26 Apr. 2013, Center for Western Studies, Augustana University, Sioux Falls, S.Dak.

17. Charles A. Smith, *A Comprehensive History of Minnehaha County, South Dakota: Its Background, Her Pioneers, Their Record of Achievement and Development* (Mitchell, S.Dak.: Educator Supply Co., 1949), p. 264; Gary D. Olson and Erik L. Olson, *Sioux Falls, South Dakota: A Pictorial History* (Norfolk, Va.: Donning Co., 1985), p. 123; Harry F. Thompson, ed., *A New South Dakota History*, 2d ed. (Sioux Falls, S.Dak.: Center for Western Studies, Augustana College, 2009), p. 338.

18. "Treasures of the Black Hills' Past: Honoring Our Origins" (text of Jew-

ish history exhibit), n.d., pp. 1–4, binder, "Synagogue History 2," Records, Synagogue of the Hills.

19. "History of the Synagogue of the Hills: Rapid City, South Dakota," in "Synagogue History 2," p. 2.

20. Ibid., p. 5.

21. Ann Haber Stanton, *Jewish Pioneers of the Gold Rush* (Charleston, S.C.: Arcadia Publishing, 2011), p. 98; Goering and Goering, "Keeping the Faith," pp. 41–44, 47.

22. "The Jews of South Dakota, *Mount Zion Congregation*, mtzionsf.com; Rathbun, "All Roads Led to Strool," pp. 367–75, 379–81.

23. Greta Stewart, "The Business of Being the 'Grand Dame of Sioux Falls,'" *Sioux Falls Business Magazine*, Sept./Oct. 2011, p. 17, issuu.com/sfbm/docs /september-october-2011/17.

24. Pat O'Brien, *I'll be Right Back After This: My Memoir* (New York: St. Martin's Press, 2014), p. 22.

25. Stewart, "Business of Being the 'Grand Dame'," pp. 17–18; Chad McKenzie, "Sylvia Henkin: The Grand Ol Dame of Sioux Falls," 9 Sept. 2013, *KSOO*, ksoo.com/sylvia-henkin-the-grand-ol-dame-of-sioux-falls.

26. Richard Melton, email to the authors, 4 July 2017; Kevin Woster, "HB1215 Shakes GOP's 'Big Tent'," *Rapid City Journal,* 19 July 2006.

27. Quoted in Brady Mallory, "The Person behind the People's Parade," 11 Mar. 2016, *KELO*, keloland.com/news/article/featured-stories/the-person-behind-the -peoples-parade.

28. "2 Hub, Two Area Judges Elected," *Aberdeen American News*, 6 Nov. 1974, p. 13.

29. Mose S. Lindau, "An Answer to Teen-age Defender," *Aberdeen American News*, 11 Nov. 1951, p. 4; "Custody of Boy Given to Parents," ibid., 8 Oct. 1952, p. 16, and "County Judge seeks re-election," ibid., 22 Apr. 1956, p. 7.

30. "Ye Shall Know the Truth," ibid., 5 Nov. 1966, p. 6.

31. Bob Johnson, "Many Duties Assigned County Court Judge," ibid., 17 May 1953, p. 19.

32. "Feinstein Seeking School Post," ibid., 17 Apr. 1962, p. 3, and "Feinstein Not Asking Re-Election," ibid., 26 Apr. 1970, p. 10.

33. William C. Wertz, "New Pair of Shoes for a McGovern Victory," ibid., 13 July 1972, p. 1.

34. "Convention Presented Impressions," ibid., 16 Aug. 1972, p. 7.

35. Fran Venderveld, "Pred's—A Success Story Spanning Nearly 50 Years," ibid., 15 Aug. 1965, p. 24.

36. News items, ibid., 7 Dec. 1951, p. 13, 28 Jan. 1952, p. 5; "Mickelson to Speak at Dinner," ibid., 12 Aug 1952, p. 12.

37. Quoted in "Dr. Kertes Leaving for Medical Reasons," ibid., 27 Sept. 1964, p. 17.

38. "Young Church People Invited to Synagogue," ibid., 20 Jan. 1954, p. 6.

39. "Premack Wins Book of Golden Deeds Award," ibid., 3 Feb. 1991, p. 4E; "Press Release," 29 Oct. 2009," United States Commission on Civil Rights, www .usccr.gov/press/2009/PR-10-29-09SD.pdf.

40. Don Hall, "Texas Snowbird Named First Lady of Aberdeen," *Aberdeen American News*, 3 Mar. 1996, p. 6E.

41. Jacqueline Bueno, "Trump's Palm Beach Club Roils the Old Social Order," *Wall Street Journal (Florida Journal)*, 30 Apr. 1997, p. F1.

42. Obituaries and news stories frequently connect B'Nai Isaac members to various Masonic groups. Julius Premack's obituary, for instance, highlights his involvement with Yelduz Shrine, Scottish Rite, and the Aberdeen Masonic Blue Lodge, as well as his role in B'Nai Isaac and B'Nai B'rith. "Local and Area Deaths," *Aberdeen American News,* 21 Mar. 1983, p. 7. One of Mose Landau's campaign announcements notes his involvement in "several Masonic groups" ("Race for Bench is Assured," ibid, 17 Mar. 1974, p. 33).

43. Shaff and Shaff, *Paving the Way*, pp. 98–99, 154.

44. Karen Psiaki, "Stanford Adelstein: Jewel of the Hills," *Black Hills Faces* 12 (Winter 2016): 13.

45. Adelstein, email to Ann Stanton, Synagogue of the Hills, 31 Dec. 2003, and "History of the Synagogue of the Hills," both in "Synagogue History 2"; Adelstein, interviews by Zimmer and Abrahamson, 16 Dec. 2015 and 25 Jan. 2016, copies in Zimmer's possession; Stephen Lee, "Roving Rabbis Bring Hanukkah to South Dakota Capitol," *Capital Journal,* 17 Dec. 2014 capjournal.com/news /roving-rabbis-bring-hanukkah-to-south-dakota-capitol/article_1b4781fa-8673 -11e4-b8bc-f7b29c7694de.html; Adelstein to Murray Polner, 15 Dec. 1978, Folder 40, "American Israel Public Affairs Committee (AIPAC) 1978," Box 2, NWEC Archive; Gilbert Kollin to Barbara Blass, 17 Oct. 1977, Folder 150, "Synagogue of the Hills, 1977"; Adelstein to Larry Blass, 20 Aug. 1978, and Joan Levine to Adelstein, 20 Sept. 1978, both Folder "SMA Correspondence July–Dec. 1978," Box 2, NWEC Archive.

46. Adelstein to Polner, 15 Dec. 1978.

47. Jon K. Lauck, John E. Miller, and Edward Hogan, "Historical Musings: The Contours of South Dakota Political Culture," *South Dakota History* 34 (Summer 2004): 164.

48. Adelstein, interview, 25 Jan. 2016.

49. Greta de Jong, *You Can't Eat Freedom: Southerners and Society Justice after the Civil Rights Movement* (Chapel Hill: University of North Carolina Press, 2016), p. 80; "National Advisory Council on Economic Opportunity" (memorandum), n.d., Folder "Council on Economic Opportunity," Box 15, NWEC Archive.

50. Adelstein, interview by Zimmer and Abrahamson, 17 Nov. 2015, copy in Zimmer's possession; Shaff and Shaff, *Paving the Way,* p. 58; Timothy J. Sullivan, *New York State and the Rise of Modern Conservatism: Redrawing Party Lines* (Albany, N.Y.: SUNY Press, 2008), pp. 36–37. *See also* John A. Andrew III, *The Other Side of the Sixties: Young Americans for Freedom and the Rise of Conservative Politics* (New Brunswick, N.J.: Rutgers University Press, 1997); Sean Wilentz, *Age of Reagan: A History, 1974–2008* (New York: HarperCollins, 2008); Steve Fraser and Gary Gerstle, eds., *The Rise and Fall of the New Deal Order, 1930–1980* (Princeton, N.J.: Princeton University Press, 1989).

51. Adelstein, interview by Zimmer and Abrahamson, 5 Jan. 2016, copy in Zimmer's possession.

52. Adelstein, interview, 29 Feb. 2016; Daniel Adelstein, interview by Zimmer, 11 Sept. 2016, copy in Zimmer's possession. On Rockefeller, *see* Richard Norton Smith, *On His Own Terms: A Life of Nelson Rockefeller* (New York: Random House, 2014).

53. Adelstein, interviews, 17 Nov. 2015, 29 Feb. 2016; Nelson A. Rockefeller to Adelstein, 14 Feb. 1974, Box 1, Folder 14, "South Dakota," Nelson A. Rockefeller Gubernatorial Records, Series 16 (FA362), Rockefeller Archives Center, Sleepy Hollow, New York.

54. Adelstein, interview, 29 Feb. 2016; "Phil G. Schroeder," Black Hills Knowledge Network, bhkn.rapidcitylibrary.org/bhkn/KnowledgeNetwork; *Your New Rapid City Public Library, 1972–1982* (n.p.: Nauman Printing, 1982), pp. 1, 7; Shaff and Shaff, *Paving the Way,* p. 234; Adelstein, interview, 25 Jan. 2016; Adelstein, "Some Not-So-Recent Rapid City Healthcare History," 17 Jan. 2013, way2gosd.com; "Operational Flow Chart," July 1980, "RCRH Board Committees," July 1980, and "Rapid City Regional Hospital," all Box 5, Service Unit Director, NWEC Archive; Rapid City Service Unit, to Area Director, Aberdeen Area Indian Health Service, 18 May 1976, Folder 143, "Rapid City Regional Hospital, Inc. Correspondence, Etc. 1978," Box 4, NWEC Archive; Adelstein, interviews, 16 Dec. 2015, 5 Jan. 2016, 29 Feb. 2016; "Arthur P. LaCroix," Black Hills Knowledge Network, bhkn.rapidcitylibrary.org/bhkn/ KnowledgeNetwork. *See also* Thomas & Associates, "Rapid City Regional Airport Proposed Runway Improvement Project Needs and Alternatives: An Historical and Data Report," 23 Dec. 1981, and "Rapid City Flood Disaster Program, Urban Renewal Project, Project #SD-R3, Rapid City South Dakota," 27 Mar. 1975, pp. 10–11, both in Local History Room, Rapid City Public Library, Rapid City, S.Dak.

55. Adelstein, interviews, 17 Nov. 2015, 29 Feb. 2016; Edmund F. Kallina, Jr., *Courthouse over White House: Chicago and the Presidential Election of 1960* (Orlando: University Press of Florida, 1988), p. 59; J. V. Yaukey, *The Governor's Scepter: Vignettes of South Dakota Governors from Byrne to Kneip* (n.p.: Hayes Bros., 1976), pp. 23, 61–63; Robert Thompson, "Ralph E. Herseth: 1959–1961," in *Over*

a *Century of Leadership: South Dakota Territorial and State Governors,* ed. Lynwood E. Oyos (Sioux Falls, S.Dak.: Center for Western Studies, Augustana College, 1987), p. 169; William O. Farber, "Archie Gubbrud: 1961–1965," in *Over a Century of Leadership,* pp. 175–76.

56. Adelstein, interview, 29 Feb. 2016; "Please Vote for Stanford M. Adelstein" (pamphlet), Box 65, NWEC Archive; *Gubernatorial Elections, 1787–1997* (n.p.: Congressional Quarterly Incorporated, 1998), p. 142; John Searle, "South Dakotans Leave Convention for Another," *Rapid City Journal,* 29 July 1960; Thompson, "Ralph E. Herseth," p. 177. Farber, "Archie Gubbrud," p. 177. In an email to Zimmer on 27 May 2017, Adelstein claimed that this phone-bank scheme was the first "get out the vote" effort in South Dakota.

57. "Stanford M. Adelstein, . . . Rapid City, South Dakota, 57701," Folder 2, Box 32, NWEC Archive; Jeff Stingley, "1983–84 Political Plan of the South Dakota Republican Party, March 1983, Overview" and "Specific and Broad Tasks Needing Consideration by South Dakota Republican Party in 1983–1984," both Folder 141, "Republican State Central Committee 1983," Box 22, ibid.

58. Adelstein, interview by Zimmer, 12 Dec. 2016, copy in Zimmer's possession.

59. Lalley, "Politics of Pragmatism," p. 319.

60. Adelstein, interview, 12 Dec. 2016; "Governor Janklow's South Dakota Department of Transportation Review Task Force, 27 Feb. 1996," pp. 6–7, 19–25, and Curt Jones and Ron Wheeler to Janklow, 24 Feb. 1996, both Folder "DOT Task Force 1996 #1," Box 106, Richardson Collection, William J. Janklow Gubernatorial Papers, University of South Dakota Archives and Special Collections, Vermillion; South Dakota Legislative Research Council, "Reorganization of the Department of Transportation," Issue Memorandum 96–25, 7 Aug 2000, p. 4, copy in Zimmer's possession; Wheeler to Kay Jorgensen, 18 June 1996, Folder "DOT Task Force 1996 #1."

61. Bill Harlan, "Election Defeat Sparks Dem Defection," *Rapid City Journal,* 7 Nov. 2000.

62. Quoted in Arthur W. Janklow, "True Contributor," *Rapid City Journal,* 4 June 2000.

63. Ibid.

64. Joyce Hazeltine, "Hazeltine Says District 32 Lucky to Have Adelstein," *Black Hills Pioneer,* 29 Oct. 2008; Denise Ross, "Adelstein Spends Record on Campaign," *Rapid City Journal,* 3 Jan. 2001; Ray M. Graff, "Adelstein Using Push Poll to Persuade Voters," *Black Hills Pioneer,* 29 Oct. 2008.

65. Jonathan Ellis, "Health Problem Forces Stan Adelstein to Resign from State Senate," *Sioux Falls Argus Leader,* 1 Jan. 2014; Adelstein, interview, 12 Dec. 2016; Cory Heidelberger, "Why Some Republicans Still Hate Republi-

can Stan Adelstein," *Madville Times,* 5 Jan. 2014, madvilletimes.com/2014/01
/ why-some-republicans-hate-republican-stan-adelstein.

66. Emilie Rusch, "Smoking Ban Supporters Hope for Senate Victory," *Rapid City Journal,* 28 Feb. 2009; Denise Ross, "Bill to Include Jews, Muslims in Marriage Law," ibid., 30 Jan. 2002.

67. Quoted in David Montgomery, "Menorah Adds Hanukkah Symbol to Capitol Display," ibid., 13 Dec 2009.

68. Kevin Woster, "Adelstein Draws Fire on Award," *Rapid City Journal,* 20 Apr. 2006; Ellis, "Health Problem."

69. Adelstein to Daugaard, 30 Dec. 2013, printed in Corey Heidelberger, "Adelstein Resigns from South Dakota Senate, Citing Health," *Madville Times,* 30 Dec. 2013, madvilletimes.com/2013/12/adelstein-resigns-from-south-dakota -senate-citing-health.

70. Dimont, *Jews, God, and History*, p. 421.

71. Adelstein to Polner, 15 Dec. 1978.

RYAN BURDGE

6 | KARL E. MUNDT AND THE PROBLEM OF RURAL ECONOMIC DEVELOPMENT IN SOUTH DAKOTA

. . .

Rural flight, or rural exodus, is not a new concept. It is most often brought up in the context of nineteenth-century industrialization, when Western society shifted from the reliance on the family unit for subsistence to wage work in mills and factories. The United States experienced a second instance of rural exodus in the postwar period of the 1940s and 1950s, when farm populations began to decline due to increased automation in the agricultural sector and the lack of industrial development in rural states.[1] Many inhabitants of the heartland states, particularly South Dakotans, saw this flight as a threat to their way of life as small towns withered, shops disappeared, and making a living became a daily struggle. It was not until President Lyndon Baines Johnson's Great Society speech in May 1964 that many began to take the widespread issues of poverty seriously, and fewer still recognized the unique characteristics of poverty that the nation's rural communities faced. United States senator Karl E. Mundt was one of those who did. He had made it his career goal to advocate for the needs of South Dakota and its rural communities, pushing for development projects that changed the landscape of his home state. He played a role in two major developments within South Dakota, the Missouri River Basin development project and the Interstate Highway System, which aimed to alleviate many of the issues that the state's rural communities were suffering.

Even though fighting poverty through economic development became the goal of President Johnson's administration (1963–1969), the president's efforts were focused almost entirely on the nation's urban centers, and few of his programs brought progress to rural states. By the 1960s, South Dakota was facing a crisis, as the agricultural economy began to stagnate and emigration to urban states began to increase. Senator Mundt positioned himself as an advocate for rural issues on the national stage. His efforts appeared to be for naught, however, as administrations continued to ignore issues of rural development, opting instead to focus on urban blight and unrest, causing the states to institute their own development programs. Near the end of the 1960s, this emphasis left South Dakota unsure of its future, its position in the national economy, and the path it would need to take to prosperity.

Immediately following World War II, sixty-seven percent of South Dakotans were living in rural areas, making it the most rural state in the nation. However, the state's rural population had been on the decline since the 1930s, with a peak of 391,000 people counted in the 1930 census. By 1960, this population was nearly cut in half and still declining. This de-population resulted from several factors, including the increased mechanization of agriculture and the lack of a developed manufacturing sector for displaced farmers to turn to. The postwar period saw a massive increase in the number of agricultural tractors being developed and sold. Just as Jethro Tull's seed drill revolutionized English agriculture with regards to speed, efficiency, and consistency in planting seeds, the combustion engine tractor increased farmer's productivity in plowing, cultivating, and working the land. By 1944, the tractor had surpassed horses and mules as the farmer's primary productivity asset, and by the early 1950s, the production and sales of tractors had reached their all-time peak. Farmers who mechanized and automated their processes, using sophisticated tractor technologies, eventually pushed out the smaller farmers who were still relying on manual tools and horsepower.[2]

The lack of a developed manufacturing center led to the scarcity of opportunities for young educated professionals during this period, as those residents age eighteen to thirty-four with high school diplomas and advanced degrees left for better opportunities in other regions, otherwise known as a "brain drain."[3] South Dakota's primary industry was agriculture, and little or no development occurred in the state's financial or business sectors to retain educated white-collar workers, who fled to growing urban and suburban centers. The severity of the economic situation in the state was not lost on state officials or federal representatives, such as Senator Karl Mundt, who remained keenly focused on the issues facing South Dakota in the postwar period.

Mundt represented South Dakota in Congress from 1939 to 1973, serving ten years in the House of Representatives and twenty-four years in the Senate. Born in Humboldt, South Dakota, in 1900, Mundt was the only child of an entrepreneurial businessman, who moved often between Pierre and Madison.[4] While attending high school in Madison, Mundt took an interest in speech and politics, becoming active on the school's debate team as well as running for class president every year he attended. When he was sixteen, Mundt and a friend attempted to enlist in the United States Army to fight in World War I, only to be turned away at the recruiter's office for being too young. Mundt refocused on his studies, graduated from high school in 1919, and attended Carleton College in Northfield, Minnesota. He continued to participate in speech and debate, joined the staff of the student publication *Middle Border*, and spent his college summers earning a living as a traveling salesman.

After finishing a degree in economics in 1923, Mundt became principal and teacher at Bryant High School outside Watertown and was appointed superintendent soon after. As teacher and administrator, he was a staunch advocate for education, especially for young men, in an era when education was largely considered unnecessary for boys who were expected to work the family farm. Mundt put his oratorical skills to work and published a series of booklets to promote the benefits of a well-rounded education, which he determined to be the foundation of a fair start in life.[5] It was during his time at Bryant that he became known regionally for his entertaining, but also poignant, speeches. He set himself apart by speaking about issues of government and politics, a change of pace for crowds accustomed to hearing about virtuous Christian living. In 1927, Mundt and his wife, Mary Moses, left Bryant to return to Madison for positions at Eastern State Normal School (now Dakota State University). He taught psychology and economics, and she taught drama and French.

After being heckled for a short speech he gave following a 1932 campaign event for Senator Royal C. Johnson, Mundt became interested in taking a more active role in South Dakota politics. Despite the wishes of the college administration, he continued giving political speeches, and in 1933, he established the South Dakota Young Republican League. After turning down an offer from the South Dakota Republican Party to be its candidate for the 1934 governor's race, he announced his run for United States Congress in January 1936. Raised in rural South Dakota, Mundt had assimilated many values associated with a "rural identity," including individualism, a strong sense of community, and tight social bonds. Billing himself as a constitutional progressive, he opposed President Franklin D. Roosevelt's New Deal, favored agricultural program reform, supported worker's rights, and opposed *isms* that sought to create an all-powerful central state.[6] Mundt's campaign rhetoric centered on reforming and streamlining government, making a government that worked "for the people" and for farmers in particular. His slogan for the 1936 campaign, "A Fair Chance for the Farmer," was attached to a platform that focused on limiting agricultural imports, opening crop insurance markets, promoting water conservation, and reducing the costs and penalties associated with farm loans.[7]

Mundt narrowly lost the 1936 election to incumbent Democratic congressman Fred H. Hildebrandt. Following the election, Mundt refocused his efforts by reducing his duties at Eastern State to focus full-time on public speaking. In 1938, he challenged Democratic farm leader Emil Loriks for the First Congressional District seat and won. He changed his campaign slogan to "A Fair Chance for a Free People" and shifted his platform to promoting limited federal government, which he believed to be the path to liberty and prosperity. He outlined his vision for America in a speech at a 1938 Executives' Club luncheon in Chicago. Outlining "The America I Want," Mundt espoused his support for democratic self-governance, a constitutional balance of power with limited and decentralized government, and an economic balance of power governed by open and free markets.[8] These principles would define his career.

As a freshman representative, Mundt made a concerted effort to stay in touch with his constituents and became the first congressman from South Dakota to publish a weekly newsletter, *Your Washington and You*, which he later disseminated through radio and television. During his House years, Mundt established himself as a conservationist, an advocate for South Dakota farmers, a backer of fiscal responsibility, and a supporter of American neutrality. Mundt was re-elected four times before seeking a vacant Senate seat in the 1948 election year. He championed the causes of cutting government waste and promoting the agricultural economy. He made a name for himself serving on the House Un-American Activities Committee, investigating government corruption, getting involved in the Alger Hiss case in the 1940s, and presiding over the Army–McCarthy hearings during the Red Scare of the 1950s.[9]

By the 1960s, the American public had become less concerned about communism and more concerned about their own welfare and economic security. Republicans lost forty-eight seats in the House and thirteen in the Senate in the 1958 midterms and then lost the 1960 presidential election, leaving legislative and executive branches in the control of the Democrats. Following the 1960 election, the Republican Party rallied behind senior Republicans who positioned themselves in opposition to New Deal Democrats, criticizing what they considered to be outdated and unnecessary federal spending programs that had little or no real effect on American prosperity. Senator Mundt took the opportunity to turn his attention back to the issues that initially got him interested in politics—agriculture and the farm economy—and endorsed projects that he believed would benefit South Dakota's farmers.

One of the largest national development projects of the period was the Pick-Sloan Missouri Basin Program, a proposal by the United States Army Corps of Engineers and the United States Bureau of Reclamation. The purpose of the project was to provide irrigation, flood control, and electricity to some of the more remote areas located within the basin area. Better flood control was necessary after the region experienced three devastating floods in 1943, 1944, and 1947, and bringing irrigation to five million acres of semi-arid land would be beneficial to farmers. South Dakota would see the lion's share of development. Prior to 1960, South Dakota representative Francis H. Case had been instrumental in coordinating dam projects between the Bureau of Reclamation and the Army Corps of Engineers, ensuring that dams within the state would be designed for both irrigation and flood control. Senator Mundt supported the projects along with Case, but it was not until after the latter's death in 1962 that Mundt took on a bigger role in lobbying for the program.[10]

In spite of its benefits, the Missouri River Basin development program had its critics. Conservationists expressed worry that the river dam system would be more destructive to South Dakota's natural land formations than it would be helpful to the state's farmland. The largest element of the project, the Oahe Dam and irrigation system, attracted the most criticism. The community of Mobridge, about one-hundred miles upriver from Pierre and the dam site, was worried that new road and bridge construction would leave their small community further isolated from the rest of the state. It was Senator Mundt who calmed their fears, traveling to Mobridge with Lewis A. Pick and Glenn Sloan, who had initially proposed the project. They explained to the community that the Oahe Dam would bring with it a network of irrigation canals throughout the region, a point previously unexplained. In his speech in Mobridge, Senator Mundt claimed that the town would experience an economic boom unlike anything its citizens had ever experienced before. Following the visit of the three men, the *Mobridge Tribune* published a front-page article giving its support for Missouri River Basin development and Oahe Dam.[11]

In early 1957, funds for the Oahe irrigation program were in danger because of a supposed lack of interest in the project among South Dakotans and an administration that was pushing spending cuts across the board. As construction on the Oahe Dam was wrapping up, the Bureau of Reclamation threatened to pull federal funding for the Oahe Irrigation Unit unless interest was shown in continuing the feasibility studies for the plan. Concerned citizens raised the issue that South Dakota might lose its water rights if the irrigation plan did not move forward. On 16 January 1957, the South Dakota Reclamation Association met to discuss the Oahe irrigation plan. The association issued twenty-one resolutions related to water reclamation and conservation within the state, reiterating the state's interest and support for the Oahe Irrigation Unit, as well as for maintaining South Dakota's sovereignty and administration of its valuable water resources. The South Dakota Reclamation Association also asserted its support for the Oahe Irrigation Unit in an area that had been neglected—the development of recreational usage for the reservoir the new dam would create.[12]

The rising costs of the dam construction and the irrigation project made it unlikely that the Senate would approve appropriations for continuation of the program, and rumors were floating that the United States Bureau of Reclamation did not support the project. Senator Mundt leveraged his senior position on the Senate Appropriations Committee to ensure that the irrigation project was fully and properly funded. In his testimony to the committee, Mundt provided evidence of overwhelming support for the project in the form of letters and testimony from South Dakota citizens and municipal councils. Mundt also wanted to make certain that the final costs of water to the farmers would be reasonable, a point overlooked in previous evaluation reports of the program. He made it clear that supporting development of the state's agricultural economy would benefit the entire region, increase food production, stabilize the environment through flood control, and increase municipal access to clean water supplies for all citizens. When the project temporarily halted, South Dakota state legislators stepped up as well, creating a plan for a water conservancy district that covered the entirety of South Dakota, further divided into sub-districts to allow local jurisdictions to create and plan their own irrigation projects in anticipation of the loss of federal funding. This measure passed in a referendum by an eighty-five percent margin in the 1960 general election. Meanwhile, the debate continued at the federal level. It was not until 1963 that the House and Senate passed appropriations of $16 million for the project, and appropriations were increased to $120 million in 1964.[13]

The Missouri River development project changed the geographic face of the heartland. However, no project changed the landscape of American life and society in such a profound way as the federal Interstate Highway System, born out of the Federal-Aid Highway Act of 1956, signed into law by President Dwight D. Eisenhower on 29 June 1956. President Eisenhower had pushed Congress to pass a highway act from the time he took office in 1953, citing safety, national defense, and economic investment as reasons that an interstate system was necessary. One of the crucial debates concerned the funding of the new system. The United States had entered a recession following the Korean War in 1953 and was only just recovering in 1956, slumping again in 1957 and 1958. To ease the fears of fiscal conservatives within Congress, the project was funded with a Highway Trust Fund, facilitated primarily by a small increase in the federal gasoline tax.[14]

Three revolutions in geographical organization have occurred within South Dakota. The first was the section-line grid, in which towns were laid along straight lines dividing the state on the map. The second was the impact of the railroad, which influenced developments in settlement and urban planning as much as it did interstate commerce. The Interstate Highway System was the third and had an impact similar to the railroad.[15] The highway system was not constricted in the same way that the railroad had been; rail transportation required depots in established towns and cities to operate effectively. By contrast, the highway had no such limiting factors, other than the imperatives of topography. In a state such as South Dakota, with its vast wide-open spaces and landscapes, there were few restrictions in routing the interstate. A boon for highway planners, this vastness was a potential downside for some communities; the planners could essentially pick and choose which towns would prosper and which would be marginalized.

The interstate highway plan for South Dakota originally included only one east-west throughway, Interstate 90, which would lie perpendicular to the north-south throughway, Interstate 29, running along the western edge of Minnesota through Jasper and Pipestone. The planning for Interstate 90 followed South Dakota's east-west orientation, enforced by the natural division of the Missouri River and reinforced by the layout of the railroads. Senators Mundt and Case worked at the federal level, securing funding for additional mileage within South Dakota and ensuring that the interstate would have the greatest net positive impact on the state. While Senator Case is often credited with securing the funding for the interstate miles, Mundt also worked to ensure that the final routes of the interstate aligned with the interests of South Dakotans.[16]

Mundt recognized that highways of all types remained vital to local communities. An illustrative incident in May 1965 involved the destruction, by flood, of Highway 14A running north-south through Spearfish Canyon between Spearfish and Cheyenne Crossing. The chambers of commerce of Spearfish, Deadwood, and Lead adopted resolutions supporting the rebuilding of the highway but with a caveat that made it different from other beautification projects going on at the time. Rather than building an improved, larger 14A, the chambers asked that 14A be rebuilt exactly as it had been, preserving the scenic beauty of the canyon. Mundt relayed the town's demands to the Bureau of Public Roads. The Denver Federal Highway Regional Projects Office was dumbfounded at the request, noting that it was uncommon for localities to demand roads be built to previous specifications rather than making improvements.[17] Rex Whitton at the Bureau of Public Roads was more than happy to accommodate their request, authorizing $1,755,300 for 14A's reconstruction and an additional $88,350 for the reinforcement of bridges at Whitewood Creek. In 1966, the United States Department of Transportation would be created, with a mandate to consider the effects that new highway development would have on historic sites and scenic landscapes.

As public works projects that were changing the landscape of South Dakota were underway, residents were still reeling from the economic slump of the 1950s. President Johnson's Great Society speech in 1964 at the University of Michigan, outlining the plan for his administration's War on Poverty, was generally well received nationally, resulting in the passage of the Economic Opportunity Act of 1964 and the establishment of the Office of Economic Opportunity. The act created several programs intended to streamline federal funding for education and job training in areas with high populations of unemployed and working poor. Many people in rural states, however, doubted that the administration's policy would meet their needs. As federal officials focused on ending poverty and developing urban areas, many inhabitants of rural areas expressed concerns about the declining state of their society. A rancher in Bonesteel wrote to Mundt about the declining beef market. A dairy farmer in Humboldt lamented the closure of shops, the lack of inventory at wholesale suppliers, and increasing bankruptcies and foreclosures. A woman in Pierre described the situation there as a depression. However, Johnson and his officials reasoned that the programs created by the Economic Opportunity Act, particularly the Head Start and Community Action agencies, were enough to meet the needs of the rural poor. Some officials at the United States Department of Agriculture (USDA) did not agree and involved themselves in the planning of the Community Action Program.[18] Senator Mundt also began formulating a supplemental plan to Johnson's War on Poverty with the intention of channeling more aid to rural communities that were in a state of decline.

The importance of developing and maintaining the nation's rural communities did get some representation in the Johnson administration through Secretary of Agriculture Orville Freeman, former Minnesota governor and founding member of the Minnesota Democratic-Farmer-Labor Party. In January of 1967, Freeman gave a speech at a conference sponsored by the National Association for Community Development, addressing issues facing the nation's poor. At the time, half of the nation's population living under the poverty line were situated in rural areas. Freeman argued that the problems facing rural and urban areas were linked. As opportunities declined in rural areas and the unemployed fled to urban centers to find work, urban communities likewise became overcrowded and unable to support the influx of new migrants, further reducing opportunities for everyone. Freeman's solution was to promote industrial development in rural areas in order to provide jobs for the unemployed and economic development for small-town America. Freeman may not have been far off from a solid solution, as Gallup polls at the time suggested that Americans preferred "Town & Country" living to metropolitan sprawl and the uniformity of suburbia. Freeman called for information to be handed out to businesses on the benefits of relocating to rural states. He believed that it was the USDA's responsibility to promote a more prosperous future for all Americans, one free of congested, densely populated urban centers and polluted air and waters.[19]

Mundt kept a close eye on Freeman and the developments in the Department of Agriculture, and he agreed with the secretary's vision for the future of the nation. Bills had been passed in prior years designed to aid economic development in rural areas, namely the Area Redevelopment Act of 1961, the Public Works and Economic Development Act of 1965, and the Appalachian Regional Development Act of 1965. While these measures did funnel resources into underdeveloped rural regions, they had little effect in promoting the permanent and sustainable communities needed to attract and retain populations in those areas. A close friend of Mundt's, Second District representative E. Y. Berry, joined Mundt's efforts to offer greater representation to rural South Dakotans, ensuring that the Johnson administration would not ignore their interests. In March of 1965, Berry published an open letter to his constituents attacking Johnson's poverty plan, citing *U.S. News & World Report* that the Johnson administration had planned for the "liquidation of 2.4 million farmers."[20]

In a March 1967 press release, Mundt announced that he was seeking cosponsors for a joint resolution to establish a commission to study population movements in the United States and any problems or issues resulting from those migrations. Mundt aimed to find out why population movements were trending in the way that they were and to propose recommendations for both reversing the loss of the nation's rural populations and reducing the influx of populations to metropolitan areas. The outline of Mundt's resolution looked at eight points of study that would culminate in what he determined to be "balanced economic development." They included socio-political factors affecting geographic location of industry, the factors necessary for industry to operate successfully outside of urban areas, federal government methods to encourage more balanced development nationwide, ways to provide public services most efficiently based on population densities, the efficiency of government on differing patterns of population concentration, the advantages of balanced economic development on public interest, the role of government in promoting geographic balance, and the practical ways in which the federal government could most efficiently disperse its expenditures.[21] With his proposal, Mundt was instrumental in furthering the efforts that Freeman had started. Over the next two years, Mundt worked to ensure that the struggle for rural America would not be forgotten in Congress.

Mundt drafted a resolution based on his concept of balanced economic development, introducing it as S. J. 64 on the Senate floor on 6 April 1967 with fifteen cosponsors: twelve Republicans and three Democrats from various regions across the nation, including Kentucky, Tennessee, Arizona, and West Virginia. In his remarks, Mundt reinforced his conviction that national economic policy should be more balanced and not leave the rural populations on the fringe. Mundt was adamant that his resolution was not about taking funds away from the urban renewal programs of the Johnson administration but was about striking a social and geographic balance in development throughout the nation. He reiterated the relationship between urban migration and urban blight that Freeman had spoken about in the previous months. The text of the resolution established a bipartisan Commission on Balanced Economic Development. Its twenty members would be composed of four members each from cities with populations of (1) one million, (2) between one-hundred thousand and one million, (3) between ten thousand and one-hundred thousand, and (4) less than ten thousand, as well as four member specialists as experts in their respective fields. The goal of the commission would be to conduct a two-year, multidisciplinary study to make a recommendation to the Johnson administration on how to best direct national policy on economic development.[22]

With the declining populations of rural communities and the shrinking number of farmers participating in the agricultural economy, industrial development was the next best option for rural areas. In addition to S. J. 64, Senator James Pearson of Kansas introduced the Rural Job Development Act on 21 July 1967. Cosponsored by Mundt, the bill featured a few tax incentives to bolster growth and development of industry in rural areas. It increased investment credits for rural businesses in machinery and provided additional credits for new building construction. In addition, businesses located in rural areas would receive tax deductions for hiring low-income workers. After congressional sessions ended that week, Mundt put out a press release to South Dakota newspapers outlining S. J. 64 and his support for Pearson's bill. Mundt believed that a partnership between federal, state, and local governments and private industry would help these measures succeed. In total, congressmen from eighteen different states cosponsored Mundt's and Pearson's bills. The crisis facing rural America was being recognized nationwide, and a senator from South Dakota was spearheading the effort to repair it.[23]

The following spring, the assistant secretary of the USDA, John Baker, spoke at a conference on Appalachia and the American Future in Charleston, West Virginia. Baker reinforced the notion that people follow jobs, citing businesses that had chosen to build locations in rural communities, including 3M, IBM, and Douglas Aircraft. These businesses derived many advantages from locating in rural communities. One plant manager claimed that his workers were more productive because they did not have to fight traffic to get to work. Less congestion resulted in improved work habits and attitudes, and businesses in rural communities had better and more fruitful communications with local governments. The availability and affordability of land was a major benefit as well. Baker, in quoting William Beverly Murphy, chief executive officer of Campbell Soup Company, suggested that the issues businesses faced in operating in urban areas were problems that they had created for themselves. With the technological advances in travel and communication, there was no practical reason for a business to choose an urban location over a rural one.[24] Lyndon Johnson seemed to agree with Baker, who quoted the president as saying, "So many times when I have . . . seen the wreckage on the television film late at night of our towns burning—I have just wondered if we could have spent a small proportion of the money . . . in helping to keep people living on the farm."[25] The Johnson administration seemed committed to working with Mundt and Pearson in shifting the economic focus of the nation from metropolitan to rural areas. Unfortunately, 1968 was an election year, and there was no guarantee that the next administration would have the same commitment as President Johnson, who was not seeking re-election.

Soon after President Richard M. Nixon took office in 1969, Mundt began polling the new administration on their views concerning rural economic development. President Nixon's campaign had focused on foreign affairs, especially ending the war in Vietnam, and he did not seem concerned with domestic policy. In a letter to Mundt, Nixon's assistant Bryce Harlow outlined the administration's view on economic development, confirming that Nixon did not care to focus on domestic economic policy. The letter laid out four administrative directives, including a pilot program to encourage the unemployed to move to areas where jobs currently existed and the establishment of a national database of job vacancy statistics, both assigned to the Department of Labor. A review of the value of regional development programs and possible reforms in the Economic Development Assistance Act, both under purview of the Secretary of Commerce, filled out the administration's policy directives. Harlow dismissed Mundt's request for a special commission on rural economic development, claiming that the Nixon administration's policies on the subject adequately addressed the need for rural-urban balance.[26] Representatives of rural districts would have to find other avenues of bolstering opportunities for their constituents.

The push for development in rural communities did not die with the Nixon administration's apathy, although Mundt was not involved in any future developments, as he suffered a debilitating stroke in late 1969. Nonetheless, regional and local governments began developing their own programs to bring assistance to rural areas. In April 1971, a letter from Lynn Muchmore, director of South Dakota's State Planning Agency, crossed the desk of Mundt's assistant, Robert McCaughey, outlining a commitment made with the Mountain-Plains Federal Regional Council to finance a new program that they titled Model Rural Development. The goal of the program was to increase the responsiveness of state and federal agencies to the needs of rural areas. Despite the reported enthusiasm of residents who would be affected by the program, representatives in Washington, D.C., were still hesitant to support a program that demanded such flexibility.[27]

The outline of the Model Rural Development program focused on revising how South Dakota planned for the allocation of federal development funds. The new planning structure would be titled the Comprehensive Operational Planning System, and its stated goals were to ensure that programs would address specific problems, promote comprehensive planning, remain flexible, and keep local citizens and government involved. The system would be comprised of eight components, the District Planning and Development Committee (DPDC) and its subcommittees, a catalyst unit for relaying information between citizens and the committee, and the Mountain-Plains Federal Regional Council. Arguably, the DPDC was to be the lynchpin for the entire program. It was made up of one commissioner from each participating county, one member from each county's planning commission, the mayors of each first-class city within the district, three members from American Indian reservations, ten additional members selected by the aforementioned members, and *ex officio* membership of the DPDC subcommittees. By executive order of Governor Richard Kneip, South Dakota was divided into six multicounty development districts. Of these, District 1, comprising ten counties in East River from Lake and Moody north to Codington and Deuel, was chosen as the pilot district for the Model Rural Development Program. Planners had chosen the district because it contained a representative combination of small towns and large nonmetro areas.[28] The program began immediately, and by the time Mundt's assistants were reading about it, projects in District 1 were already underway.

The first report on the Model Rural Development Program's actions in the pilot district came out in January 1972. Among the projects described were the Parent Resource for Information, Development and Education (PRIDE) Program, an area beautification program focused on collecting junked vehicles, a drug education program, and an expansion of Manpower (employment agency) programs. A notable project was the proposed establishment of a multicounty housing authority. Project managers at the United States Department of Housing and Urban Development, weary of funding small development projects in lieu of large ones, had suggested it so that they could build thousands of housing units at a time. If a rural area, such as District 1, could make a singular request for development funding that covered multiple counties, it would thus increase its chances of receiving federal funds. In addition to the success of some of these programs, the report stated that a second district of eleven counties West River would be added to the program. The region was so enthusiastic about joining the program that several cities pledged free office space and utilities to staff of the Model Rural Development Program's committee members.[29]

The July 1972 report of District 1 suggested that the first year of the program was a resounding success. By pooling resources and streamlining the planning structure, the most-rural areas of the state greatly increased the amount of funds they received from federal programs, as well as their effectiveness in project execution. The DPDC expanded the scope of its efforts, as well as the number of agencies bringing projects to it. Among the added and expanded initiatives were a youth employment service, sewer and water planning under the Federal Housing Administration (FHA), and certification as an area-wide planning organization from the FHA's parent office, the Department of Housing and Urban Development. By the September 1972 report, the DPDC had established and improved its PRIDE area beautification program, increased funding from the Department of Housing and Urban Development, and expanded its education programs at American Indian schools within District I. The DPDC had also consolidated its accrued knowledge and programs into planning modules that could be printed and distributed to localities wanting to submit plans to the committee. The planning modules included Demographic and Economic Base Analysis, Transportation, Governmental Services, Recreation, and Natural Resources, among others. By pooling their resources and streamlining aid request process, the district received aid that it might never have received given the Nixon administration's blasé attitude toward rural development. The South Dakota's Model Rural Development Program served as an example to surrounding states that needed the same kind of developmental assistance, and the program continues today, with six active planning districts covering sixty-one of the state's sixty-six counties.[30]

The importance of agricultural economy to South Dakota cannot be overstated, and seeing to its welfare is often a bipartisan effort between state Republicans and Democrats. South Dakota has always been primarily Republican, largely due to the GOP's favorable positions towards the agricultural economy and conservative values. Senator Mundt's ability to tap into these values during his campaigns allowed him to enjoy a long congressional career. South Dakota Democrats have enjoyed some success by tapping into those same values, and the 1970s saw both Senate seats filled with Democrats. George McGovern retained his seat in 1974 after he lost his presidential bid to Richard Nixon, and James Abourezk took over Mundt's seat in 1973. McGovern's career, with its focus on foreign policy, offered a contrast to Mundt's. As the United States ended its involvement in Vietnam and entered another recession in 1973, however, McGovern spoke out on tax policy and the farm economy, proposing new personal income tax credits that resembled policies that Nixon and Reagan later instituted and new controls over foreign beef imports. Abourezk, who positioned himself as antiestablishment, did not enjoy much success with his initiatives in office. By 1981, Republicans would regain both Senate seats. As Abourezk retired in 1978, opening the way for Congressman Larry Pressler to capture Mundt's old seat, while McGovern lost to James Abdnor two years later when Ronald Reagan captured the presidency. Abdnor and Pressler both positioned the farm economy as the cornerstone of their campaigns and stressed the notion that the Democratic Party was out of touch with the needs of South Dakotans.[31]

The postwar period saw unprecedented changes in America and South Dakota. As the nature of the agricultural industry and economy evolved and shifted, so too did the nature of politics in the rural United States. Many considered the New Deal policies of the 1930s to be no longer beneficial or necessary for rural development, and farmers demanded policies that would allow them to expand their operations. Senator Karl Mundt brought the issues that rural communities faced to national attention and supported programs that provided the framework necessary for South Dakotans to determine their own paths to success. This framework included irrigation development that gave farmers easier and steadier access to fresh water for their crops and an interstate highway system that increased their ability to travel. The Johnson administration's War on Poverty, although it increased aid to rural communities, was ineffectual in developing programs that rural communities needed to reverse the ongoing decline. The Nixon administration's neglect exacerbated the problem, but it resulted in many of the heartland states taking the initiative for creating their own programs for development, with minor support from the federal government. It is difficult to say if that is the sort of progress that Mundt had envisioned when he first took office in 1938, but the Model Rural Development Program certainly represents a government program that worked for South Dakotans.

NOTES

1. Marcus D. Gross, "Post-war Rural Development," *Papers of the Twenty-Eighth Dakota History Conference* (1996): 171.

2. U.S., Department of Commerce, Bureau of the Census, *The Seventeenth Census of the United States,1950* (Washington, D.C.: Government Printing Office, 1950); Gross, "Post-war Rural Development," p. 171; Carolyn Dimitri, Anne Effland, and Neilson Conklin, "The 20th Century Transformation of U.S. Agriculture and Farm Policy," United States, Department of Agriculture, *Economic Information Bulletin*, no. 3 (June 2005): 6, ers.usda.gov.

3. Gross, "Post-war Rural Development," p. 172.

4. Scott Heidepriem, *A Fair Chance for a Free People: Biography of Karl E. Mundt, United States Senator* (Madison, S.Dak.: Leader Printing Co., 1988), pp. 3–4. The details of Mundt's life and career come from this source.

5. Mundt, *Value of an Education*, copy in Box 1208, Folder 1, Karl E. Mundt Archives, Dakota State University, Madison.

6. Janel M. Curry, "Community Worldview and Rural Systems: A Study of Five Communities in Iowa," *Annals of the Association of American Geographers* 90, no. 4 (2000): 707–8; Heidepriem, *Fair Chance,* p. 20.

7. Mundt, *It's Time for A Fair Chance for the Farmer* (pamphlet), 1936, copy in Box 1602, Mundt Archives.

8. *The Executives' Club News,* 7 Oct. 1938, Box 1205, Folder 2, ibid.

9. Heidepriem, *Fair Chance*, p. 32.

10. "Program for Land and Water Resources Development of the Missouri River Basin, Missouri Basin Inter-Agency Committee," 1949, Box 666, Folder 1, Mundt Archives; Jean Rahja, "Fresh Water on the South Dakota Prairie," *Papers of the Thirty-Third Annual Dakota Conference* (2001): 562–63.

11. Peter Carrels, *Uphill against Water: The Great Dakota Water War* (Lincoln: University of Nebraska Press, 1999), pp. 21–22.

12. "Resolutions of the Nineteenth Annual Convention of the South Dakota Reclamation Association, Pierre, S.Dak., January 16, 1957," Box 396, Mundt Archives.

13. Mundt, "Statement on Oahe Irrigation Unit," Folder 2, ibid.; Adam R. Eastman, *Oahe Unit, James Division, Pick-Sloan Missouri Basin Program*, United States Bureau of Reclamation (Washington, D.C., 2008), p. 10.

14. Dwight D. Eisenhower, Speech to Congress, 22 Feb. 1955, The American Presidency Project, www.presidency.ucsb.edu/ws/index.php?pid=10415; Jim Wilson, "Interstate Highway System," *Papers of the Forty-Second Annual Dakota History Conference* (2010): 142.

15. Wilson, "Interstate Highway System," p. 142.

16. John E. Miller, "Traveling the Road of Change: Historical Forces in the Development of South Dakota Transportation," *South Dakota History* 41 (Summer 2011): 289.

17. Chambers of Commerce of Deadwood, Lead, and Spearfish, Resolutions, 6 July 1965, K. S. Chamberlain to John Emmett Olson, n.d., and Rex E. Whitton to Karl E. Mundt, n.d., all Box 232, Folder 1, Mundt Archives.

18. Mrs. Donald Baldwin to Karl E. Mundt, 17 Feb. 1964, Folder 6, Mrs. Ed Begeman to Karl E. Mundt, 10 Nov. 1964, Folder 8, Mrs. G. F. Barnes to Karl E. Mundt, 19 Apr. 1964, Folder 7, all Box 1002, Mundt Archives; David Torstensson, "Beyond the City: Lyndon Johnson's War on Poverty in Rural America," *Journal of Policy History* 25, no. 4 (2013): 598–99.

19. Freeman, "Address at National Association for Community Development Conference, 30 Jan. 1967," Box 569, Folder 8, and Freeman, "Remarks before representatives of rural-oriented industries, May 13 1968" both Box 569, Folder 7, Mundt Archives.

20. Berry, Letter to constituents, Mar. 1965, Box 1013, Folder 9, ibid.

21. Mundt, Press Release, 17 Mar. 1967, Box 569, Folder 7, ibid.

22. Ibid., 6 Apr. 1967, Box 1425, Folder 2.

23. Pearson, on Rural Job Development Act, 90 Cong. Rec. 19629–31 (21 July 1967); Mundt, Press Release, 24 July, Box 1425, Folder 2, Mundt Archives.

24. Baker, "Address at conference on Appalachia and the American Future, 22 Apr. 1968," Box 569, Folder 7, Mundt Archives.

25. Johnson, quoted ibid.

26. Harlow to Mundt, 26 Apr. 1969, Box 1425, Folder 1a, ibid.

27. Muchmore to Mundt, 20 Apr. 1971, Box 305, Folder 2, ibid.

28. South Dakota Planning Agency, "South Dakota Model Rural Development Proposal," 31 Mar. 1971, Box 305, Folder 2, ibid.

29. First District Model Rural Development Program, Monthly Report, Dec. 1971, Box 381, Folder 7, ibid.

30. Ibid., July, Sept. 1972, Box 1082, Folder 3; South Dakota Planning Districts, Map, denr.sd.gov/des/gw/Sourcewater/Planning_District_Map.pdf.

31. Jon D. Schaff, "A Clear Choice: George McGovern and the 1972 Presidential Race," in *George McGovern: A Political Life, A Political Legacy*, ed. Robert P.

Watson (Pierre: South Dakota Historical Society Press, 2004), p. 130; Mark A. Lempke, "Senator George McGovern and the Role of Religion in South Dakota Political Culture," in *The Plains Political Tradition: Essays on South Dakota Political Culture*, Vol. 2, ed. Jon K. Lauck, John E. Miller, and Donald C. Simmons, Jr. (Pierre: South Dakota Historical Society Press, 2014), p. 171.

MATTHEW PEHL

7 | GENDER POLITICS ON THE PRAIRIE
THE SOUTH DAKOTA COMMISSION ON THE
STATUS OF WOMEN IN THE 1970S

. . .

In March 2006, South Dakota Governor Mike Rounds signed into law what *The New York Times* called "the nation's most sweeping state abortion ban."[1] The law, which prohibited abortion in all cases except to preserve the life of the mother, was a flamboyant provocation clearly designed to trigger a legal confrontation and a possible reversal of the United States Supreme Court's 1973 *Roe* v. *Wade* decision. In 2008, anti-abortion activists in South Dakota launched yet another assault on *Roe* v. *Wade*, this time placing abortion restrictions on a ballot initiative. Once more, in 2014, the South Dakota statehouse considered what would have been one of the most stringent abortion restrictions in the country, preventing any abortion after seven weeks of pregnancy and, in what many critics saw as biased and misleading language, seeking to prevent the "dismemberment or decapitation of certain living unborn children."[2] This flurry of anti-abortion politics burnished the state's national image as a conservative hotbed of pro-natal family values and, almost by definition, a staunch opponent of the allegedly twin evils of permissiveness and feminism. As Carly Thomsen notes, the fact that anti-abortion activists chose South Dakota as the intended launch pad for a *Roe* v. *Wade* challenge, despite the state's low abortion rate, "cannot be dislodged from broader cultural assumptions about the anachronism of the rural . . . Midwest."[3]

The problem with this narrative of intransigent gender conservatism is that none of these laws ever took effect. The 2006 law, while embodying a certain stylishly fervent family-values politics, was forced onto a referendum, where voters rejected it. A truer reading of South Dakota's aggressive twenty-first-century gender traditionalism is to see it, not as an essentialist and timeless characteristic of the state, but as the political outcome of a deeply emotional, hotly contested, and ultimately paradoxical struggle over the meaning of women's equality and the legacy of feminism. The conclusion of this struggle was not preordained in the early 1960s, when the strains of what might be called an agrarian interpretation of second-wave feminism began stirring in South Dakota. On the contrary, the political moment seemed responsive to forces of change. In 1963, President John F. Kennedy signed the Equal Pay Act—the first explicit congressional action on behalf of women in many years—and supported the creation of a Presidential Commission on the Status of Women. Kennedy encouraged states to follow suit, and Governor Nils Boe took heed, establishing the South Dakota Commission on the Status of Women (CSW) in 1963.[4]

The CSW was designed to serve as a fact-finding commission, tasked with researching and publicizing the particular problems encountered by wage-earning women. It certainly was not created as a formally feminist organization. Indeed, most South Dakotans would have looked askance at a state agency that took any part in challenging the deeply rooted and widely appreciated complementary gender system of the typical family farm—that is, the notion that men and women each had necessary, but often separate and unequal, roles to serve and duties to perform in a virtuous society. Lacking any grounding in a social movement or critical political philosophy, the CSW instead functioned as an agent of what I would term "knowledge activism." The women who came to operate the CSW did not intend to revolutionize gender roles, but they recognized that societies can only legislate on issues about which they are informed; and, critically, there are some issues—such as domestic violence, marital rape, and systemic gender wage-gaps—about which society might prefer to remain ignorant. After all, if an issue is not public, it cannot become political and, hence, subject to change. As a nonpartisan, empirically based, fact-finding body, the CSW could push government to respond to the particular problems of women without appearing to challenge the basic underpinnings of relations between the sexes.[5]

For a brief moment in the 1970s, the knowledge activism of CSW seemed to be visibly altering the fabric of state and society. While its profile in the 1960s was quite modest, between 1973 and 1977, the CSW emerged as the political and institutional embodiment of second-wave feminism in South Dakota. In those years, it vastly broadened its vision, public presence, and scope of activities. Many commissioners maintained strong ties with liberal feminist groups such as the National Organization for Women (NOW) and took an active part in lobbying for—or, in the case of commissioners who were also legislators, sponsoring—the Equal Rights Amendment at both the state and national levels. Over time, commissioners discovered that, while gender inequality might express itself most directly in workers' paychecks, its reach was systemic. Thus, CSW not only investigated workplaces, but it also considered the economic difficulties that married homemakers, single women, and widows faced. It shone a spotlight on women's struggles in obtaining job training but also on women's artificially limited access to credit and capital. The organization acknowledged the particular difficulties that American Indian women in South Dakota confronted. In the process, the CSW held conferences and produced booklets to remind women of their rights and to raise consciousness about the nature of gender inequality. Tellingly, the CSW clearly accepted the personal-is-political claim of 1970s-era feminism, meaning that political and economic equality for women would only be possible when there was equal protection for women under the law in the private realm of families, marriages, and relationships. Spurred by this insight, CSW proved crucial in pushing for the construction of women's crisis centers, rape support groups, and wholesale revisions to the state's battery and sexual assault laws.

In the mid-1970s, however, the political chemistry of the state swung abruptly and decisively against liberal feminism, which advocated for women's individuality and autonomy, often at the expense of traditional gender identities. Indeed, the same period that produced the CSW also witnessed the rise of a powerful antifeminist movement—one that would come to shape the political and cultural identity of the Midwest, even as the practical legacy of feminism (such as the continually increasing number of women in professional, governmental, and educational fields) quietly transformed the region. Antifeminism was rooted in a profound rejection of liberalized abortion and perceived threats to traditional family life, which, in South Dakota, meant family life on the farm. In 1978, Republicans won elections at all levels of government; consequently, the CSW found itself populated with antifeminist conservatives and, shortly thereafter, defunded. The state legislature even rescinded its early, enthusiastic ratification of the Equal Rights Amendment. As elsewhere throughout the nation, the antifeminist counterinsurgency helped fuel the rise of conservatism within the state, a transformation that might well be considered the most enduring legacy of the 1970s.[6]

South Dakota feminism was distinct from the gender-equality movement in other regions of the country; it reflected idioms and structures of thought rooted in the history and culture of the region. From the nineteenth and into the twentieth century, women were indispensable to the settlement and development of the rural Midwest because, as historian Mary Neth has shown, farming depended upon a family labor system. Whereas an industrial wage system more easily developed hierarchies that segregated men's work from women's work, farming required the reciprocal labor of both. Gender roles in the Midwest developed less around ideas of the "separate sphere" than around the notion of "complementarity": men had specific jobs to do, but they also required the complementary work of women. Both sexes were interdependent, if unequal. Paula M. Nelson has demonstrated that this idea of complementarity meant that women in West River South Dakota were active figures in their communities, engaged in any number of public endeavors; indeed, the idea helps explain why western states were at the vanguard of woman suffrage. By the postwar period, this legacy of complementary farm women had produced what historian Jenny Barker Devine describes as "agrarian feminisms," or efforts by rural women to simultaneously claim public space and defend their agricultural inheritance. Devine astutely observes that, while rural midwestern women took an increasingly active part in public life in the 1960s and 1970s, they "rejected the feminist label associated with a movement for radical or wage-earning women because feminism, as portrayed in the media and popular discourse, was incompatible with their goals of maintaining a family farm."[7]

Still, complementarity was not quite the same as equality, and the daylight between these positions became clearer in the 1960s and 1970s. Complementarity might provide security and satisfaction within a family labor system, but it offered little comfort to the increasing number of women who, by choice or necessity, worked for wages. It hardly clarified why women should only be hired as low-paid secretaries and take direction from higher-paid men. Complementarity could seem especially obsolete to divorced or single women, and numbers of both were rising in the 1970s. Finally, complementarity rang hollow to intelligent and ambitious women who aspired to a career in the professions, even if they remained traditional in their personal lives. These economic critiques were central to the emerging movement of second-wave feminism, often linked to Betty Friedan and her landmark 1963 book *The Feminine Mystique*, and provided the impetus for much of the CSW's work.[8]

South Dakota feminism emerged as a fusion of the older legacy of the complementary farm wife and the newly emerging concerns of second-wave feminism. Eschewing ideological or systematic debates, South Dakota feminists highlighted the pragmatic and everyday unfairness of women's lives. Little interest was expressed in the more radical ideas associated with women's liberation, which posited a rejection of the very premise of rural life. As Lona Crandall of the Sioux Falls chapter of the National Organization for Women (NOW) made clear in 1973, her group sought "no part of any extreme radical movement in any sense of the word."[9] South Dakota women, insisted NOW activist Mary Lynn Myers, were "not radical at all." Instead, feminism was "very much economically based—pragmatically we were concerned about equal employment opportunity, equal pay for equal work, childcare for working women who needed to support their families —a lot of very basic economic issues."[10] Surely, feminists argued, ordinary citizens could recognize that a gender pay gap or women's lack of access to professional education seemed wrong. This basic unfairness, they claimed, was simply un-South Dakotan. Women's equality did not repudiate the social order but addressed common-sense standards of fairness—what Crandall called equal justice. By the early 1970s, these ideas formed the philosophical bulwark of CSW, and the organization appeared to be on the upswing.

Political currents and generational transitions both played a role. The late 1960s are often depicted as disastrous for Democrats and a crisis-period for liberalism as a political philosophy, but in South Dakota the Democratic tide was still swelling. In 1972, South Dakota had two Democrats in the United States Senate (George McGovern— the 1972 Democratic presidential nominee who ran one of the most explicitly leftist campaigns in United States history—and James Abourezk), a Democrat in the House (Frank Denholm), a Democratic governor (Richard Kneip), a Democratic majority in the state legislature, a vigorous CSW, and arguably the nation's most progressive state

Division of Human Rights, led by Mary Lynn Myers.[11] The election of Democrat Richard Kneip as governor in 1970 would prove especially significant in reviving the dormant CSW. Expressing his position to Lee Ellen Ford, a legislative consultant in Indiana who was investigating women's commissions across the country, Kneip stated unequivocally, "I firmly support and encourage efforts to achieve a changing attitude toward the status of women." Moreover, the governor continued, "Legal equality is not enough; the greater problem lies in equality as a reality." In other words, Kneip envisioned not only the defense of existing rights but an active effort to change conditions and expand rights. As he pointed out to Kay Burgess, one of his choices to revitalize the CSW, he had appointed 123 women to various state boards and commissions during his first year in office (84 were new appointees; the remainder were reappointments).[12]

Kneip's desire to reinvigorate the CSW with new appointees eager to push for substantial social change raised expectations among younger and more liberal women and seemed to expose generational and political tensions. When Kneip appointed Burgess, a Keystone businesswoman and fervent Democrat, in 1971, her response was warm but blunt, "I sincerely trust that this committee will command more stature under your administration than in previous years." Burgess flatly warned, "Unless your Status of Women committee is more meaningful, I am entirely too busy to waste my time and energy on conversation."[13] Like other South Dakota women in the 1970s, Burgess wanted action. The next year and a half would prove to be key transitional years for the committee, as Burgess's activist orientation came to define the character of the CSW.

In April 1972, the CSW hosted a major conference in Pierre called "The World of Work." The conference reveals much about the CSW's evolving self-conception. As an agency charged with researching and informing—not actual lobbying or bill-writing—the CSW viewed conferences as an appropriately nonpartisan forum for addressing women's issues, and it intended the event to provide policymakers with information about women's employment opportunities and offer suggestions for policies that might promote fairness and equity. CSW member Burgess no doubt agreed with this general goal, but another aspect of the conference struck her more forcefully: none of the presenters were women. To her, this lack represented a persistent pattern of women's disempowerment all across state government: symbolic gestures might be offered to them, but women remained barred from actual positions of respect, power, or authority.[14] Other women shared Burgess's perspective. Just months after the World of Work conference, Connie Bowen wrote CSW Chair Winifred Echleberger to complain about "the deplorable situation in state government personnel, where women with qualifications equal to those of men in high positions are invariably secretaries." Bowen urged the CSW to support "affirmative action" to promote women in state government.[15] In the meantime, Burgess resigned from the committee in protest.

The imbroglio over Burgess's resignation offers insight into the shifting nature of gender politics in 1972.[16] Women such as Burgess were inspired by a more assertive, activist vision of feminism than the concerns that initially prompted the creation of CSW in the early 1960s, and they sensed that the time had come to press their case. They had legitimate reason for optimism. Slowly, women were gaining visibility in political institutions; while only two women served in the statehouse before 1972, an additional six were elected by the end of the year (three Democrats and three Republicans).

More significantly, the Equal Rights Amendment (ERA) was gathering support and raising feminists' expectations across the country. As commissioner Ruth Alexander would later write, the ERA was the "center ring" and "the key issue for feminists in the seventies."[17] Suffragist Alice Paul had originally proposed the ERA in 1923 to amend the federal constitution to provide equal rights under law and prohibit discrimination "on account of sex"; it was simple in language and profound in implications, adding a constitutional imprimatur to the concept of gender equality. In March 1972 (just one month before the CSW conference), Congress overwhelmingly approved the amendment and forwarded it to the states for ratification. In South Dakota, the ERA met with strong approval. In public hearings, Republican state senator Oscar Austad even hailed it as "the emancipation proclamation of the twentieth century." In February 1973, the South Dakota legislature endorsed Austad's view, ratifying the amendment by a vote of twenty-two to thirteen. For feminists coalescing around the CSW, the momentum seemed to be with their cause.[18]

Burgess's colleagues on the commission certainly realized that times were changing. For Frances ("Peg") Lamont, a longtime CWS member and later a Republican state senator, the new tenor of women's rights activism threatened to cloud the commission's fundamental purpose. Writing to Burgess, Lamont corrected her misunderstanding regarding the lack of female presenters at the World of Work conference: women had, in fact, been invited to present, but scheduling conflicts prevented them from attending. More to the point, Lamont held, the gender of the presenters was irrelevant. "We are not doing a women's lib conference," she declared. "It is a high level communication of information," and CSW utilized whoever was best qualified.[19] Lamont's distinction is highly revealing. "Women's lib," to Lamont and other South Dakota women's rights activists, held pejorative connotations, raising the titillating specter of sexual libertines burning their bras and denouncing the myth of the vaginal orgasm as part of the patriarchal conspiracy. As historian Beth Bailey has astutely observed, women who invoked the term "liberation" implied that they "sought more than equal rights in the existing society" but rather pursued "fundamental change."[20] The CSW, in contrast, was committed precisely to women's equality within society: as voters, workers, students, and even housewives. Its methods were empirical, impartial, nonpolitical (at least in theory), and informational. It advocated for women's rights through the mechanism of knowledge activism, but it eschewed the transformative, even revolutionary, implications of liberation.

Still, the profile of CSW was changing. Following another CSW conference in November of 1972, Vermillion attorney Ina Litke politely wrote to Governor Kneip to criticize the leadership of Governor Boe's Republican appointee Winifred Echelberger. Litke suggested that Echelberger be replaced to "improve the image of the committee." There is little doubt what Litke had in mind. "An active, progressive [Commission] on the Status of Women would be appreciated by many in South Dakota—not only women," she added, clearly implying that the current CSW was neither particularly active nor progressive. Connie Bowen agreed with Litke. After she wrote to Kneip with an identical complaint, the governor's assistant, Ted Muenster, responded that he, too, felt "a woman of younger vintage and more modern attitudes" should replace Echelberger.[21]

This pressure had the desired result. By 1973, a core group of younger, highly educated, ambitious, and talented women had emerged to provide leadership and energy for the CSW. Ann Thompson, a young attorney from Pierre who had lobbied for the ERA, was appointed chairperson; Lorraine Collins, a freelance writer and civic activist from Belle Fourche, would take over the chairpersonship after Thompson moved on. Ruth Alexander, a professor of English at South Dakota State University, remained involved throughout the decade. Linda Miller, a young teacher from Sioux Falls, was elected to the statehouse in 1972 and was soon appointed to CSW; her friend Loila Hunking was also elected to serve in Pierre and became the last chairperson of CSW. Lona Crandall and Mary Lynn Myers formed a remarkable mother-daughter partnership; while Crandall hosted the Sioux Falls chapter of NOW and served on CSW, Myers had participated in NOW's "Women's Liberation Strike" in Chicago before becoming, at age twenty-six, director of the state Division of Human Rights, which enforced equal-opportunity laws. Winifred Echelberger was moved out of the chairpersonship, though she remained involved with the committee, as did Lamont.[22]

Also in 1973, the state legislature approved a measure giving CWS statutory recognition, chartering it with a mission to "make studies and conduct research into the status of women . . . and suggest ways in which women may reach their potential and make their full contribution as wage earners and citizens."[23] Suddenly flush with legislative approval, a respectable budget, a supportive governor, a staff person, and several active new committee members, CSW entered the mid-1970s as the state government's institutional conduit for South Dakota feminism. As Ruth Alexander recalled, "the heady excitement of gathering with other women from across the state" to address long-recognized but little-acknowledged inequalities provided the group with a surge of energy.[24]

Commissioners had good reason to feel that their activism was needed. Throughout the 1970s, women constituted around 35 percent of the state's labor force, but, like those in many states, South Dakota women dominated a narrow range of often poorly paid occupations: nursing, retail, teaching, or other pink-collar work. In the early 1970s, women constituted only 17 percent of medical school students and 19 percent of law school students. As Nancy Schuette of the University of South Dakota Medical School ruefully noted in 1974, "I was always told little girls become nurses, not doctors."[25] Well into the 1970s, in fact, South Dakota newspapers segregated their "help wanted" notices by gender.[26] Bottled into a handful of jobs that conflated gender with skills, women earned a shocking 53.5 percent of "similarly employed" men—despite the fact that, in 1966, the state had adopted an "equal pay statute" and allowed female employees to sue their employers for lost wages. Still, in 1977, 40 percent of full-time women workers earned under three thousand dollars a year, and one-third of female-headed single families in the state lived in poverty. For the CSW, remediating these disparities and advancing women's economic security was the master key to social and political equality.[27]

CSW's attention was broader than wage-earning women. In the mid-1970s, it also concentrated on the economic perils that confronted stay-at-home wives. "The career of homemaking," CWS commissioner and researcher Mary Ellen McEldowney concluded, "has many economic disadvantages. The major one is that homemakers earn no salary in a society that measures success in dollars and cents." The choice of the word "career" to describe homemaking reveals much about the feminist analysis. McEldowney and her colleagues on the CSW were arguing that homemaking was work; that work in modern American society carries an economic value; and that homemakers, due to law and custom, stood to lose much of the value of their labor whenever their marriage ended, either through death or divorce. While wives were theoretically entitled to a "right to support" (a common point, especially among antifeminists), McEldowney argued that the "meaningful test of this legal right is whether a court will enforce it," and, in fact, almost no court would intervene in any marriage where both spouses remained joined in the same household. Any arrangement in which rights to equality for half of the party depended upon the generosity and magnanimity of the other half might be judged thin.[28]

Neither were housewives guaranteed protection through inheritance, insurance, or alimony. If a woman was widowed and her husband had no will, property would be automatically split between the widow and the children; if a marriage produced two or more children, a widow could receive no more than one-third of her husband's estate. While a husband might will a larger portion of his estate to his wife, in the 1970s, South Dakota was also one of the few states in which a woman could be totally disinherited in the husband's will (without notice). Due to congressional action in 1974, widows might claim some annuity rights to a husband's pension, but only if he was actually retired at the time of death. Social Security was similarly unreliable; it paid only if couples had been married for more than twenty years and then only after the husband had retired or died. As Laurie Shields, a member of the NOW task force on older women and an organizer from the Alliance for the Displaced Homemaker, told CSW commissioners in 1976, homemakers could easily fall between the cracks of welfare, social security, the paid labor force, and the law.[29]

Working along a similar vein in 1974, the commission launched a major investigation into the problem of women's credit discrimination. The credit issue was significant to the CSW, both practically and symbolically. Without access to modern financial instruments, few women could survive outside the orbit of a larger family. While women were legally entitled to equal consideration for loans and credit cards, in reality, financial institutions routinely placed women at a significant disadvantage. As the CSW demonstrated through its statewide survey of banks, credit bureaus, and retail stores, most financial institutions automatically placed a wife's credit history in her husband's file when she married, thus transforming the wife from an individual with her own financial experience to an economic extension of her husband. She did not build her own credit record; indeed, some credit bureaus simply refused to create a separate file for a married woman, even when asked. Therefore, if they were widowed or divorced, women—who already faced the problem of earning almost half of men in the labor force despite higher levels of education—faced daunting barriers to obtaining mortgages, car loans, or credit cards. This issue was not abstract for South Dakota feminists. Mary Lynn Myers, director of the state Division of Human Rights from 1972 to 1978, was repeatedly denied a mortgage because creditors would not count her income along with her husband's. After her career in public service ended in 1978, Myers became the first female loan officer at a Sioux Falls bank.[30]

There were powerful cultural and symbolic reasons for CSW researchers to target credit discrimination. As RoJean Madsen wrote in her report to the commission, "The myth that women are not competent or responsible in economic or financial matters pervades our society." As much as the CSW hoped to open practical opportunities for women, it also wanted to challenge the ideas and assumptions that permitted inequalities to fester in the first place. Feminists faced the delicate task of exposing a sexist structure of thought that seemed, to many men, to be couched not within any inherent hostility toward women but within a common-sense understanding of how the world worked. When a clerk in a large South Dakota chain store refused to take an order unless it was placed in a man's name, she was simply following store policy. When an unmarried South Dakota woman was ridiculed when she applied for a mortgage, the reason seemed obvious to the banker who turned her down: what woman needs a house if she does not have a family? When a lender was asked how women might improve their chances of acquiring credit, he no doubt felt he gave good advice when he responded, "be careful who you marry." Women not only faced the problem of accessing credit as individuals; they faced the challenge of not being *thought of* as individuals.[31]

Thus, even as economic fairness remained at the heart of the commission's agenda, the women were interested in more than bread alone. Indeed, while the CSW strictly avoided association with "women's lib," it inevitably discovered that the lines between equality and liberation could blur. As historian Sara Evans pointed out, distinctions between "liberal" feminists and "radical" liberationists were often rhetorical and permeable rather than rigid and impassable.[32] As pragmatic as South Dakota feminists were, they nevertheless came to understand that political and economic equality necessitated a reshaping of the state's broader culture and its prevailing gender ideology. As Ruth Alexander put it, the commission aspired to "arouse the consciousness and conscience of the male power structure over the inequities women face in South Dakota."[33] The commission's first quarterly newsletter in 1974 featured a column called "Consciousness Razor," which might sharpen the reader's thinking on gender issues. Likewise, on the eve of International Women's Year (1975), the commission solidified arrangements with over forty local South Dakota newspapers to publish a regular information column for women readers called "Did You Know?" Over the next five years, the commission published dozens of columns that were read throughout the state on topics ranging from farm life to job training programs.[34]

Raising consciousness required more than sobering statistics and the legalese of policy eggheads. Like all genuine social movements, feminism needed to encourage, inspire, and provoke: in short, it needed a narrative. To this end, in 1975, the CSW threw itself into the task of preparing a series of books, pamphlets, speakers, and slide shows celebrating the heritage of South Dakota's female pioneers. The commission urged its supporters to collect family stories, conduct interviews with elderly suffrage leaders, and comb the state archives to find images and documents that illustrated women's legacy in the state. By early 1976, the commission had produced a thirty-minute slide show examining women's experiences in the state from the 1850s through the 1920s; microfilmed the papers of Aberdeen suffragist Matilda Joslyn Gage; compiled a bibliography of women in the state; and purchased seventy-five volumes for the state library, including the classic works of suffrage activists. By the end of the year, the CSW had produced a history of pioneer women and another booklet chronicling the history of the woman suffrage movement in South Dakota.[35] Of all her work with the commission, Ruth Alexander later recalled, "the reclaiming of our heritage has seemed to me to be the most significant and long-lasting."[36] While not overtly political, the CSW's historical preservation projects sent a subtly powerful cultural message. They provided feminists with a purposeful sense of context, continuity, and connection within a dramatic and unfolding tale of freedom—and the comfort of knowing that their own efforts did not exist in a vacuum—while reminding men that they did not own history.

Perhaps the popular phrase "the personal is political" captured the most far-reaching and significant insight of 1970s-era feminism. Women's bid for political and economic equality was inextricably predicated upon equity in the so-called private or personal realm of sexuality, family, child bearing, and marriage. Nothing illustrates how deeply this quintessentially feminist analysis of women's needs had permeated the CSW than the committee's investigation of sexual abuse and domestic battery, which began in April of 1978. Indeed, the CSW itself acknowledged that exposing domestic battery "requires investigation in an area regarded as private and sacred," but the impact of the Women's Liberation Movement had demonstrated the necessity of such work. While the evidence was scattered and often underreported, the CSW concluded that domestic abuse in the state was widespread, sadly noting, "For many women . . . battering is an accepted way of life." Especially for women in isolated rural communities, the burden of leaving an abusive relationship was higher than the threat of staying. This fact partially reflected the economic difficulties that many single women confronted, but more broadly, it reflected the unspoken social norms of the state. Although divorce rates in America were surging in the 1970s, divorce, especially for women, remained taboo and shameful even in the case of abuse. For many South Dakotans, the "failure of a marriage implies failure as a woman." These messages were quietly reinforced across the field of social experience. A minister told one woman to forgive and pray for her husband while he beat her. A mother told her daughter that the abuse she suffered was her fault. A number of abused women reported difficulty dealing with police; one social worker, asking police why they under-reported domestic abuse, was told, "We thought you wanted a count of those who did not deserve the beating." Through its exposé of this "conspiracy of silence," CSW was able to advance the case for legal reform and, throughout the late 1970s and early 1980s, South Dakota passed a series of new measures protecting women from domestic abuse, martial rape, and stalking.[37]

Despite these significant successes, the political tide turned quickly and decisively against the CSW in the late 1970s. While feminism's promise of pragmatic, legal fairness was relatively uncontroversial, the movement's insistence on women's equality and advancement in their own right—rather than in their presumed nature as mere complements to men—*did* challenge normative gender categories that were buried so deeply in Great Plains' culture as to seem self-evident and natural rather than invented and created. As one social worker from western South Dakota observed, the dominant culture of the region remained decidedly male-oriented; women, meanwhile, were socialized to be "dependent, childlike, and wanted domination."[38] Some men were openly derisive about feminism's critique of this culture. At a women's liberation symposium in Brookings in the early 1970s, one male participant openly averred: "A woman who is equal is not a woman. I believe in the woman behind the man."[39] Likewise, when University of South Dakota students considered the impact of feminism, male students were caustic. "The idea of a unisex culture is really rather repugnant to me," one male student said. Feminists sought to "bolster their own egos at the cost of men's masculinity. What they don't realize is that men, in the long run, are going to be the dominant ones, and if they continue like they are, they are just asking for trouble." For these men, feminism seemed to be challenging not only the law but the natural ordering of society.[40]

Within this environment, no issue proved more galvanizing for antifeminists than the sudden politicization of abortion after 1973. When the Supreme Court overturned state-level anti-abortion laws in the 1973 case of *Roe* v. *Wade*, many South Dakotans reacted with shock and anger that exploded in the state like a culture bomb. The court decision invalidated an existing South Dakota law, and as the state worked to find an appropriate legal response, Governor Kneip's office was inundated with correspondence from constituents. Kneip, a Democrat but also a devout Catholic, spoke strongly against abortion, a position that drew some criticism. Kathleen Holt, for instance, urged the governor to reconsider his support of new abortion restrictions "since it is a religious issue." She continued: "The stand of the Methodist, Congregational, Presbyterian, et al., is very different from your churches' [*sic*] stand! . . . A woman should have a choice!!"[41] But the overwhelming majority of correspondence indicated deep shock regarding the Supreme Court decision and supported strong measures to restrict abortions in the state. Gil Colussy of Rapid City blamed profiteering doctors and "hoped and prayed that you [Kneip] have the guts to stand up against these promoters of murder who are lining their own pockets with money from doing abortions." Mrs. Walter Mulle of Meckling described abortion as "mass murder" and caustically suggested that women who received the procedure should be sterilized to prevent future abortions.[42]

As South Dakota grappled with the implications of *Roe* v. *Wade*, a growing constituency—both male and female—came to see liberalized abortion as the logical and diabolical end of a far-ranging assault on the sanctity of the American family. Women "libbers," Mrs. Gerald Ailts wrote in the *Sioux Falls Argus Leader*, "reject marriage and motherhood," which is why they pressed for federal day care centers and abortion on demand. "We believe," declared the "Non-Vocal Majority" to the *Rapid City Press* in the early 1970s, "that development of persons with the family unit to be the key to personal and national well-being."[43] In the mid-1970s, Ruth Karim, a Pierre housewife, founded South Dakota Right to Life (SDRTL) to lobby against abortion and advance an antifeminist vision of women's rights. By 1979, SDRTL had established twenty-eight chapters across the state and counted roughly two-thousand members.[44] Significantly, in 1978, newly elected Republican governor William ("Bill") Janklow appointed Karim to the CSW, a decision indicative of the increasingly conservative and anti-feminist tenor of state politics more generally.[44]

The emerging conservative movement concluded that feminism threatened the family unit and thereby endangered the nation it-self. The perception that the American family was changing and that South Dakota families were especially vulnerable was not unreason-able. Around the country, the introduction of no-fault divorce laws in the 1970s led to a historic peak in divorce levels. Media depictions of the generation gap and the youth counterculture furthered the sense of family crisis. And the sudden public appearance of a gay rights movement after 1969 confirmed that traditional definitions of gen-der and sexuality were shifting.[45] More to the point, many rural South Dakotans sensed that the traditional family and community life were changing—even if they personally remained happily married, het-erosexual, and close to their teenagers—because the state's overall demography suggested an uncertain future. The increasingly mecha-nized and capital-intensive nature of post-WWII farming meant that fewer small family farms could survive. Indeed, in 1970, only twenty-five percent of the state's population lived on farms. Meanwhile, over the mid-century decades, fourteen percent of South Dakota's young people left the state and forty-three counties experienced population loss during the 1970s.[46] Because rural life was deeply linked to both a family economy and a broader ideology of Jeffersonian virtue, femi-nist concerns that might be understood in terms of common-sense social equality became increasingly drawn into a culturally fraught, personalized, and polarizing struggle. Every issue that involved gen-der equality came to be seen as a referendum on morality, decency, and the family.

The ERA, supported so warmly in the state in 1973, came under renewed scrutiny as a national Stop ERA movement organized to pre-vent the amendment's ratification. By 1976, South Dakotans were con-sidering a rescission of their ratification vote. That year, Republican Les Klevan of Sturgis, with the backing of Karim's SDRTL, introduced HJR 510, which linked the ERA with abortion and would have made the amendment an issue on the next state ballot. As correspondence to Governor Kneip indicates, the early-1970s concept of feminism as a pragmatic issue of basic fairness was steadily eroding, and a new understanding of feminism as a cultural threat was gaining adherents. Leroy Schneider's response was typical. When the ERA was approved in 1973, "I more or less shrugged my shoulders," he wrote in 1976, "thinking 'sure, women should have equal rights.'" But after hearing the antifeminist critique of the ERA, he worried about what the amendment "would do to women and the family structure," now judging the ERA a "grave mistake." Amy Olson claimed, "Women stand to lose a great deal and our whole culture will degenerate" if the ERA was adopted. While such opponents were receptive to the general idea of fairness and pay equity, they consistently viewed the amendment as a loss, rather than a gain, of rights. In particular they worried about women losing the right to support from a husband and exemption from military service.[47]

Although Governor Kneip defended the ERA, and HJR 510 was defeated, the battle exposed the shakiness of the ERA's support in the state, and the fault line it created would grow ever more pronounced. Indeed, South Dakota seemed like such promising territory for rescission that Phyllis Schlafly, the embodiment of the national Stop ERA movement, visited the state in 1977. With some misgivings, Mary Lynn Myers, head of the state Division of Human Rights, debated Schlafly on the ERA at a public forum in Huron. Myers contends that she won the debate on the merits, but she acknowledges that Schlafly's presence had a debilitating impact on feminism in the state.[48]

Nobody in South Dakota combatted the ERA with the ferocity of Kitty Werthmann, the state-level chairperson of Schlafly's Stop ERA. Born in Austria, Werthmann had lived under both Nazi and Communist regimes before marrying an American doctor and moving to Pierre. In the ERA, Werthmann claimed to discern the glimmerings of totalitarianism, and she campaigned tirelessly to overturn its ratification. Like Karim, Werthmann viewed the passage of the ERA and the liberalization of abortion as basically interrelated issues. As she toured the state to denounce the ERA, Werthmann gathered a small but determined group of followers who viewed themselves as defenders of "true" South Dakota values, standing against an antidemocratic liberal elite that was imposing feminism on an unsuspecting and vulnerable populace. Writing to the *Daily Capital Journal*, Joy Cook articulated this perspective when she praised Werthmann's courage and pointedly asked why the local media refused to report on her activities. "Frankly," Cook declared, "I'm sick of reading about . . . the perverted sex gangs and their activities, the women libbers that tear down the American life style and promote abortion every chance they get, . . . the government programs and policies that degenerate our society and all the biased news coverage that the American public is subjected to."[49] To Werthmann and her allies, sexual libertinism and feminism were interlinked, were rooted in the growth and corruption of the liberal state, and were supported by a compliant intellectual class.

The CSW was not a lobby group for the ERA, and it certainly had never taken anything like an activist position on abortion. However, the majority of CSW members were personally committed to the ERA, and some, including Ann Thompson and Linda Miller, had lobbied for it. From these personal links, antifeminists such as Karim and Werthmann created a powerful narrative that characterized CSW as a partisan and elitist government agency in cahoots with murderous abortionists and family-hating feminists. In early 1979, as another state vote on ERA rescission approached, the CSW found itself caught in a political and cultural crossfire it could not control. In October 1978, the CSW and the newly formed South Dakota Women's Caucus called a meeting to discuss the embattled future of the ERA. Werthmann and fifty of her supporters wanted the group to debate the adoption of an anti-ERA plank.[50] According to Werthmann, the chairperson of CSW at that time, Loila Hunking, demanded that all attendees pledge to work one hundred percent against any effort to defeat the ERA. When Werthmann's group refused, they were asked to leave the meeting, she claimed. "Needless to say," Wethmann wrote to a state senator from Sturgis, "we were most disgusted."[51]

Facing a resurgence of conservative Republicans in state government after the elections of 1978, the CSW had already seen its budget slashed and influence diluted. Ultimately, it was the pressure of antifeminist women such as Karim and Werthmann that doomed the commission. In her letter to state Senator William Grams, Werthmann made the point directly: "Please stop funding the Commission on the Status of Women and in so doing, avoid wasting the TAXpayers' money."[52] In January 1979, public hearings began to consider cutting the last thirty-one thousand dollars of the CSW budget. It was, as a reporter for the *Argus Leader* noted, "one battle in an emotional war . . . with the issue of abortion savaging both sides."[53] Ruth Karim testified against CSW, arguing that her "personal experience" with the commission suggested to her that the group was not, in fact, a neutral, fact-finding group working in the public interest but instead took a "one-sided" approach in favor of both the ERA and abortion.[54]

Following this confrontation, CSW was defunded, the ERA rescinded, and feminism vilified in the state. Subsequently, feminism became a totem of regional politics, often and successfully invoked as a symbol of alien, arrogant, urban, secular, antifamily, big-government liberalism. At the same time, the basic historical force that has propelled the transformation of gender roles over the last century and a half—the integration of women into the paid labor force—continued unabated. Surprisingly, for a state with such a long history of women's work taking place primarily on family farms, South Dakota had the seventh-highest rate of female participation in the paid labor force in 1990; yet, largely because of the extreme gender segregation of the economy, the actual earnings of South Dakota women ranked forty-second in the nation. The story in 2015 remained much the same. By that date, over sixty-five percent of South Dakota women worked for wages, but the average woman working in Sioux Falls or Rapid City earned eleven-thousand dollars less than men. Overall, South Dakota women earned seventy-six cents for every dollar earned by men, a phenomenon that cut across all industries.[55]

The ways in which feminism played out in real lives is more complex than anything that could be captured in polarizing political catchphrases. Juanita Buschkoetter, the young Nebraska woman whose life and marriage anchored the documentary film *The Farmer's Wife* (1998), exemplifies these complexities (though her experience is not, of course, representative of all rural families). Throughout the film, Buschkoetter lives a pinched, precarious economic life as a "complement" to her farmer husband, Darrel. But she had married for love and *chose* her life on the farm when a more comfortable life in the suburbs of Omaha or Sioux Falls could certainly have been available to her. As the film poignantly reveals, Darrel is no omnipotent patriarch; he must work for wages on another person's farm to support his own dream of rural independence. More significantly, he comes to rely, first, on Buschkoetter's ability to communicate with bankers and bureaucrats on behalf of the family farm and, later, as she enrolls in community college and earns wages of her own, with the increasing possibility that farm life is no longer viable and that his wife will become the family breadwinner.[56]

Reflecting on Juanita Buschkoetter's changing circumstances in the film, writer Kathleen Norris tellingly observes: "When rural women decide to pursue an education and career training, they often face terrific obstacles from the people closest to them. A mother-in-law might make pointed remarks about attempting to reach above one's proper station in life, a husband might feel so threatened as to resort to violent means of keeping her a wife at home."[57] Traditional feminism would view Buschkoetter's growth as a vindication: because women have gained equal rights to education and work, both men and women benefit. But the human experience of this newfound freedom is bittersweet. Buschkoetter pursued her education not to *escape* her marriage and her husband's farm but to defend and support them. She was not chasing individual liberation but family survival. For the Buschkoetters, as for many rural midwesterners, aspirations for lives rooted in the traditionalism of the past are uncomfortably and inextricably intertwined with the economic and political forces of liberal modernity.

NOTES

The author wishes to acknowledge the generous support of the Charles and Jane Zoloudek Faculty Research Fellowship at Augustana University. Portions of this essay were written in conjunction with a Methods and Philosophy of History course at Augustana University in the spring of 2016. The author wishes to thank his students, especially Adam Anderson, Carolina Beck, Matthew Housiaux, Kamryn Miller, Sophia Silverman, and Cole Silvertson.

1. Monica Davey, "South Dakota Bans Abortion, Setting Up a Battle," *New York Times,* 7 Mar. 2006, p. 1.

2. Tara Culp-Ressler, "South Dakota Is Considering One of the Harshest Abortion Bans in the Nation," thinkprogress.org/health/2014/02/13/3287541/south-dakota-harsh-abortion-ban/. *See also* ballotpedia.org/ South_Dakota_Abortion _Ban,_Initiative_11_(2008).

3. Carly Thomsen, "The Politics of Narrative, Narrative as Politic: Rethinking

Reproductive Justice Frameworks through the South Dakota Abortion Story," *Feminist Formations* 27 (Summer 2015): 5.

4. For a useful overview of 1970s feminism, *see* Ruth Rosen, *The World Split Open: How the Modern Women's Movement Changed America* (2000; Tantor ebook, 2012). On Kennedy's commission, *see* Dorothy Sue Cobble, *The Other Women's Movement: Workplace Justice and Social Rights in Modern America* (Princeton: Princeton University Press, 2005).

5. For an overview, *see* Ruth Ann Alexander, "South Dakota Women Stake a Claim: A Feminist Memoir, 1964–1989," *South Dakota History* 19 (Winter 1989): 544–49.

6. Much has been written about the rise of conservatism in the 1970s. For an introduction, *see* Bruce J. Schulman and Julian E. Zelitzer, eds., *Rightward Bound: Making America Conservative in the 1970s* (Cambridge: Harvard University Press, 2008).

7. Neth, "Gender and the Family Labor System: Defining Work in the Rural Midwest," *Journal of Social History* 27 (Spring 1994): 563–77; Nelson, *After the West was Won: Homesteaders and Town-Builders in Western South Dakota* (Iowa City: University of Iowa Press, 1986); Devine, *On Behalf of the Family Farm: Iowa Farm Women's Activism since 1945* (Iowa City: University of Iowa Press, 2013), pp. 9–10.

8. For connections between Friedan's writing and women's economic issues, *see* Daniel Horowitz, "Rethinking Betty Friedan and the *Feminine Mystique*: Labor Radicalism and Feminism in Cold War America," *American Quarterly* 48 (Mar. 1996): 1–42.

9. Quoted in *Sioux Falls Argus Leader*, 13 May 1973; this newspaper clipping and many other relevant clippings are contained in "Newspaper clippings," Box 1, the Papers of the National Organization for Women (NOW), Vermillion (S.Dak.) Chapter, Archives & Special Collections, University of South Dakota (USD), Vermillion.

10. Myers, interview with author, Sioux Falls, S.Dak., 31 Mar. 2016, recording in author's possession.

11. Jon K. Lauck, "'It Disappeared as Quickly as it Came': The Democratic Surge and Republican Comeback in South Dakota Politics, 1970–1980," *South Dakota History* 46 (Summer 2016): 95–140.

12. Kneip to Ford, 2 June 1971, and Kneip to Burgess, 13 Apr. 1972, both in "Status of Women," Box 39, Richard Kneip Papers, Archives & Special Collections, USD.

13. Burgess to Kneip, 13 Aug.1971, ibid.

14. Kay [Burgess] Valdes to Kneip, 22 Apr. 1972, ibid.

15. Bowen to Echelberger, 28 Nov. 1972, ibid.

16. Kneip to Burgess, 13 Apr. 1972, ibid.; [Burgess] Valdes to Kneip, 22 Apr. 1972.

17. Alexander, "South Dakota Women," p. 549.

18. Matthew Housiaux, "The Equal Rights Amendment in South Dakota," pp. 6–7, paper in author's possession.

19. Lamont to Burgess, 13 Apr. 1972, Kneip Papers.

20. Bailey, "She 'Can Bring Home the Bacon': Negotiating Gender in the 1970s," in *America in the 70s*, ed. Beth Bailey and David Farber (Lawrence: University Press of Kansas, 2004), p. 110.

21. Litke to Kneip and Muenster to Bowen, 1 Dec. 1972, both in Kneip Papers.

22. Alexander, "South Dakota Women," pp. 544–45; Myers, interview; Linda Lea (Miller) Viken, interview with author, Sioux Falls, S.Dak., March 11, 2016; Collins, Resume, 29 June 1974, File "Lorraine Collins," Box 3, CSW Papers, South Dakota Department of Social Services, #85-180, State Archives Collection, South Dakota State Historical Society (SDSHS), Pierre.

23. "An Act," Binder 3, HB645, Commission on the Status of Women, #2003-080, State Archives Collection, SDSHS.

24. Alexander, "South Dakota Women," p. 545.

25. Quoted in student newspaper, *Volante* (USD, Vermillion), 2 Apr. 1974.

26. Myers, interview.

27. "Where We're At," *South Dakota Commission on the Status of Women (SDCSW) Newsletter* 3 (Aug. 1977): 3.

28. McEldowney, "The Legal Status of Home-Makers in South Dakota," Homemakers Committee, National Commission on the International Women's Year (Washington, D.C., 1977), pp. 3, 24, copy in "Family Law," Box 7, CSW Papers.

29. Ibid., pp. 11–20; "Laurie Shields Represents Homemakers," *SDCSW Newsletter* 2 (June 1976): 2–3.

30. RoJean Madsen, "South Dakota Women and Credit: A Study," CSW (Pierre, S.Dak., Summer 1974); Myers, interview.

31. Madsen, "South Dakota Women and Credit," pp. 9, 15.

32. Evans, "Beyond Declension: Feminist Radicalism in the 1970s and 1980s," in *The World the Sixties Made: Politics and Culture in Recent America*, ed. Van Gosse and Richard R. Moser (Philadelphia: Temple University Press, 2008), pp. 52–65.

33. Alexander, "South Dakota Women," p. 545.

34. A full run of the "Did You Know?" columns, along with agreements to publish with South Dakota newspapers, are in Box 3 (unprocessed), Ruth Ann Alexander Papers, H. M. Briggs Library, South Dakota State University, Brookings.

35. "CSW Preserves Women's Heritage," *SDCSW Newsletter* 2 (Feb. 1976): 1, 3.

36. Alexander, "South Dakota Women," p. 547.

37. Joyce Eckbald, "Conspiracy of Silence: A Report on Spousal Abuse in South Dakota," CSW (Pierre, Nov. 1979), pp. 20, 25, 28–29.

38. Ibid., p. 30.

39. Quoted in unidentified news article, "Newsclippings," Box 1, NOW Papers.

40. Quoted in Carol Petrik, "Men Predict Women's Liberation Is Doomed Cause," *Volante*, 20 Oct. 1970. The author gratefully acknowledges Carolina Beck for discovering this source.

41. Holt to Kneip, Mar. 1973, "Abortion," Box 171, Kneip Papers.

42. Colussy to Kneip, 23 Apr.1973, and Mulle to Kneip, 2 Apr. 1973, both ibid.

43. Letter to the editor, *Sioux Falls Argus Leader*, 14 Feb. 1973, and "Women's Lib Challenged," *Rapid City Press*, n.d., both in "Newsclippings," Box 1, NOW Papers.

44. "Testimony of Ruth Karim," Jan. 1979, "ERA," Box 3, Alexander Papers.

45. Especially insightful on these issues are Natasha Zaretsky, *No Direction Home: The American Family and the Fear of National Decline* (Chapel Hill: University of North Carolina Press, 2007), and Robert O. Self, *All in the Family: The Realignment of American Politics since the 1960s* (New York: Macmillian, 2012).

46. R. Douglas Hurt, *The Big Empty: The Great Plains in the Twentieth Century* (Tucson: University of Arizona Press, 2011), pp. 177, 195.

47. Leroy Schneider to Kneip, 30 Jan. 1976, and Amy Olson to Kneip, 19 Jan. 1976, both in "ERA," Box 173, Kneip Papers.

48. Myers, interview.

49. Letter to the editor, *Daily Capital Journal*, n.d., clipping in "ERA," Box 3, Alexander Papers.

50. Viken, interview.

51. Werthmann to Senator W. Grams, 21 Oct. 1978, in "ERA," Box 3, Alexander Papers.

52. Ibid.

53. "Hearing Reflects War between Women," *Sioux Falls Argus Leader*, 28 Jan. 1979.

54. "Testimony of Ruth Karim."

55. Ann Mari May and Robert H. Watrel, "Occupational Segregation of Women on the Great Plains," *Great Plains Research* 10 (Spring 2000): 171; "South Dakota Gender Wage Tops $11,000," South Dakota Dashboard, www.south dakotadashboard.org/south-dakota-gender-wage-gap-tops-11-000; "South Dakota," Status of Women in the States, statusofwomendata.org/explore-the-data/state-data/south-dakota/.

56. *The Farmer's Wife*, David Sutherland Productions, 1998.

57. Norris, "On 'The Farmer's Wife,'" pbs.org/wgbh/pages/frontline/shows/farmerswife/essays/norris.html.

CORY M. HAALA

8 | REPLANTING THE GRASSROOTS

REMAKING THE SOUTH DAKOTA DEMOCRATIC
PARTY FROM MCGOVERN TO DASCHLE,
1980–1986

• • •

On 18 October 1980, amid a bitter reelection campaign, George McGovern walked into West Sioux Hardware in Sioux Falls to purchase a pheasant hunting license, a tradition for any candidate for office in South Dakota. Though the clerk recognized him as the state's three-term United States senator, she informed him that because he lacked a valid South Dakota driver's license, she could not sell him the permit. It was perhaps the penultimate indignity the 1972 presidential candidate would have to endure. His opponent, West River congressman James Abdnor, quipped, "It shows he's not out in South Dakota a great deal." Though a local game official helped him secure a license, it was another strike against the scion of prairie populism.[1] Painted as out-of-touch, McGovern succumbed to the final indignity of defeat just a week later, when Abdnor thrashed him by twenty percentage points, ending a decade of Democratic dominance in South Dakota.

McGovern's defeat was the final blow for Democrats during an era of surging conservatism in South Dakota, which began in the late 1970s. Former state attorney general William ("Bill") Janklow's election as governor (1978) and Larry Pressler's capture of outgoing Democratic senator James Abourezk's seat (1978) were the first major victories of the Reagan Revolution in South Dakota. The state had been ripe for the New Right movement made up of "states' rights federalists, moral traditionalists, and business interests."[2] Historian Jon K. Lauck—echoing McGovern after his 1980 defeat—argued that the fall of the South Dakota Democratic Party (SDDP) in the 1970s was due to "the essential conservatism of South Dakota," noting that to be generally electable Democrats must "be seen as moderate," tap into "an animated farm vote," and rely "on Republican mistakes and a fortuitous convergence of helpful factors."[3] Others have highlighted the rise of evangelical conservatism, which pushed South Dakota's political culture to the right.[4] South Dakota voters during the late 1970s demonstrated, as historian Jon D. Schaff has argued, that the state's "default partisan allegiance is to the Republican Party." In this model, South Dakota is an inherently conservative state that adheres to family values and individual enterprise, while Democratic success is anomalous and the state party is ineffectual or wholly absent.[5] These findings are supported, moreover, by Democrats' failure to win a statewide race between 2008 and 2018 and by the fact that over the last 125 years, Republicans have won 83.2 percent—437 of 525—of elections for partisan, statewide offices.[6]

The model, however, ignores the fact that from 1986 until 2004, two-thirds of South Dakota's congressional delegation was Democratic, implying either an incredibly long anomaly or that South Dakota does, in fact, have some affinity for liberalism. Historians have noted that the "agrarian aspect of South Dakota political culture [still gave] Democrats an opening for success."[7] Indeed, even the immense gains the South Dakota Republicans made in the early 1980s may have been due to an exceptionally conservative national climate. A 1981 report by University of South Dakota political science professor Alan Clem noted that national anti-incumbency trends were reflected in South Dakota: three-term Democratic governor Richard Kneip was no longer governor; Jimmy Carter was unpopular; and McGovern himself had recognized that his 1980 reelection bid would be a major challenge. Democrats retooled their message between 1980 and 1986, led primarily by Congressman Tom Daschle, who would become the standard-bearer for the Democratic Party in South Dakota during the 1980s and 1990s. During the years between McGovern's defeat and Daschle's Senate victory, South Dakota Democrats returned to agrarian populism, downplayed social liberalism, embraced voters' preference for individual enterprise, and pitted the state's interests against "unfair" external forces, particularly the federal government. While the party itself struggled to win votes due to its own institutional weakness, Democratic candidates such as Tom Daschle projected more pragmatic, centrist Democratic politics than George McGovern's strident progressivism.[8]

The 1980 elections demonstrated just how disconnected and disorganized leading South Dakota Democrats and the state party had become. McGovern had long identified with his constituents and colleagues as a Prairie Populist, stating, "we never thought that farmers were getting a good enough deal."[9] In 1978, after the GOP routed the Democrats from every state-level partisan office except the East River congressional seat and a public utilities commissioner, McGovern wrote outgoing Democratic governor Harvey Wollman, "You are mindful, as I am, of the serious challenges ahead for the South Dakota Democratic Party."[10] Moreover, as one *Yankton Press and Dakotan* editorial noted, "There were times that even candidates on the Democratic ticket sensed that there was a 'lack of direction.'"[11] South Dakota Republicans framed Democrats as out-of-touch and loyal to national liberalism not South Dakotans. In a 1979 telegram to McGovern and Daschle, Janklow accused the two of taking money from out-of-state labor unions, reminding them, "You got your voters from South Dakota farmers and ranchers."[12]

South Dakota Democrats struggled to adapt to changing voter preferences. In the 1980 West River congressional primary, the messages of Pennington County Democratic Party chairman Tom Katus and incumbent Public Utilities Commissioner Ken Stofferahn embodied the growing split in the South Dakota Democratic Party (SDDP). Katus embraced government action and called for a "total commitment to an alternative energy program," while Stofferahn tapped South Dakotans' resentment of the federal government, highlighting its inability to deal with inflation. McGovern, more tellingly, faced a stiff challenge from Larry Schumaker, a pro-life native of Britton who returned to South Dakota from his residence in Texas to highlight McGovern's ultra-liberal tendencies.[13] McGovern won only 62.5 percent of the vote as Schumaker's backers targeted conservative Democrats in "farming groups, gun-owner clubs, national defense groups, and right-to-life organizations."[14]

McGovern's inability to reframe debates over issues important to South Dakotans reflected the general weakness of the Democratic Party. At the outset of the 1980 election cycle, McGovern was one of six veteran liberal senators targeted and eventually defeated by the National Conservative Political Action Committee (NCPAC).[15] By June, McGovern's adviser George V. Cunningham reported that two hundred fifty thousand dollars "in NCPAC negatives... have been effective in turning voters away from you—both in the Democratic Party and certainly among GOP and Independents."[16] McGovern was vulnerable to assertions that he was more of a Washington insider than a South Dakotan. The NCPAC was confident enough of victory to withdraw in August after spending one hundred and fifty thousand dollars on the race, citing Abdnor's wide lead over McGovern. Seizing on the influence of PACs, McGovern finally began to campaign hard in October and painted Abdnor as beholden to big business. Political observers soon noted that McGovern was making up the twenty-six-point gap by attacking Abdnor's negative campaign and unwillingness to debate.[17]

McGovern remained in a weak position because of the increasing prominence of the abortion issue, emblematic of social issues traditionally important to South Dakota. In October, McGovern took his wife Eleanor and their children to Watertown for their thirty-seventh wedding anniversary to combat his antifamily image. He complained, "It's just the frustration of my life that I'm the one labeled as antifamily when I've been married for 37 years, have five children and four grandchildren, and my opponent is a bachelor."[18] McGovern's defense of federal farm programs was less effective in appealing to voters than it had been in previous elections, prompting comment from the *Fort Pierre Times*: "It's obvious from McGovern's newfound philosophy that he's in political trouble. He's always been able to return to South Dakota six months before the election in the past and whip up public opinion to his side." The newspaper dubbed McGovern "South Dakota's senior chameleon" for shifting his positions during an election-year.[19] Especially across the western two-thirds of the state, McGovern was now considered a Washington liberal.

The 1980 elections marked the end of the SDDP's 1970s coalition and demonstrated the need for the party to rebuild. In 1980 only freshmen United States Congressman Tom Daschle and Public Utilities Commissioner George Kane won elections for the Democrats. Registered Democrats fell from 45.9 percent of the electorate in 1978 to 45.1 percent in 1980; Republicans increased from 45.6 percent to 46.1 percent. McGovern won just 62 percent of his traditional base of moderates and independents, while West River congressional candidate Ken Stofferahn won 68 percent of registered Democrats' votes. Meanwhile, Daschle won 4 percent more of the vote than the total number of registered Democrats. Indicative of his moderate appeal, Daschle outpolled McGovern by 33,838 votes.[20] McGovern and the SDDP suffered from the breakdown of their old coalition of "family farmers, Democrats, small-town Catholics, and moderate Republicans."[21] This phenomenon was not uniquely South Dakotan, but it ended the Democratic surge in the state during the 1970s.

During the two years between McGovern's defeat and Daschle's 1982 victory, the SDDP struggled to define its mission and lacked the resources for widespread grassroots campaigning. Leading Democrats proposed different explanations for the party's demise. Former governor Richard Kneip blamed the party's inability to take hardline platform positions, while his successor Harvey Wollman believed that voters merely wanted "the status quo and the good old days" but would come back to the Democratic Party when they wanted change. Still others believed that a lengthy and contested primary between Roger McKellips and Wollman for the Democratic gubernatorial nomination in 1978 left the party leadership factionalized and voters turned off to Democratic politics.[22] McGovern campaign manager George Cunningham cited a lack of "professional horsepower in the state to run a strong campaign," while McGovern argued that South Dakota was "essentially a conservative state."[23] Former Democratic congressman Frank Denholm later reflected, Democrats "couldn't stand political prosperity. They were too selfish. Everyone had to have their own campaign and they couldn't do things together."[24]

To overcome these internal divisions, the SDDP sought to regain political momentum in order to remain relevant. South Dakota's reduction to one at-large congressional seat meant that the 1982 election would likely pit two-term Democrat Tom Daschle against Abdnor's successor in Congress, Clint Roberts, the first-term GOP representative and longtime Republican state senator from Presho. Noting the traditional weakness of state Democrats in West River counties, Clem observed that the Democratic Party would need to court the western half of the state aggressively.[25]

The new leadership of the SDDP charted a new course for the party in the 1980s. Facing crippling debts incurred in the 1970s, state party chair Loila Hunking spoke in 1981 of the need to "demonstrate to the press, the public, and ourselves that the Democratic Party is indeed alive and well and on the comeback trail in South Dakota."[26] The SDDP, Hunking later recalled, "was in such a mess they decided that even a woman could do a better job than what had been done."[27] Others such as South Dakota Young Democrats president Bob Abbott demanded consistency: "Some people think it is a sporadic organization —here today, gone tomorrow. . . . As long as these attitudes continue, the Young Democrats will never evolve into an active training ground for the future leaders in South Dakota."[28] Meanwhile, McGovern joined the Coalition for Common Sense, a PAC organized to fight extremist groups across the nation, and focused on national politics. He did, however, argue in June 1981 that Democrats "must be willing to accept some element of compromise for the good of both the party and the nation."[29] It was a curious about-face for the uncompromising progressive, but it demonstrated shifting winds within the party, especially at the local level.

Slowly, an embrace of pragmatism developed within the SDDP, despite the resistance of some hard-core McGovern supporters.[30] In a February 1981 editorial, Cunningham argued that the SDDP needed "a good deal of voter education, dissemination of information and a solid organizational structure . . . built around a pragmatic rethinking of what the party really stands for."[31] In June 1981 meetings led by Hunking, prominent Democratic leaders including Harvey Wollman, members of Daschle's Washington staff, and state senators Roger McKellips, Jake Krull, and Lars Herseth vowed to pursue grassroots organizing and called for a rethinking of party positions.[32] Daschle rejected the idea that the party could "hope to regain the allegiance of voters here in South Dakota . . . by trying to pretend we are more Republican than the Republicans." Instead, he argued, the party needed to reassert itself as the "champion of the most competitive sector of our entire economy, the family farm." Blaming the old guard of the Democratic Party for blind idealism, he challenged the state party to "help them attain that life, not by giving it to them with somebody else's tax dollars, but by providing the environment in which they have a fighting chance to earn it."[33] Daschle emphasized a balanced budget amendment and aid to farmers, attacking the Reagan administration for defending the wealthy.[34]

Daschle's articulation of views more moderate than McGovern's blended populist pragmatism with an economically progressive, socially ambivalent, or conservative, brand of liberalism committed to local issues. The SDDP offered little infrastructure to advance that vision, however, and remained small and in debt. Moreover, Governor

Janklow's populism continued to stymie the SDDP in state-level politics. In 1980, he guided the state's purchase of the Milwaukee Road's rail lines in South Dakota, passing a temporary one-cent sales tax to fund the purchase and creating a railroad authority to improve and manage over thirteen hundred miles of track. Amid Reagan-era fiscal conservatism and distrust of government, Janklow's purchase of the railroad and his luring of Citibank to the Sioux Falls area by loosening state interest-rate restrictions reflected South Dakotans' preference for local benefits over inherent conservatism. Polls conducted by the Daschle campaign in December 1981 reflected South Dakotans' overwhelming approval for the governor's pragmatic brand of leadership. In Pierre, Democrats remained a weak opposition party, outnumbered in the state legislature seventy-four to thirty-one. Yet the plans for Daschle's 1982 campaign provided a blueprint for the state party, using local issues to frame how Democrats could better address average citizens' needs.[35]

By the 1982 elections, the SDDP clung to one congressional seat while struggling to identify and support viable candidates. Running Sioux Falls state senator Mike O'Connor for governor and lining up behind Daschle, the SDDP hoped that it could be "the party of George McGovern, Tom Daschle, and Richard Kneip."[36] O'Connor called for counties across the state to take the initiative in rebuilding the party: "For too long we have watched as individual Democratic campaigns became strong by performing the tasks traditionally done by the party. We must resist the temptation to allow this erosion of party strength. Our strength as a party is served as we render political service to our Democratic candidate(s), not vice versa."[37] As Daschle and the SDDP hit the campaign trail during 1982, only the congressional race captured significant voter attention.

Daschle avoided the mistakes that plagued McGovern in 1980 and ran an aggressive, pragmatic campaign. When the new Mid-America Conservative PAC announced in July 1981 that it planned to spend up to thirty-five thousand dollars to attack Daschle's voting record, the congressman struck back, calling them "the sorriest spectacle in politics today."[38] Polls revealed ambivalent views in the public as voters expressed confidence in Reagan's economic policies but harbored a strong sense that his policies discriminated against poor and working people. Party leaders saw a need to avoid McGovern's mistakes: "Abortion is a potentially serious problem. Probably the best response is to avoid it."[39]

Daschle needed to make inroads with more-conservative West River voters. His lack of name recognition declined from forty-two percent unfamiliar in April 1981 to eleven percent by December, and across the state, he had a sixty-four percent favorable rating. Daschle's campaign team crafted a populist image for the candidate. He co-chaired a joint meeting with Canadian lawmakers to secure markets for local wheat, promoted the Earth Resources Observation and Science (EROS) Center near Sioux Falls, and solicited feedback from voters as he helped draft farm legislation. Daschle was on the campaign trail taking the message to the voters, but the SDDP struggled to formulate organized opposition to the state Republican Party.[40]

In September 1982, Hunking appointed longtime Democratic activist Marilyn Teske of Pierre as executive director of the party. During the 1982 State Fair, Teske and the SDDP passed out ten thousand newspapers attacking Janklow for lambasting senators and "being a puppet of the Reagan Administration." O'Connor distanced himself from the action—wanting, in his words, to run a positive campaign. Janklow, meanwhile, had been tipped off by "Democratic friends in Sioux Falls."[41] Attacking the popular incumbent created the same perception of meanness that had dogged McGovern. The episode, a departure from Hunking's stated attempts to rebuild the party "without taking on Governor Janklow, [or] chastising him in the press," backfired.[42] The SDDP wildly underestimated Janklow's popularity among South Dakotans; his style of pragmatic populism transcended party affiliation.

As South Dakota Democrats struggled to gain their footing against Janklow, however, the rapidly declining fortunes of family farms across the Great Plains provided them with ammunition against the federal government and allowed them to reposition themselves as champions of the South Dakota farmer. National conservatives had tied McGovern to Jimmy Carter's 1980 embargo on grain shipments to the Soviet Union, damaging McGovern in the eyes of South Dakota's farming bloc. As the average real value of farmland dropped by twenty-nine percent between 1980 and 1984 and net farm numbers declined by four percent between 1978 and 1982, agrarian discontent led activists to pin the blame for the farm crisis on federal policy. Farmers from forty-four states sued Secretary of Agriculture Richard Lyng, then his successor John Block.[43] By the 1970s, scholar Catherine Mc-Nicol Stock noted, "A growing number of white men in rural America had come to believe that [corporate friendly] liberalism had little or nothing to offer them."[44] As prices for a bushel of corn dropped nearly one dollar to $2.52 a bushel and soybeans plummeted two dollars to $5.80 a bushel in 1984, South Dakota farmers sought federal redress for economic wrongs as Reagan joked that he should "keep the grain and export the farmers."[45] In fact, in 1982 O'Connor had run for governor partially on a platform of Great Plains states establishing a grain exporting cartel similar to the Organization of Petroleum Exporting Countries (OPEC). While eight states signed an agreement to act on his program, which was endorsed by candidates such as Daschle and Wollman, it presaged mixed successes for South Dakota Democrats.[46] Agrarian anger at the federal government enabled the rise of Democrats to national positions, but Republicans often vented their anger at the state level, stunting the rise of the state Democratic Party.

At the federal level, Daschle positioned himself as a South Dakotan against the out-of-touch federal government. In an October speech at the National Farm Crisis Day Rally in Nevada, Iowa, Daschle attacked "any farmer who believes the October promises of those who have helped David Stockman and John Block destroy the farm coalition," accusing the administration's budget handlers of demanding a "foreclose first" policy while allowing oil companies to exploit tax loopholes. Daschle joined the SDDP's concern with fighting the national GOP message and rural voters' concerns over Reagan's economic policies. He extended that message to environmental issues, appealing both to environmentalist Democrats and ranchers and farmers who depended on the Missouri River.[47]

Daschle's largest break from McGovern's 1980 strategy was his stance against abortion, reflecting some of the traditionally conservative elements of South Dakota political culture. Attacking both his opponent and "other groups from out-of-state" in an October 1982 letter to his constituents, Daschle decried "outright lies" that he favored abortion, experimentation on fetuses, and sex crimes, hammering home the fact that he was a Catholic and a "life-long South Dakotan . . . not in favor of abortion."[48] Daschle's position reflected his avoidance of stances on social issues and his emphasis on his status as a South Dakotan.

A series of East River debates in the early summer demonstrated how Daschle pitted South Dakota against the Republican-dominated federal government and positioned Democrats as the ones responsive to voters' needs. Daschle tied opponent Clint Roberts to the Reagan administration's tax cuts and asked the voters if they felt the benefits of those cuts.[49] After Roberts canceled an October debate due to medical issues, Daschle continued face-to-face meetings across the region; Janklow and Senator Larry Pressler provided lukewarm support for Roberts; and Reagan concluded his campaign swing for Republicans without visiting South Dakota. Daschle won the race to the center. One *Sioux Falls Argus Leader* editorial wryly noted, "Some who know Daschle well think he has some Republican blood in him and is anything but a flaming liberal."[50] Yet, cynicism aside, Daschle succeeded in making the most important point in South Dakota politics—that he was best for South Dakota.

As Daschle solidified his coalition, though, the SDDP floundered. Legislative coordinator Scott MacGregor excoriated the executive board in early October for failing to get various legislative districts to commit one thousand dollars per district to statewide advertising campaigns. O'Connor demanded that counties and legislative districts assume more authority for the campaigns in July, but just two months later, the party continued to perform those tasks. Teske subsequently announced that because fundraising did not pick up in September, they were reducing staffers to half-time in October, had lost volunteers, were not printing the *Democratic Forum* that month, and were giving up their word processors.[51]

As voters went to the polls in 1982, it was a tale of two Democratic parties: the well-organized and well-funded Daschle campaign and the flagging SDDP. Voters expressed appreciation for Governor Janklow's "take-charge" style, as he thrashed O'Connor, 71 percent to 29 percent. Daschle held off a surprisingly close challenge from Roberts, winning a greater percentage of voters East River (56.3 percent) than Roberts did West River (52.8 percent). The party stumbled badly in the state legislature, losing a seat in the senate and five more in the house.[52] Considering that a Daschle survey from December 1981 found that 51 percent of South Dakotans did not consider Republicans' domination of state offices problematic, it was clear that party balance "was not an important criteria."[53] Hunking stepped down as state chair to seek elected office in Sioux Falls, and the only other Democrat elected to statewide office, Public Utilities Commissioner Dennis Eisnach, tore into the party for failing to "take the lead in going into the counties and developing those basic functions of a political organization and I don't mean just raising money."[54] The SDDP diagnosed its own weakness in the 1982 election cycle but lacked the infrastructure to address those shortcomings. Daschle succeeded thanks to his incumbency and his well-organized, populist campaign. O'Connor and Eisnach shared his vision but faced a formidable foe in Janklow. Eventually, they hoped, the SDDP could model the Daschle strategy.

As the farm crisis deepened ahead of the 1984 elections, the SDDP developed a more locally focused electoral strategy around agricultural issues. Newly elected state chair Bob Williams, a state senator from Aberdeen, and other officials took to the campaign trail alongside Daschle in 1983, increasing party visibility and opposition to the Reagan administration. In March, Williams announced his plans to "revitalize our state party organization from the ground up."[55] Winning policy battles helped: while Janklow and the Republicans maintained their supermajority, Janklow supported a Democrat-backed agriculture and small business bill. Daschle declared his belief that the party was "on the upswing," noting increased party organization and more local candidates running against Republicans.[56]

The 1984 elections would not be easy, however, as Democratic gains would be tested against popular Republican incumbents. The SDDP took the opportunity to shore up its structural deficiencies and lay the groundwork for three statewide races in 1986. Political observers had already noted that while Democratic United States Senate candidate George Cunningham knew South Dakota voters from his time as McGovern's campaign adviser, incumbent senator Larry Pressler was a well-liked moderate.[57] Asking Richard Kneip, Harvey Wollman, and George Cunningham all to answer the question "How can a Democrat win in 1984?", the *Democratic Forum* received different answers. While Wollman called for a candidate with "the capacity of a George McGovern and the hometown-boy believability of Tom Daschle," Cunningham and Kneip both asked for a candidate who could forge "immediate association with the Democratic Party in every way possible," would "share with Democratic officials [any] thoughts on basic issues affecting the people of South Dakota," and "be able to unify the Democratic Party [as] . . . a credible alternative to the incumbent." "Realistically," to Cunningham, "the basic Democratic goals in the 1984 election are to reelect Congressman Daschle and PUC Commissioner Ken Stofferahn while increasing Democratic representation in the State Legislature." Tellingly, in his response on the Senate race—before he even won the nomination—he hoped for a "modest chance of success."[58]

Daschle, meanwhile, continued to solidify his statewide coalition, having locked up moderate voters in advance of the 1984 election. Feted by the Rapid City Chamber of Commerce for his vote against legislation that would have taxed small businesses and invoking his support for rural electrification before an East River co-op, Daschle canvassed the state, reminding voters of his commitment to South Dakota issues. His Republican opponent, Dale Bell of Spearfish, a longtime Reagan-admirer-turned-director-of-public-affairs for the State Department of Health and Human Services, offered little resistance. Attacking Daschle via punch-card advertisements and soliciting clergy help in recruiting their congregations, Bell drew the ire of both the press and Daschle. By State Fair season, the incumbent had doubled Bell's standing in the polls. Daschle continued to craft his campaign around local issues, announcing his intention to sue Secretary of Agriculture John Block for refusing to support South Dakota farmers during spring flooding.[59]

While Daschle appeared safe, the SDDP recognized their generally weak position in 1984. Bob Williams bemoaned, "The reason so many Republicans keep getting elected is because Democrats are voting for them." Still, Williams challenged the notion that South Dakota was a clearly Republican state, blaming "the occasional creation of factions within the party" for Democratic problems and emphasizing the "need to put our differences behind us and work together to support the entire Democratic ticket."[60] Former congressional candidate Bob Samuelson announced that the party had been "closet Democrats too long," and Wessington Springs state representative Jim Burg challenged the party to publicize how Republicans in the state legislature blocked tax-reform policies at every turn. While Williams backed off his earlier goal of electing ten to fifteen new legislators, the SDDP re-committed to addressing local issues and gently pushed solutions of government intervention to address the fiscal shortcomings of the Reagan and Janklow administrations.[61]

Defeats in 1984 belied a stabilized South Dakota Democratic Party. Once again, it lost another seat in the state senate, and Cunningham lost his bid for the United States Senate by the largest margin in South Dakota history. Former congressman Frank Denholm recalled that Cunningham, "didn't even get the Democratic vote," including Denholm's.[62] A prominent figure from McGovern days, Cunningham represented little of the emerging Democratic coalition within South Dakota. At the state level, though, Democrats won two of the three statewide elections. Daschle lost just one East River county and came within thirty-two hundred votes of Bell in West River. Stofferahn easily won as Public Utilities commissioner, and the Janklow-endorsed measure to combine the offices of State Treasurer and Administration of Public Lands was narrowly defeated. More importantly, the party raised a record one hundred eighty-five thousand dollars in 1984, nearly doubling the contributions of 1983, allowing it to modernize its offices, support more candidates, and build more county offices in 1985.[63] Prominent legislators such as McKellips and Herseth vowed to "[push] our own proposals instead of just reaction to the governor and Republican leadership," including the establishment of an export-trading company by the state and implementation of a low-interest loan program to small businesses, ranchers, and farmers.[64] South Dakota Democrats, still struggling to reverse course, developed a fund-raising and campaign network based on local issues and tapped into winning candidates who could deliver on those promises in the next election.

Tom Daschle's populism led the way for the SDDP. In 1986, the party committed statewide to a campaign on agricultural issues and against the federal government, forcing Republicans to downplay their ties to the federal government. Ahead of the campaign, Daschle told staffers, "We cannot afford the luxury of scattershot involvement in a broad range of issues" and demanded an offensive strategy that would not let conservatives dictate the terms of the campaign.[64] After his "no" vote on the 1985 farm bill because it did not increase farm income, Daschle proposed a new farm program ahead of the 1986 elections, calling for federally guaranteed loan levels for wheat and corn, interest buy-downs for farmers, and guarantees for commercial lenders who forgave farmers' debt.[65]

The election and Daschle's campaign gave the SDDP a candidate to rally the state's Democratic base around, bolstering the party's prominence in the process. Daschle announced his candidacy for Abdnor's Senate seat and his intention to seek a seat on the Senate Agriculture Committee on 6 March 1986. County-level Democratic Party committees hosted Announcement Day Parties across the state, with over four thousand supporters in attendance.[66] Daschle's campaign planned to get out the vote in areas of South Dakota where he traditionally polled weakest. One memo from the Daschle campaign advocated that he spend thirty percent of his campaigning "with the emphasis placed on the Black Hills region rather than the less populated, more conservative West River." Moreover, the memo called for "grass roots visibility with minimum staff participation," noting, "South Dakota, as a legacy of the McGovern-Abourezk days, has a strong [get-out-the-vote] tradition despite its weak state party."[67] The SDDP now sought to tap this tradition and revive voters' affiliation to the Democratic Party.

Frustrated voters demanded visible leadership, and South Dakota Democrats stepped into that role. In 1985, Daschle told his Washington staff that the SDDP required "an improved role in party leadership in South Dakota."[68] With the credit crunch of the farm crisis gripping the state, the SDDP had every opportunity to appeal to the rural vote. As irate farmers rallied on the steps of the state capitol on 25 February 1985, SDDP leaders turned out in full force to channel that anger toward joining the party. Daschle, Herseth, leaders of the South Dakota Farmers Union, and others addressed over six thousand people, calling for a moratorium on foreclosures, immediate credit for farmers, and a tax rebate for all South Dakotans. They attacked Republicans for being opposed to any alternatives, noting that the GOP killed Herseth's tax rebate proposal in committee, effectively "[showing] the weakness of any possible arguments they might have."[69]

With a new chair, C. Red Allen of Yankton, and vice-chair, Marion Zenker of Rapid City, the SDDP tied Republicans' recalcitrance to the flagging economy, particularly in agriculture. Zenker's first message observed: "For many years, Democrats have directed their loyalty to very worthwhile individuals such as Kneip, McGovern, Daschle, etc. . . .

We need to go beyond and develop a loyalty to the Democratic philosophy itself."[70] State Senator Roger McKellips sponsored a bill that transported the entire legislature to Washington, D.C., in late February 1985, earning the state and particularly the SDDP a great deal of media attention. Reagan did not meet with the contingent, but their presence helped the Daschle-sponsored Farm Emergency Credit Act (FECA) through the House with bipartisan support (though it failed in the Senate). Upon returning to Pierre, Lars Herseth introduced a resolution requesting that Reagan sign the FECA. It failed in the lower chamber before Republicans amended it to a weaker call to "speak to President Reagan in much more general terms, basically asking him to 'work with the Congress on the farm crisis.'"[71] Democrats even defeated an attempt to repeal one of the party's triumphs of the 1970s, the Family Farm Act, which prevented large corporations from buying up South Dakota farmland.[72] Approaching the 1986 elections, the SDDP had thus highlighted their ability to defend the average South Dakotan, especially by pitting their efforts against federal policies.

The SDDP continued to suffer from organizational—especially financial—weakness as it sought to promote its new leadership around the state. By August 1985, money was tight—the issue of *Democratic Forum* scheduled earlier in May had been scuttled for lack of funds. The party paid off its debts by May 1986, but funding problems restricted the party's ability to advertise its message. It was a handicap the SDDP could ill afford during an election cycle in which the farm crisis made Republicans vulnerable for the first time since the Watergate scandal. Institutionally, though, the SDDP shored up its ability to recruit and coach candidates. Red Allen's most important contribution as state chair was creating the Democratic Constitutional Officers for the Citizens of South Dakota, chaired by Harvey Wollman and vice-chaired by George Kane, designed to enable experienced politicians to coach and advise potential candidates.[73] The SDDP also chose Steve Jarding, then also a manager on the Daschle Senate campaign, as the SDDP executive director. Jarding, who went on to manage several more successful campaigns in right-leaning states across the country, presented an eighteen-point plan centered on aggressive marketing, voter registration drives, and increased fundraising for the state party between 1986 and 1988, culminating in a "parity in voter registration by 1990."[74]

With the at-large House seat, Senate seat, and governorship all up for consideration in the 1986 election, a more coherent SDDP attacked Republicans' failure to address specific South Dakotan economic issues and pushed a strong slate of candidates. State senators Jim Burg and Tim Johnson contested in the primary for Daschle's former United States House seat, each promising to speak for the average South Dakotan and revitalize family farms, while Herseth, Kneip, and Stofferahn all threw their hats into the ring for governor. Kneip renounced his support for a state income tax, which hurt his popularity in the 1970s, and ran on his reputation as an efficient manager, while Herseth promised to appoint a farmer as secretary of agriculture and noted his record in the state legislature along with an extensive volunteer network. The victorious primary candidates, Herseth and Johnson, won the East River vote by wide margins, gathering just enough support in the west to protect their majorities.[75]

While Daschle, Johnson, and Herseth represented the strongest trio of Democrats the SDDP had run in a decade, their reputations were increasingly divorced from party identification. Leading up to the election, the GOP had passed Democrats in the number of Minnehaha County registrations since 1984. Jarding spun the party's struggles as a positive, noting, "The Democratic Party is offering what many observers think are the most electable candidates in years." Yet the SDDP struggled to attract a larger number of South Dakota voters, especially in local elections.[76] Loyal to responsive, locally based politicians such as Daschle, Johnson, and Herseth, rather than to the party structure, South Dakota voters continued to split tickets.

Daschle's Senate campaign benefited from the defeat of term-limited Governor Janklow in the 1986 Republican primary. The erratic but popular governor had posed a potential challenge to Daschle because he ran on an even greater populist message. Janklow had butted heads with state Republicans on a number of occasions when the state senate refused a moratorium on farm foreclosures during the 1985–1986 legislative session and both houses overrode his veto of a bill removing high-school foreign-language requirements. Janklow, notorious among Democrats and appreciated among South Dakotans generally for his pragmatic governorship, also established an agricultural development authority to aid farmers, though the state legistlature removed limits on the amount banks could charge.[77] As Janklow considered challenging Senator James Abdnor in the primary, Daschle's campaign initially found it "hard to imagine we can best Bill [Janklow] in a traditional way on effectiveness" and found its candidate "vulnerable—just as Abdnor is—to an anti-Washington populist appeal."[78]

This anti-Washington sentiment both laid the foundation for discrediting Abdnor and left the farm vote skeptical of the GOP ahead of the 1986 elections. The *Wall Street Journal* took note of Janklow's challenge, highlighting the split in the Republican Party as the "frontier politician" challenged the "stoic incumbent." State GOP chairman Joel Rosenthal admitted he "would be happier if I didn't have this problem," as Janklow attacked Abdnor as one of the "inept" and "gutless" politicians in Washington.[79] Janklow extended his criticism to the entire congressional delegation, noting: "They've got thirty-one years of seniority in the United States Congress. What have we got for that?"[80] Abdnor trailed both Daschle and Janklow in early polls, but he took to the campaign trail in October 1985 with a media blitz aimed at eroding Janklow's support. Reagan all but endorsed Abdnor at a fundraiser in late October 1985, and Abdnor lashed out at critics who declared him a master of obscurity in the Senate. By December, an *Argus Leader* poll found Abdnor leading Janklow 60 to 33 and Daschle 51 to 46, and Daschle leading Janklow 53 to 43. Janklow declared his candidacy in late December, and the GOP campaign turned ugly as both candidates questioned the other's credentials, record, and demeanor. While Abdnor's reputation took a hit, his representation of the more conservative, West River elements of South Dakota put the onus on Janklow to explain why he should replace an incumbent senator on the ticket. Janklow attacked Abdnor, citing many of the weaknesses the Daschle campaign had discussed and calling public attention to a fractured party.[81]

The vote split along river lines: Abdnor defeated Janklow 54.5–45.5, winning sixty-one percent of the vote in the west while gaining just forty-eight percent of the vote in the east. Commentators had noted Democrats registering as Republicans for the 1986 primary. For example, in Shannon (now Oglala Lakota) County, three hundred and sixty people became Republicans, and in Pennington and Davison counties, close to one hundred people joined Republican voters. Abdnor won all three counties but now faced a daunting challenge from an in-

PLAINS POLITICAL TRADITION

flamed rural electorate skeptical that he represented their interests in Congress.[82] Even though internal conflicts beset the Republicans, by June they emerged with a proven candidate who had beaten a grassroots liberal before. However, they faced a more organized and militant Democratic Party.

During the 1986 campaign, the SDDP developed its new identity as an organized and vocal opposition to Republicans. Johnson and Herseth ran moderate campaigns appealing to South Dakotans' pocketbooks, and while Daschle and Abdnor settled into a mudslinging campaign centered on negative fundraising letters and jockeying on farm issues, Daschle held the upper hand in polls. As in 1980, Abdnor's campaign called for only two debates, due to his speech impediment and limited debate ability, while Daschle's demanded at least six, charging that Abdnor wished to hide behind Reagan.[83] In the gubernatorial race, Janklow campaigned for George S. Mickelson, tying the GOP candidate to his own populist reputation. "I don't think I have ever met a farmer who said 'Janklow, you didn't try to do anything for us,'" the former governor said, promising that Mickelson would do the same. In August, Herseth held a 30 to 21 point lead among decided voters, but forty-nine percent remained undecided.[84] Johnson, meanwhile, opened up a quiet lead on his opponent, keeping farmers' issues at the forefront and bemoaning how "our politics have become so personalized."[85] While Herseth's moderate appeal on his record faced a daunting challenge given Janklow's support of Mickelson, Johnson could present himself as above moral reproach and as a ceaseless advocate for South Dakota farmers. Populism won in 1986, and the Democrats were better prepared.

Daschle's campaign in the West River and the SDDP's embrace of rural issues paid dividends beyond party affiliation. In September, Rapid City businessman Steve Johnson, a former treasurer for Abdnor, announced that he would form a statewide committee called Republicans for Daschle "to move forward with individuals, above and beyond party politics." Tellingly, Johnson supported Mickelson for governor.[86] Reagan arrived in South Dakota to stump for Abdnor, which Abdnor feared "could hurt him among farmers," an issue compounded when Abdnor missed the rally because voting commitments demanded he stay in Congress.[87] Meanwhile, Daschle hammered Abdnor's obscurity in the Senate, noting, "The state ranked among the top in federal dollars lost in several categories."[88] Stumping on his record in Washington as an outsider, Daschle transcended party loyalty by pitting state interests against the federal government.

The year 1986 signaled the SDDP's future reliance on populist, agricultural-oriented liberalism. Daschle defeated Abdnor 52–48, Johnson thumped Bell by a nearly three-to-two margin, and Herseth lost a narrow contest to Mickelson, 52–48. The Democrats gained two seats in the state senate and nine in the house. Though the Republicans still held a 71–34 advantage across both houses in Pierre, it was a strong showing for the Democrats, who counted twenty-four thousand fewer registered voters than the Republicans.[89] Daschle won nine-thousand fewer votes in West River than Johnson, but as a *Rapid City Journal* reporter noted in the aftermath of the election, Daschle "did well enough in the West River counties to protect the lead he gained in more populous eastern counties."[90] It helped Johnson that South Dakota voters rejected Dale Bell for the third time, but as commentators described Johnson's political views as "an echo of Daschle's," his larger vote totals undoubtedly reflected the down-ballot success of the agrarian populism of the SDDP's top candidate.[91]

Contrary to notions of "essential conservatism," the marked turnaround in the SDDP in 1986 demonstrates that, while agricultural issues are central to Democratic success, pragmatic, liberal populism plays a large role in South Dakota political culture. To be sure, internal Republican conflict in the 1986 primary affirms the notion that GOP blunders contributed to Daschle's Senate victory.[92] Janklow's primary defeat, though, reflects the fact that South Dakota Republicans' choice of an ideologically sound candidate was partially beaten by the Democrats' embrace of pragmatism centered around local issues, a marked pivot away from the more strident progressivism of George McGovern. We can better understand, as Frank Denholm noted, why "the best time for the Democrats to win are when the Republicans are in control," especially of the federal government.[93] Highlighting the weakness of the Republican Party in 1986 neglects the reconstruction of the SDDP—it is vital to recognize that Democrats in South Dakota function as a check on essential conservatism. While as Jon K. Lauck observes, it "helps the Democrats' cause to be seen as moderate," Jarding's get-out-the-vote strategies and Johnson's observation, "We're door-knocking in towns that have never been door-knocked in before," helped Democrats succeed with rural voters in 1986.[94] The SDDP recruited new voters, followed its prominent candidates to a more moderate, pragmatic platform, and ran competitive candidates in more districts.

Even amid Daschle's victory, however, we can see South Dakotans swing toward the Reagan-era preferences for individual entrepreneurship and antifederalism. Daschle's campaign manager had to admit that the Democrats' struggles in persuading voters in Mitchell and their struggle to win Minnehaha County with only fifty-six percent of the vote reflected the state's entrenched conservatism.[95] The centrist nature of the new SDDP, embodied by the Daschle-Johnson coalition, reflected the fact that the South Dakota Democratic Party, running its strongest slate of candidates in 1986, hitched its cart to left-center politics, agrarian populism, and an outsider reputation. While successful at sending candidates to Congress, this pivot crippled the party's ability to win local elections in South Dakota. Daschle's career would end during similar anti-incumbent and perhaps anti-Democratic sentiment, just as McGovern's did, but more importantly, the coalitions that he and Johnson marshalled help our understanding of South Dakota and midwestern liberalism. Jon K. Lauck's interpretation of Daschle's defeat by John Thune in 2004 concluded that Daschle won "when he abandoned the politics of Peter, Paul, and Mary; his defeat came when he embraced it again."[96] This finding, at least today, rings true: South Dakota Democrats lose when their interests appear to align with national liberalism rather than local needs.

Regardless, conclusions that South Dakota remains essentially conservative diminish the importance of an internally cohesive and politically pragmatic South Dakota Democratic Party within the state's political culture through the 1980s. The party's decline, especially from 1976 to 1980, left a divided party that lacked the funds, candidates, or platform to campaign competitively. With prominent candidates such as Daschle and Johnson and a better-organized party structure, the SDDP rebuilt its statewide prominence. Bob Williams, Lars Herseth, and George Cunningham—along with others such as Richard Kneip and Harvey Wollman—reimagined the ideological and strategic goals of the party and applied Daschle's politics to McGovern's campaigning. Their efforts made the Democrats' ability to seize on the farm crisis possible. The SDDP returned to its grassroots in

1986, gaining two strong voices in Washington for decades to follow. Future studies of the state's political culture may gauge the efficacy of that strategy into the 1990s, but they need to reckon with the undercurrent of grassroots, liberal populism in South Dakota.

NOTES

1. "McGovern pursues in-state license," *Sioux Falls Argus Leader*, 28 Oct. 1980.

2. Jonathan Rieder, "The Rise of the 'Silent Majority,'" in *The Rise and Fall of the New Deal Order*, ed. Steve Fraser and Gary Gerstle (Princeton, N.J.: Princeton University Press, 1989), p. 263. *See also* John E. Miller, "Setting the Agenda: Political Parties and Historical Change in South Dakota," in *The Plains Political Tradition: Essays on South Dakota Political Culture* [Vol. 1], ed. Jon K. Lauck, John E. Miller, and Donald C. Simmons, Jr., eds. (Pierre: South Dakota Historical Society Press, 2011), p. 94; Matthew Pehl, "The Frustrations of Organized Labor in South Dakota and the Making of a Conservative Coalition in the Midcentury United States," in *The Plains Political Tradition: Essays on South Dakota Political Culture*, Vol. 2, eds. Lauck, Miller, and Simmons (Pierre: South Dakota Historical Society Press, 2014), pp. 120–21.

3. Lauck, "'It Disappeared as Quickly as It Came': The Democratic Surge and the Republican Comeback in South Dakota Politics, 1970–1980," *South Dakota History* 46 (Summer 2016): 139–40.

4. Mark A. Lempke, "Senator George McGovern and the Role of Religion in South Dakota Political Culture," in *Plains Political Tradition*, Vol. 2, p. 172.

5. Schaff, "The Politics of Defeat: Senate Elections in South Dakota," in *The Plains Political Tradition* [Vol.1], pp. 313–14.

6. Eric Ostermeier, "Seeing Red: A Brief History of Republican Domination in South Dakota," *Smart Politics*, 29 Mar. 2013, editions.lib.umn.edu/smartpolitics /2013/03/29/seeing-red-a-brief-history-of/.

7. Schaff, "Politics of Defeat," pp. 313–14.

8. Clem, "The 1980 Election in South Dakota: End of an Era," *Public Affairs* 80 (Mar. 1981): p. 6–7. On the new forms of populism, *see* Michael Kazin, *The Populist Persuasion: An American History* (Ithaca: Cornell University Press, 1995), pp. 278–80.

9. McGovern, "Letter from Washington: The Challenge of Farm Legislation and Programs," 25 Sept. 1978, copy in William Janklow Papers, I. D. Weeks Library, University of South Dakota (USD), Vermillion.

10. McGovern to Wollman, 19 Dec. 1978, Box 21, Senator George McGovern Papers, George and Eleanor McGovern Library and Center for Leadership and Public Service, Dakota Wesleyan University, Mitchell, S.Dak. On the election, *see* Lauck, "'It Disappeared,'" pp. 137–38.

11. "Will Somebody Please Explain?" *Yankton Press and Dakotan*, 15 Dec. 1978.

12. Janklow to McGovern and Tom Daschle, 27 July 1979, Box 60, Janklow Papers.

13. "Stofferahn-Katus square off for Second District Seat," *South Dakota Demo News*, Apr. 1980, p. 1, copy in I. D. Weeks Library, USD (all editions of *South Dakota Demo News* and the later *Democratic Forum* were accessed through this collection); Richard Michael Marano, *Vote Your Conscience: The Last Campaign of George McGovern* (Westport, Conn.: Praeger, 2003), p. 27.

14. Harry Johns, PAC Finance Chairman, "Larry Schumaker for Senate . . . '80," 19 Apr. 1980, Pt. 2, Box 3, McGovern Papers. Statistics can be found in South Dakota, Secretary of State, "Official Election Returns and Registration Figures for South Dakota: General Election, 7 Nov. 1978," and "Official Election Returns and Registration Figures for South Dakota: Primary Election, 3 June 1980," sdsos.gov/elections-voting/election-resources/election-history/election-history-search.aspx. Unless otherwise noted, all electoral statistics are accessed from this website.

15. "McGovern will fight back with Common Sense," *Dubuque Herald-Telegraph*, 12 Nov. 1980, p. 19. The other five senators were Birch Bayh of Indiana, John Culver of Iowa, Gaylord Nelson of Wisconsin, Frank Church of Idaho, and Warren Magnuson of Washington. Considering the career trajectories of Bayh, Culver, and Nelson, research into the Reagan Revolution's effects on liberalism in the Midwest is needed, especially into how state parties reacted to the loss of such prominent figures.

16. Cunningham to McGovern, "The 1980 Election—Where we stand now," 9 June 1980, Box 7C, McGovern Papers.

17. Tena Andersen, "NCPAC withdrawal pleases both sides," *Sioux Falls Argus Leader*, 4 Oct. 1980; Wayne King, "McGovern, Long a Target, Finds Rewards in Taking the Offensive," *New York Times*, 20 Oct. 1980, p. D11; Anthony Lewis, "Abroad at Home: Backlash in South Dakota," *New York Times*, 14 Oct. 1980, p. A23. Abdnor received a large amount of negative press in October for his connections to the NCPAC, including being called a "statesman" by a Ku Klux Klan Imperial Wizard. *See* Raasch, "Abdnor files suit against the NCPAC," *Sioux Falls Argus Leader*, 28 Oct. 1980, and Jack Anderson, "McGovern spattered by out-of-state mud," *Sioux Falls Argus Leader*, 14 Aug. 1980.

18. Quoted in Chuck Raasch, "McGovern clan to combat anti-family image," *Sioux Falls Argus Leader*, 31 Oct. 1980, clipping in Box 21, McGovern Papers.

19. Editorial, "South Dakota's senior chameleon," *Fort Pierre Times*, 11 July 1980.

20. "Official Election Returns by Counties for the State of South Dakota: General Election, November 7, 1978; "Official Election Returns and Registration Figures for South Dakota: General Election, November 4, 1980." In 1980, registered

Republicans outnumbered Democrats 206,411 to 202,062 of a total 447,508 registered voters; in 1978, Democrats outnumbered Republicans 193,375 to 191,766 of a total of 420,818 registered.

21. Steven A. Stofferahn, "The Persistence of Agrarian Activism: The National Farmers Organization in South Dakota," in *Plains Political Tradition*, Vol. 2, p. 230. For general histories of conservatism in the 1980s, *see* Sean Wilentz, *The Age of Reagan: A History, 1974–2008* (New York: HarperCollins, 2008); Laura Kalman, *Right Star Rising: A New Politics, 1974–1980* (New York: W.W. Norton, 2010); or Rick Perlstein, *Invisible Bridge: The Fall of Nixon and the Rise of Reagan* (New York: Simon & Schuster, 2014).

22. Chuck Raasch, "Demo problems in S.D. run deep," *Sioux Falls Argus Leader*, 14 Dec. 1980. Jon Lauck makes a similar case for the ideological divisions within the SDDP in "It Disappeared,'" pp. 134–35.

23. Cunningham to McGovern, "The 1980 Election;" McGovern quoted in Judy Allen, "McGovern to launch new career after farewell tour of South Dakota," *Mitchell Daily Republic*, 4 Dec. 1980.

24. Frank Denholm, interview by Jon K. Lauck, 8 Sept. 2015, Brookings, S.Dak., transcript, p. 35.

25. Clem, "The 1980 Election," p. 7; Schaff, "Politics of Defeat," p. 319; Tim Schreiner, "McGovern's song wrong key for constituency," *Sioux Falls Argus Leader*, 10 Nov. 1980.

26. Hunking, "From the State Chair," *Democratic Forum* 1 (May 1981): 3. Hunking went on to serve as the first woman on the Sioux Falls City Commission in 1983. *See* Dorene Weinstein, "The Legacy of Loila Hunking," *Sioux Falls Argus Leader*, 6 Sept. 2014, argusleader.com/story/life/ 2014/09/07/legacy -loila-hunking/15225209/.

27. "Oral history interview with Loila Hunking" (transcript), by Lisa Pruitt, 30 Mar. 1994, SDOHP 3004, p. 7, Oral History Center, USD.

28. Abbott, "Robert Abbott—Young Demos President," *Democratic Forum* 1 (May 1981): 4.

29. McGovern, "For the Democrats, a Return to Grass Roots," ibid. (June 1981): 3. *See also* "McGovern finds support for coalition," *Siouxfalls This Week*, 13 Nov. 1980, clipping, Box 21, McGovern Papers.

30. McGovern, "Policies Democrats Should Pursue," *New York Times*, 3 Apr. 1982, p. 25. In a draft of this op-ed, McGovern himself affirmed that he was "one ex-office holder who is content to remain out of step" (McGovern, "On Being Out of Step," 10 Sept. 1981, Box 7A, McGovern Papers).

31. Cunningham, "Rebuilding challenge seen for Democrats," *Sioux Falls Argus Leader*, 8 Feb. 1981.

32. Hunking, "From the State Chair," *Democratic Forum* 1 (July 1981): 1–2.

33. Daschle, "Democratic Dilemma," ibid. (Aug. 1981): 1–2.

34. Carole Pagones, "War on Poverty Ended . . . We Lost," ibid. (Nov. 1981): 1–3; Daschle, "Shell Game," ibid., p. 2.

35. Hunking, "From the State Chair," ibid. (Aug. 1981): 3; David Montgomery, "Five ways Bill Janklow changed South Dakota," *Rapid City Journal*, 13 Jan. 2012; Penn & Schoen Associates, "Congressman Tom Daschle Survey Analysis," 22 Dec. 1981, p. 8, Box 1, DA 3.1, Thomas A. Daschle Papers, Archives and Special Collections, Hilton M. Briggs Library, South Dakota State University, Brookings.

36. Mike O'Connor, "Governor O'Connor '82," *Democratic Forum* 2 (May 1982): 3.

37. O'Connor, "O'Connor Asks Counties to Assume Political Power Base," ibid. (July 1982): 2.

38. Quoted in David Enger, "Remember NCPAC? MACPAC targets Daschle," *Sioux Falls Argus Leader*, 8 July 1981.

39. Quoted in Penn & Schoen, "Congressman Tom Daschle Survey Analysis," pp. ii–iii.

40. Ibid., pp. 2–3; "Daschle to Head Regional Wheat Talks That Could Benefit South Dakota Wheat Growers," 3 May 1981, "Daschle Invites Committee Chairmen to Visit EROS Center," 27 Apr. 1981, and "It Matters Most at Times Like These," n.d., all clippings in Box 24, DA 1, Daschle Papers.

41. "Demo Paper uses headline barrage to attack Janklow," *Sioux Falls Argus Leader*, 31 Aug. 1982, and "There goes that Governor, again!" *Democratic Forum* 2 (Sept. 1982): 3. *See also* "Teske Named Exec. Director," *Democratic Forum* 1 (Sept. 1981): 2.

42. "Oral history interview with Loila Hunking," p. 7.

43. Charles W. Calomiris, R. Glenn Hubbard, and James H. Stock, "The Farm Debt Crisis and Public Policy," *Brookings Papers on Economic Activity* 2 (1986): 441; Thomas L. Dobbs, "Implications of the Farm Crisis for Rural Communities in South Dakota," in *South Dakota Cooperative Service Extension: Economic Newsletter* 220 (20 Apr. 1985): 1–2; Kathryn Marie Dudley, *Debt and Dispossession: Farm Loss in America's Heartland* (Chicago: University of Chicago Press, 2002), pp. 180nn1–2.

44. Stock, *Rural Radicals: Righteous Rage in the American Grain* (Ithaca, N.Y.: Cornell University Press, 1995), p. 150. Dudley, *Debt and Depression*, pp. 99, 102, also notes suspicion of government programs among farmers in rural western Minnesota—a region socioeconomically similar to eastern South Dakota.

45. Quoted in Jessica Giard, "1980s Series: Farm Crisis Unites a State," *Mitchell Daily Republic*, 14 Feb. 2014.

46. O'Connor-Danekas Ag Advisory Group, press release, 22 Oct.1982. Box 67, Roxanne Barton Conlin Papers, Iowa Women's Archives, University of Iowa, Iowa City.

47. "Daschle Keynotes National Farm Crisis Day Rally in Nevada, Iowa"

(press release), 2 Oct. 1982, Box 24, DA 1, Daschle Papers. Daschle attacked the *Sporhase* v. *Nebraska ex rel. Douglas* ruling of 1982 and fought off false accusations by his opponent that he wished to turn the Ellsworth Air Force Base into a "greenbelt." *See* "Address by Congressman Tom Daschle, delivered before the Western States Water and Power Consumers Area Fall Conference," Mitchell, S.Dak., 20 Sept. 1982, Box 18, DA 1, Daschle Papers, and David Hoffman, "The 1982 Elections: Incumbent vs. Incumbent," *Washington Post,* 15 Oct. 1982, washingtonpost.com/archive/politics/1982/10/15/the-1982-elections-incumbent-vs-incumbent/cb97bfb5-6290-4c77-8579-1465533c13cc/. Clint Roberts further blundered when he insinuated that Indian reservations be eliminated. *See* George Pierre Castille, *Taking Charge: Native American Self-Determination and Federal Indian Policy, 1975–1993* (Phoenix: University of Arizona Press, 2006) p. 57.

48. Daschle, letter on pro-life record, n.d., Box 26, DA 1, Daschle Papers.

49. Scott Heidepriem to Daschle, 17 May 1982, and Cindy Dwyer to Daschle, "Debate w/Roberts at SDSU," n.d., Box 26, DA 1, Daschle Papers.

50. Dave Kranz, "Editorial," *Sioux Falls Argus Leader*, Oct. 1982, clipping, Box 26, DA 1, Daschle Papers.

51. McGregor, "Update—1982 Democratic Majority Committee," Oct. 1980, and Teske to County Officers, Executive Board, and Legislative Candidates, 7 Oct. 1982, both Box 26, DA 1, Daschle Papers.

52. "Official Election Returns and Registration Figures for South Dakota: General Election, Nov. 2, 1982"; Penn & Schoen, "Congressman Tom Daschle Survey Analysis," pp. 11–12.

53. Penn & Schoen, "Congressman Tom Daschle Survey Analysis," p. 38;

54. Eisnach, "Thoughts from Dennis Eisnach, Public Utilities Commissioner," *Democratic Forum* 3 (Jan. 1983): 2. *See also* Hunking, "Letter from the State Chair," ibid., p. 1–2.

55. Williams, "The Chairman's Perspective," *Democratic Forum* 3 (Mar. 1983): 2.

56. Bette Burg, "Huronians reject S.S. reform at Daschle meeting," *Huron Plainsman*, 7 Feb. 1983; Lars Herseth, "1983 Legislative Wrap-Up," *Democratic Forum* 3 (Mar. 1983): 3; "Daschle says Democratic Party on upswing," *Huron Plainsman*, 4 Oct. 1983.

57. "S.D. politicians jockey for 1984, 1986 position," *Sioux Falls Argus Leader*, 17 July 1983. Cunningham's path to the nomination was cleared when Wollman announced in July 1983 that he would not run for the Senate seat because of Pressler's popularity. *See* "Big boost for Cunningham," ibid., 20 July 1983.

58. All quoted in "Campaign '84, The Senate Race: How the Democrats Can Win," *Democratic Forum* 3 (July 1983): 1–3.

59. Baron Glassgow to Daschle, 7 Dec. 1983, and Daschle, "Remarks to the

East River Cooperative Annual Meeting," Sioux Falls, 5 Sept. 1984, Box 24, DA 1, Daschle Papers; Roger Kasa, "Daschle says Bell avoiding real issues," *Huron Plainsman*, 2 Sept. 1984; "Bell Crosses Foul Line with Pitch to Churches," *Sioux Falls Argus Leader*, 13 Sept. 1984; Internal memo, "State fair straw poll," 4 Sept. 1984, Box 1, DA 3.1, Daschle Papers; "Daschle gets 'no' from Block," *Aberdeen American-News*, 2 Oct. 1984.

60. Williams, "The Chairman's Perspective," *Democratic Forum* 4 (Oct. 1984): 2.

61. "Democrats look to the future," *Sioux Falls Argus Leader*, 1 Apr. 1984.

62. Denholm, interview, p. 23.

63. "Official Election Returns . . . November 6, 1984"; Williams, "The Chairman's Perspective," *Democratic Forum* 4 (Dec. 1984): 2.

64. Quoted in Williams, "Chairman's Perspective," p. 3; Daschle to Staff, untitled memo on 1985 legislative year, n.d., Box 23, DA 1, Daschle Papers. Daschle also noted that there was a "less than even chance I will run for the Senate" in 1986 but proceeded to describe what a hypothetical campaign for that office would look like.

65. Doug Cunningham, "2 see way to stave off farm crisis," *Sioux Falls Argus Leader*, 8 Jan. 1986.

66. "Charge on, Tom!" *Democratic Forum* 6 (Mar. 1986): 2; Deana Brodkorb, "Daschle would go after ag seat," *Aberdeen American News*, 8 Mar. 1986.

67. Campaign strategy memo, n.d., p. 17, Box 2, DA 3.1, Daschle Papers. *See also* "Media Plan," n.d., p. 15, ibid.

68. Daschle to Staff, untitled memo on 1985 legislative year.

69. "Farmers Rally in Pierre," *Democratic Forum* 5 (Feb. 1985): 1, 4.

70. Zenker, "The Vice-Chair Speaks," ibid. (Mar. 1985): 1–2. *See also* C. Red Allen, "The Chair's Perspective," ibid.

71. "Was It Worth It?" ibid., p. 5.

72. "Legislative Wrap-Up," ibid., p. 6; Penn & Schoen, "Congressman Tom Daschle Survey Analysis," p. 22.

73. Allen, "For Your Information," *Democratic Forum* 5 (Aug. 1985): 2; "Jefferson/Jackson Day—A Tremendous Success!," ibid. 6 (May 1986): 1; Bill Stevens, "Democratic Constitutional Officers for the Citizens of South Dakota," ibid. (Mar. 1986): 3.

74. "New Executive Director Announces Party Revitalization Plan," ibid. (May 1986): 2. Other points included "(2) Raise our century and majority club [donor] memberships to 750 members, . . . (6) Adopt a new small donor program to broaden our donor list by one-third by 1988, (7) Open a satellite state campaign office in Sioux Falls and hopefully in Rapid City, (8) Strive toward convention success and unity at our state convention, . . . (11) Broaden our relations with the national party, (12) Elect Democrats in 1986 and 1988—through the most aggres-

sive assistance program ever offered to our standard bearers, (13) Extensive public relations campaign, (14) Establish several new programs to assist the elderly, (15) Work to improve the conditions of the South Dakota farmer, (16) Broaden and expand our youth camp in the Black Hills, (17) Establish a Young Democrat group in every school district in South Dakota by 1988, (18) Set up a revolving internship program from South Dakota college students." For Jarding's personal approach to winning elections in white, predominantly conservative southern and midwestern states, *see* Jarding, Dave Saunders and Bob Kerrey, *Foxes in the Henhouse: How the Republicans Stole the South and the Heartland and What the Democrats Must Do to Run 'em Out* (New York: Simon & Schuster, 2006).

75. "Gubernatorial Candidates," *Democratic Forum* 6 (May 1986): 4–5; "Official Election Returns and Registration Figures for South Dakota: Primary Election, June 3, 1986."

76. Richard Bale, "Records: GOP gains strength," *Sioux Falls Argus Leader*, 31 Oct. 1986.

77. "Legislative Wrap-Up," *Democratic Forum* 6 (Mar. 1986): 3.

78. Ibid.; "Media Plan," pg. 5. The Daschle campaign also planned to distance Daschle from Washington to "convince voters Tom is better than Janklow" in a "race of personality. Wild Bill versus Mr. Clean. Hot versus Cool. Negative versus Positive" ("Media Plan," p. 5).

79. Quoted in David Shribman, "Republican Feud for Senate Seat in South Dakota Pits Frontier Politician against Stoic Incumbent," *Wall Street Journal*, 12 Aug. 1985, p. 1.

80. Quoted in "Janklow moves a step closer to announcing for the Senate," *Watertown Public Opinion*, 9 Oct. 1985.

81. "Abdnor leads, poll says," *Sioux Falls Argus Leader*, 5 Dec. 1985; Bob Mercer, "Abdnor begins TV ad campaign to promote his re-election," *Aberdeen American News*, 10 Oct. 1985; Todd Murphy, "Janklow letter implies: I run or Daschle wins Senate seat," *Sioux Falls Argus Leader*, 15 Nov. 1985; Mireille Grangenois Gates, "Reagan lavishes praise on Abdnor at GOP lovefest," ibid., 30 Oct. 1985; Abdnor, "Here are the tricks for staying anonymous in the U.S. Senate," ibid., 27 Nov. 1985; "Abdnor leads, poll says," ibid., 5 Dec. 1985; Todd Murphy, "Janklow to run for Senate," ibid., 21 Dec. 1985; James R. Dickenson, "Divisive South Dakota GOP Primary Set," *Washington Post,* 23 Feb.1986; John T. Dolan, "Abdnor hasn't been straight with voters about ties with group," *Sioux Falls Argus Leader*, 27 May 1986. Abdnor had taken to the campaign trail reminding voters that he "asked the Political Action Committee to leave the state during his 1980 Senate campaign" (quoted in Todd Murphy, "Abdnor: I want to keep fighting," ibid., 12 Feb. 1986).

82. "Official Election Returns and Registration Figures for South Dakota: Primary Election, June 3, 1986"; Brenda Wade, "S.D. voters switch parties for

primaries," *Sioux Falls Argus Leader*, 23 May 1986; Chet Brokaw, "Abdnor beats Janklow," *Aberdeen American News,* 4 June 1986.

83. Brenda Wade, "Daschle, Abdnor intensify farm rhetoric," *Sioux Falls Argus Leader*, 19 Aug. 1986; Jim Rasmussen, "Abdnor, Daschle debate talks break off," ibid., 28 Aug. 1986.

84. Janklow quoted in Kranz, "Janklow gives Abdnor welcome news," ibid., 17 Aug. 1986.

85. Quoted in "Candidates bombard voters with 'negative' campaign ads," *Des Moines Register,* 26 Oct. 1986.

86. Quoted in Bill Harlan, "GOP committee backs Daschle," *Rapid City Journal*, 2 Sep. 1986.

87. Quoted in Chuck Raasch, "Abdnor might miss Reagan visit," *Sioux Falls Argus Leader*, 27 Sep. 1986.

88. Quoted in Todd Murphy, "Debate smolders," ibid., 19 Oct. 1986.

89. "Official Election Returns and Registration Figures for South Dakota: General Election, November 4, 1986."

90. Bill Harlan, "Farm vote puts Daschle on top," *Rapid City Journal*, 5 Nov. 1986.

91. "Daschle, Johnson have big jobs to fill," *Sioux Falls Argus Leader*, 6 Nov. 1986.

92. Larry Pressler also noted the importance of political infighting, arguing, "No matter which party may have control at a given time, it can be assumed that a good deal of political infighting has taken place" (Pressler, "South Dakotans in the United States Senate: A Composite Portrait," *South Dakota History* 11 [Spring 1981]: 125).

93. Denholm, interview, p. 36.

94. Lauck, "It Disappeared," p. 139; Johnson quoted in Todd Murphy, "Daschle unseats Abdnor," *Sioux Falls Argus Leader*, 5 Nov. 1986.

95. Todd Murphy, "Rural revolt seen in victories," ibid., 6 Nov. 1986.

96. Lauck, *Daschle vs. Thune: Anatomy of a High-Plains Senate Race* (Norman, Okla: University of Oklahoma Press, 2007), p. 251.

EMILY O. WANLESS

9 | UNDERSTANDING
SOUTH DAKOTA'S POLITICAL CULTURE
THROUGH THE 1994 ELECTION OF
GOVERNOR BILL JANKLOW

• • •

As he was growing up in Flandreau, South Dakota, William John ("Bill") Janklow's motto was "never start a fight; finish every fight."[1] This mantra not only characterized his approach to problem solving while in office, it also reflected how South Dakotans perceived both his personality and his appeal. Holding a number of state and federal elected offices, Janklow gained a reputation for hard work, honesty, candor, and an ability to deliver what people wanted. That said, he was also considered a brash individual who did not hesitate to call out those who crossed him. When Janklow assumed the governorship in 1979, some viewed South Dakota as suffering from an inferiority complex as an agrarian state increasingly left behind in the realms of business, technology, and innovation. However, polls taken during his 1994 gubernatorial campaign indicated that large numbers of people, regardless of partisan affiliation, appreciated his ability to move the state into the modern era.[2]

South Dakota's political culture straddles the moralistic and individualistic typologies first identified in Daniel J. Elazar's classic work *American Federalism: A View from the States*. The state embraces a conservative ideology and frontier individualism of self-reliance. Its roots are in an agrarian economy, but it has evolved into a state friendly to business, big and small. Above all, it is a republican state that values citizen involvement, public virtue, and the ability to have personal relationships and access to government officials.[3] Elected state chief executive four times, Janklow was South Dakota's longest serving governor and a clear embodiment of the state's political culture.[4] In particular, his 1994 bid to return to the governor's mansion after an eight-year absence helps refine South Dakota's hybrid moralistic-individualistic classification, and his campaign serves as a case study to explain South Dakota's political tradition. Using content analysis of campaign commercials, public opinion data, campaign archives, and interviews with Janklow's aides, we can relate the success of strategically emphasized attitudes, beliefs, and issues on the campaign trail to the values important to South Dakotans.

Born in 1939, Janklow lived in Chicago until his father's death in 1949. Widowed with six children, his mother, Lou Ella Janklow, moved the family to her hometown of Flandreau, South Dakota. A high school dropout, Janklow attended the University of South Dakota for his business undergraduate and law degrees after a brief, yet successful stint in the United States Marine Corps. He began his career in law as the chief legal officer for the South Dakota Legal Services System on the Rosebud Indian Reservation, a role he served in for seven years. As a result of his time with legal aid, Janklow entered into his first political position when Democratic attorney general Kermit Sande appointed him to serve as the chief prosecutor of the state's case against the American Indian Movement. After a few years in private practice, Janklow successfully ran for the position of attorney general of South Dakota in 1974, serving one term before seeking out the governorship in 1978.[5]

On 6 June 1978, Janklow won 52 percent of the vote in the Republican primary for governor, defeating state senators Clint Roberts and LeRoy G. Hoffman. Janklow's general election opponent, Roger McKellips, defeated incumbent governor Harvey Wollman in the Democratic primary. Wollman, South Dakota's thirty-second lieutenant governor, had assumed the governorship when Richard Kneip stepped down to serve as United States ambassador to Singapore. Janklow was elected to his first of four terms as governor, 56.6 percent to McKellips' 43.4 percent. Up for reelection in 1982, Governor Janklow faced no primary opposition and won the general election against Mike O'Connor with 70.9 percent of the vote. Governor Janklow's popularity is evidenced by his results in the 1982 contest, as he earned fifty-thousand more votes than he did in his 1978 campaign and secured the largest proportion of the vote in a governor's race to date.[6]

Barred from seeking a third consecutive gubernatorial term, Janklow ran instead for a seat in the United States Senate in 1986 against fellow Republican and incumbent James Abdnor. He lost the primary to Abdnor by 10,490 votes (54.5 percent to 45.5 percent), a result largely attributed to his inability to persuade West River voters and Republican party elites of Abdnor's inadequacies.[7] Governor Janklow returned to private life and the practice of law, waiting to run again when the two terms of popular Republican governor George S. Mickelson were complete.

Janklow's desire to return to the governor's mansion in 1994 was widely known, but the manner in which he sought his return could never be imagined. On 19 April 1993, sitting governor Mickelson died in a plane crash near Dubuque, Iowa, in the midst of his second term. Upon the death of Mickelson, Walter Dale Miller assumed the office of governor and soon after announced his intentions to seek the position outright. This decision came as a shock to the Janklow campaign, as Miller had not previously expressed the desire to seek the office. Defeating Miller became the primary goal of the 1994 Janklow campaign. On 7 June 1994, Janklow defeated Miller 54 percent to 46 percent in a contentious battle for the Republican nomination. Janklow secured his third term as governor on 8 November 1994, handily beating Dakota Wesleyan University president Jim Beddow, 55.36 percent to 40.52 percent.[8]

After Janklow's failed bid for the United States Senate in 1986, many in his innermost political circles knew that his return to the governor's mansion seemed likely. Jim Hagan, political aide and friend, recounts how Janklow loved being governor: "It fit his personality and talents. He loved solving problems and loved studying a variety of issues. He was also arrogant enough to believe he was the best man for the job."[9] Prior to his death, Governor Mickelson, soon-to-be-term limited and out of office, encouraged Janklow to run again. Multiple members of Janklow's 1994 campaign staff recall the endorsement of both Mickelson and eventual primary opponent Lieutenant Governor Walter Dale Miller.[10] Of course, these endorsements came prior to Mickelson's death and the subsequent appointment of Miller to office.

Although Janklow liked Miller, he did not wait for him to step down. Interviews indicate that Janklow believed South Dakota had a number of issues that he was uniquely qualified to handle. In particular, he believed government had gotten too big, spending had grown too quickly, and too many bureaucrats were employed in Pierre and around the state. Additionally, taxes, in particular property taxes, were skyrocketing. Upon Governor Mickelson's death, Janklow saw himself as someone who could return South Dakota to a form comparable to when he had left office. One of his greatest accomplishments as governor, he believed, was helping South Dakota over its inferiority complex, positioning its citizens to accept that it was a state to be taken seriously. Campaign staffer Jim Hagan explained Janklow's appeal in this capacity: "His first two terms left South Dakota a bit exhausted and wanting a bit of a respite. But then it was quiet. South Dakota wasn't on the map."[11] When asked what was the first thing that came to mind when thinking about Bill Janklow, one 1994 voter responded with a common sentiment: "I think he'll put the state on the map again. He speaks his mind whether it's right or wrong. . . . He kind of got Citibank in here. He's more nationally known."[12] Essentially, Janklow perceived that there were a number of matters after the Mickelson era that he could handle better than Governor Miller.

An internal public opinion poll commissioned in May 1992 evidenced Janklow's intention to run, as well as his belief in his own unique qualifications. Even two years before the first campaign event, Janklow's name recognition amongst South Dakotans was extremely high and overwhelmingly positive. He was especially strong among Republicans (+59 percent favorability), older voters (+63 percent), and men (+56 percent). However, his favorability ratings with Democrats and Independents in the state were +29 and +37 percent, respectively. Regionally, his name identification was highest in Sioux Falls. In the James River and northeastern part of the state, his favorability ratings were in the upper sixties (69 percent). West River, he had slightly weaker favorability ratings (63 percent). However, the area of weakest support, the Black Hills, was still at a net positive favorability, with 57 percent to 34 percent favorable-unfavorable responses.[13]

Given this information on Janklow's appeal, coupled with Miller's decision to seek the governorship outright, two main issues faced the Janklow campaign in the 1994 Republican gubernatorial primary. First, Janklow was facing a divisive primary in which there was significant support for Miller. Second, he had to address the varying levels of support based on geography. Not only was there the traditional West River–East River divide amongst the South Dakota electorate, but the Pierre "Establishment" and corporate interest contingents had their own sets of preferences when it came to gubernatorial candidates.

To deal with these issues and to shape the message of the campaign moving forward, Janklow's strategists formulated a three-fold strategy. The campaign would be directed toward the notion that voters needed to "know ya, like ya, and trust ya . . . in that order." Towards the goal of "know ya," the campaign wanted to remind voters of Janklow's accomplishments during his first two terms and leverage the fact that he left South Dakota better off. To this end, the campaign crafted the phrase "South Dakota Advantage" and repeated it incessantly in speeches, campaign literature, and television advertisements. The South Dakota Advantage strategy included reminding voters of all the ways South Dakota was better positioned nationally and within the state as a result of the prior eight years of Janklow in office.[14] Before Janklow's tenure, an inferiority complex had hampered the state; his time as governor convinced South Dakotans that they could be big and do big things. He successfully recruited Citibank to Sioux Falls. He was innovative with the education and prison system. This skill was identified in the eulogy offered by Governor Dennis Daugaard:

> Again and again, decade after decade, Bill Janklow proved that there was nothing too arduous, nothing too ambitious, and nothing too audacious for South Dakota to achieve. . . . He taught us to be proud of ourselves. Bill often said that South Dakota has an inferiority complex. Because we are small, and because we are remote, we sometimes believe that we cannot be the first, or the best, or the most innovative. . . . Bill Janklow showed us there is nothing that South Dakota cannot achieve—because he achieved so much himself.[15]

To address ways to make voters "like ya," the campaign emphasized personal appeals over any particular issue (save maybe the property tax issue). Probably the biggest hurdle the campaign had to overcome was a significant gender gap, where perceptions of his abrasive and authoritative nature overwhelmed any support from women based on his possession of desirable leadership qualities. In order to combat these stereotypes, campaign strategy needed to emphasize his role as a compassionate, moral family man.[16]

Finally, in an effort to get voters to "trust ya," the campaign decided to create a campaign platform that highlighted issues Janklow "owned," meaning issues that voters viewed Janklow positively on or as best suited to handle, and minimize issues the former governor

TABLE 1. Content Analysis of 1992 Survey Response

Character Trait	Mentions	Character Trait	Mentions
Honesty	159	Intellect	16
Leadership	60	Financial Skills	13
Works in Best Interest of South Dakota	57	Strong Personality	13
Gets Job Done/Accomplished	42	Work Ethic/Responsible	12
Experience/Skill	37	Rural/Farming/Agriculture	11
Communicate with People/Receptive	35	Christian/Religious	10
Integrity	30	Genuine/Friendly	9
Open-minded/Unbiased	30	Innovation	7
Conviction	24	Compassion	6
Straightforward	20	Democrat	3
Republican/Conservative	19		

Source: Public Opinion Strategies, "Statewide Survey," Janklow Personal Papers, USD.

was perceived as being weaker on. If a weakness was salient enough that it could not be pushed from the spotlight, the campaign would try to transform perceptions. Governor Bill Janklow's success in getting voters to trust him was in part a result of his personality and style aligning with the personality and style that the people of South Dakota preferred. A state's political culture provides insight into how citizens think about politics and governmental institutions, including the desired qualities and character traits of elected officials. Given South Dakotans' individualistic-moralistic political culture, voters resonate with elected officials who embody conservative and pragmatic approaches to governance. Specifically, voters are looking for candidates who are perceived as problem solvers, authentically South Dakotan, and conservative with a streak of populism.[17]

Table 1 presents a content analysis of the open-ended responses that South Dakotans provided during an internal poll conducted for the Janklow campaign in 1992. As is commonly the case, regardless of office sought or election year, honesty and leadership were the most important character traits voters looked for in a gubernatorial candidate. Other character traits for a gubernatorial candidate included: "Good leadership. Somebody that doesn't promise a lot and then doesn't do it. If people make a promise they should keep it. A prom-

TABLE 2. Most Important Issues for South Dakota
Republicans, 1992

Issue	Mentions
Taxes	72
Education	32
Video Lottery	24
Abortion	22
Wages/Employment	18
Crime	6
Healthcare	4
Marijuana	2
Anti-homosexuality	1

Source: Public Opinion Strategies, "Statewide Survey,"
Janklow Personal Papers, USD.

ise is a promise. Somebody that knows how to get things done and someone who is a good leader," or simply, "honesty." Also important, voters expected a gubernatorial candidate to work in the best interest of South Dakota, with the ability to "get the job done." Frequently, respondents stated they were looking for someone "mostly honest [who] will do something for the state, basically do the right things for the people," or "someone that gets things done. One that speaks out, not afraid to speak out. Gets things done."[18]

To determine what issues to highlight and minimize in the campaign, the Janklow operation took information collected from public opinion polling on topics such as the most important issue for that election and combined it with the perceived strengths and weaknesses of Janklow versus his opponent. The first step was to identify the most important issues for voters. Table 2 identifies the issues Republican voters mentioned most often in the open-ended survey response during the primary election. The overwhelming issue for Republicans in 1994 was taxes, which received more than double the number of mentions than the next most important issue, education.

Throughout the eighties, South Dakotans had witnessed an explosion in the amount they paid in property taxes, and the public outcry against the perpetual increases reached a turning point in 1994.

Known as Dakota 1, Initiated Measure 1 proposed a cap on property taxes at $193 million. The ballot measure gained popular support as it was circulated for the requisite signatures and created a tangible position for voters to hold candidates accountable to. Public opinion regarding the property tax issue was split down the middle, with half the state's population in uproar over the growth in government and the subsequent need for increasing tax revenue, while the other half was aware that a cap in property taxes would leave local government short by about $300 million.[19] Voters' conflicting views on the issue can be seen in responses collected during an April 1994 survey for the Janklow campaign. A common response to the question of what is the most important issue was: "Whoever is against [the] income tax would be a good person." However, just two responses later, an equally common answer was: "I know they can't do everything, but I think they should be pushing for tax revision." Education, always a central issue to South Dakotans because the remote nature of the state made public education logistically and financially challenging, also resonated with voters. Responders wanted "a person who says he will do something and follow through with it . . . the problem with taxes, and his stance on education."[20]

The video lottery issue was as divisive as the property tax issue. Voters' views on the lottery ranked high in saliency; however, their diverging opinions on the matter made it a problematic issue for candidates. In 1989, South Dakota had been the first state in the nation to institute a video lottery. By 1994, it had been subject to repeal through an initiated measure, legal challenges over its constitutionality, and a referred constitutional amendment providing for its reinstatement. Voters were split over their support and gauged their preference in gubernatorial candidates in part on how the candidate stood on the issue.[21] South Dakotans were concerned about "getting the video lottery back" and wanted someone who "listens to both sides of the story. . . . To care about the people that are losing money for their video lottery." But, they also desired someone willing to "support higher education, who is not afraid to raise necessary taxes, and is against gambling."[22] Least important to voters were more progressive social welfare and privacy concerns: healthcare, the legalization of marijuana, and gay rights.

Voters were queried about how well they thought the state was han-

TABLE 3. Republicans' Biggest Concern for South Dakota, 1992

Concern	Percent Responding
POCKETBOOK/ECONOMY	
The Economy/Recession	3
State Spending on Education	1
Farm Problems	4
Government Spending	2
High Taxes/Unfair Taxes	11
High Property Taxes	16
Low Wages	5
Unemployment	4
SOCIAL	
Abortion	1
Crime	2
Education	8
Environment/Pollution	1
Healthcare	4
Racial Problems/Diversity	1
Social Security/Aid to Elderly	1
OTHER	
State Legislature	1
Too Many State Employees	—
Decline in Moral Values	1
No Problems	4

Source: Public Opinion Strategies, "Statewide Survey,"
Janklow Personal Papers, USD.

dling its most pressing issues and what their greatest concern was for South Dakota's future. Republicans' responses identified a number of problems that voters expected elected officials to handle (Table 3). While a majority felt South Dakota was going in the right direction under Walter Dale Miller, that optimism fell by eleven percent in the three months leading up to the primary election. Voters were espe-cially concerned with taxes; the two most-cited responses were issues surrounding property taxes and increasing or unfair taxes. Education was the third most-cited problem facing South Dakota.[23]

One important piece of information that Janklow strategists used to plan for the 1994 election was information cultivated from a "testing the waters" poll conducted by Public Opinion Strategies. Undertaken prior to his decision to run for governor, this 1992 poll helped the campaign calculate how the public perceived Bill Janklow, regardless of how they felt about his primary challenger. Geographically, the poll indicated that Janklow had a three-to-one favorable to unfavorable name recognition with South Dakota voters in four out of five regions. Janklow received the strongest support from the Sioux Falls area (72 percent favorable, 18 percent unfavorable), with the weakest levels of support coming from the Black Hills region (57 percent favorable, 34 percent unfavorable). There was a noticeable gap between men and women in their initial support of Janklow, especially among working women (66 percent of homemakers had a favorable opinion, while only 58 percent of working women saw Janklow in a favorable light). He received his greatest levels of public support from voters age 50–64 (79 percent favorable, 16 percent unfavorable). That said, over a majority of respondents in all age groups had a more favorable opinion of Janklow than unfavorable. Finally, as expected, voters identifying with the Republican Party viewed Janklow positively (75 percent favorable, 16 percent unfavorable). This level of support among party members was certainly promising, but even more encouraging was the fact that 59 percent of Democrats and 61 percent of Independents also viewed him favorably.[24] Early on, it was clear that his appeal as a statewide candidate was far reaching.

Ultimately, the Public Opinion Strategies 1992 poll captured what voters believed to be the most pressing issues in South Dakota, the positive attributes associated with Bill Janklow, and any concerns people had about his candidacy. Anecdotally, the open-ended responses painted a compelling picture of how a majority of South Dakotans viewed the political environment in the state and their preferences for the type of gubernatorial candidate capable of handling that environment. One voter maintained that people wanted a "strong leader who can bring South Dakota through the video lottery situation. The property tax problems. I want a governor who is concerned about private property issues." Yet another identified a successful candidate as someone who "works for the people. [Doesn't] pull the wool over our eyes. Get some of the taxes down. That's why we need the lottery. Keep education up and take care of the older people."[25] The Janklow camp emphasized these sentiments and translated them into numerous strategies for advertising, stump speeches, and campaign literature.

The Janklow campaign focused on two things: the former governors' own qualities and the contrast between his candidacy and that of the incumbent. Campaign manager Rollyn Samp sought to help voters to "know [Janklow], like him, and trust him."[26] In the 1960s as a result of the advent of television and the use of political primaries, campaigns were increasingly about the selling of the candidate, not the issue platform.[27] As such, the campaign focused on the personal, private side of Janklow, framing him as a compassionate and loving family man. They also highlighted his strong leadership style and ability to get things done, frequently citing his first two terms in office as evidence. Overall, the campaign used public opinion data to craft an agenda that emphasized issues voters not only found salient but positively correlated with Janklow. Issues that voters did not care about or did not positively associate him with were minimized.

In crafting this issue agenda, Janklow campaign managers used "head-to-head" polls that asked voters to compare candidates on specific traits and issues. In particular, the campaign looked for general themes, specific topics, and any changes in public opinion during the primary campaign. Two months before the primary, public opinion polling indicated that South Dakotans favored Janklow over Miller 50 percent to 44 percent. Both candidates were widely known, and Republican voters viewed them both favorably. When asked, "Whether you have heard of this person," 99 percent of Republicans surveyed knew of Janklow (73 percent favorable and 26 percent unfavorable/ no opinion) and 98 percent knew Miller (75 percent favorable and 23 percent unfavorable/no opinion). When asked about desired character traits, one respondent articulated a common perception of both candidates and how they would choose between Janklow and Miller: "I was going to say honesty, but that applies to both of them because I think they are both honest. So, someone who would work for the good of South Dakota."[28]

More specifically, the campaign could use the head-to-head polling

TABLE 4. 1994 Republican Party Head-to-Heads, Bill Janklow vs. Walter Dale

Category	Janklow	Miller
Knows where he wants to lead South Dakota	54 percent	22 percent
Strong and consistent	60 percent	24 percent
Represents the past	50 percent	31 percent
Shares values	36 percent	40 percent
Will put taxpayers first	49 percent	26 percent
Honest/high degree of integrity	24 percent	40 percent
Will do more for South Dakota	51 percent	27 percent
Will make a difference by fighting for South Dakota	61 percent	22 percent
A good Republican	32 percent	25 percent
Best able to solve major problems facing state	55 percent	24 percent
Cares about people like me	32 percent	40 percent
Will fight the implementation of a state income tax	66 percent	14 percent
More likely to raise your taxes	20 percent	40 percent
Best able to create jobs	57 percent	17 percent
Best able to cut property taxes	38 percent	20 percent

Source: Wirthlin Group, "South Dakota Brushfire Analysis," Janklow Personal Papers, USD.

to identify the perceived strengths and weaknesses of both Republicans. Table 4 lists Republican respondents answers to the prompt, "Is the phrase a better description of Bill Janklow or Walter Miller?" Republican voters felt the issue of taxes, working for South Dakota, and being a strong leader embodied the former governor best. For Miller, his strongest traits surrounded soft leadership qualities, such as compassion, integrity, and sharing voters' values. Fortunately for Miller, these soft leadership traits were also some of Janklow's biggest weaknesses. Miller was strongest with Janklow's soft supporters in the areas of sharing values (35 percent of Janklow's soft supporters said Miller better embodied this trait than Janklow), honesty and integrity (33 percent of Janklow's soft supporters), and caring for people (29 percent). Unfortunately for Miller, his top four traits were all under 50 percent, and Janklow was largely seen as more capable to handle the issues voters found most important (taxes, jobs, fighting for South Dakota), regardless of whether they were strong or soft supporters.

Thus Janklow trumped Miller when it came to handling important issues and getting the job done, but Miller trumped Janklow on softer leadership characteristics. The latter was especially problematic for Janklow given that the number one determinant driving the vote was perception of honesty and integrity. However, the gap between the two candidates lessened by ten percentage points from February to April, indicating that South Dakotans were willing to change their perception of the gubernatorial candidates.[29]

By April, the Janklow campaign felt comfortable with the support from his base and decided to turn its attention toward shoring up soft supporters and undecideds. To do this, campaign staff suggested that Janklow shift his focus from men under forty-five or over sixty-five living East River, particularly in Sioux Falls, to younger women and middle-aged men, higher income voters, and voters whose greatest fear was the increasing property tax rate. The staff's remaining consideration was how to handle the divide within the party. Party elites in Pierre preferred the Miller candidacy, a result of their ties to the current chief executive and the former Mickelson administration. However, when Republican voters across the state expressed a desire for the Janklow years of the past, the Janklow campaign felt they could secure the party's nomination without support from the establishment. Ultimately, the Janklow campaign largely ignored Pierre's party elites until the general election phase.[30]

As an East River resident, Janklow always found it more difficult to capture the West River vote. With the hope of attracting West River voters, the campaign announced, unusually early and before the primary, that Carol Hillard would be Janklow's running mate. Hillard had been born in Deadwood and served as councilwoman and state representative for Rapid City, the largest city west of the Missouri River in South Dakota. The strategy was to just "leave her in the Hills," recognizing the logistical concerns of hours separating the Black Hills from Sioux Falls and still garnering the support voters give a "favorite son" candidate. To increase support in the middle of the state, the campaign focused not on the establishment in Pierre but rather on the James River area. In particular, the campaign emphasized a right-to-life message by sending out a mailer targeted at German Catholics. Finally, Janklow used his business connections in Sioux Falls to lock in corporate support (and funding) from companies like Citibank. However, he also campaigned in call centers or at large businesses to interact and build support among corporations' numerous employees.[31]

Addressing the issues of the primary election, the Janklow campaign sought first to issue trespass, or focus the campaign message on the character traits and/or issues typically attributed to or "owned" by their opponents. In particular, it emphasized Janklow's softer leadership qualities as a way of combatting the perceived strengths of Miller. A theme from the beginning of the campaign was that Janklow was not just a former governor but also a compassionate family man imbued with South Dakotan values. At the same time, the campaign reinforced perceptions of Janklow as a strong leader who was most likely to fight for change. A final element of the strategy was to emphasize Janklow's determination to keep taxes low. Janklow's proposed solution to high property taxes was to reduce them by thirty percent while continuing the slogan "Putting Tax Payers First."[32]

A content analysis of Janklow's television advertisements summarizes his message for home viewers (Table 5). Rollyn Samp wrote four television advertisements that national political advertising expert Stuart Stevens then filmed. The campaign used two-day rolling poll averages to adjust their television buys, but largely, these four advertisements ran repeatedly throughout April, May, and June of 1994. Trying to persuade voters that Janklow was not as cold and calculating as some people, especially women, believed, the campaign aimed to close the gender gap with softer advertisements utilizing interviews with his children ("Big Heart") and everyday South Dakotans ("South Dakota First" and "Genuine"). Even the names of the advertisements were intended to depict the "side of Bill that 95 percent of the public didn't get to see."[33] Images showed Janklow interacting with families, children, or the elderly. They were always staged in a comfortable setting, with Janklow nowhere near an office or a business suit. The exception to this portrayal was "Promises, Promises," which substantively discussed the issue of taxation. This advertisement was also the only one to mention his primary opponent or the upcoming election. Ultimately, the advertisements appeared to have been successful, as internal polling saw the number of definite supporters increase from February to April. He defeated Miller in the Republican primary by a margin of eight percent.[34]

Name	Themes	Script Excerpt
"Big Heart"	Family, compassion, focus on individual, ability to govern and move state forward	"Bill's just got a big heart for South Dakota."
"South Dakotan First"	Bill as a person, connects with people, grassroots person, pussycat dad, team player, make a good governor	"He puts South Dakota first."
"Genuine"	Kind, considerate, cares about individuals, compassionate, genuine, honest	"I think he does listen."
"Promises, Promises"	Taxes, Walter Miller	"We always know where he [Janklow] stands."

Source: Audio-Visual Materials, Janklow Personal Papers, USD.

After the Republican primary, the Janklow campaign's largest concern was ensuring that Miller's supporters would show up on election day. Governor Janklow saw his acceptance speech at the 1994 state Republican convention, "Leadership that Cares," a "healing speech" for the party. In addition to persuading Miller's base to support his candidacy, Janklow sought to reassure Republicans of his conservative beliefs and to initiate populist appeals attractive to South Dakota Democrats. For example, Janklow took up the cause of child vaccinations, an issue of government assistance that was seen as palatable to Republicans and Democrats alike.[35]

General election strategy again evolved out of considerations regarding the state's geographic differences and voters' perceptions. As a result, the campaign emphasized Janklow's record on promoting business interests within the state and bringing South Dakota onto the national scene. In the West River area, the campaign continued to capitalize on the appeal of lieutenant governor candidate Carol Hill-

TABLE 6. 1994 Head-to-Head Polling Data

Question	Janklow	Beddow
If election held today	56 percent	37 percent
Heard of	98 percent	88 percent
Favorable impression	65 percent	48 percent
Unfavorable impression	27 percent	18 percent
Do more for South Dakota	56 percent	25 percent
A strong leader	66 percent	18 percent
Will create jobs for South Dakota	59 percent	20 percent
Is best able to deal with the property tax mess	53 percent	24 percent
Best prepare South Dakota for the future	53 percent	27 percent
Consistently oppose tax increases	49 percent	16 percent
Shares my values	41 percent	30 percent
Cares about people like me	42 percent	33 percent

Source: Wirthlin Group, "1994 General Election Public Opinion Poll," 22 Sept. 1994, Janklow Personal Papers, USD.

ard and to stress Janklow's record of producing jobs. The campaign appealed to voters in the central part of the state by highlighting social issues such as abortion and emphasizing personal connections. Strategist Rollyn Samp recalls constructing a letter-writing operation in which the campaign identified the most influential person in each county and asked them to write ten letters to their neighbors in support of Janklow's candidacy. Samp believes that more than any other state, South Dakota responds to appeals and community ties.[36]

The issues that had been important in the primary remained central in the general election. A mid-September poll conducted by the Wirthlin Group suggested that themes surrounding accomplishments, leadership, jobs, and taxes were equally important to Republican, Democrat, and Independent voters. Head-to-head polling data (Table 6) indicated that Janklow entered the race largely favored by South Dakota voters; he benefited from greater name recognition and a more favorable image than his opponent James Beddow. In contrast to Miller, Beddow was viewed less positively in all of the categories of character traits or salient issues. Similar to Miller, the margin between perceptions of the two candidates' skills or traits was closest

TABLE 7. 1994 General Election Television Advertisements

Name	Themes	Script Excerpt
"Tested"	Income taxes, property tax, tested problem solver/gets job done, acquiring jobs	"He can do more for South Dakota."
"War on West"	Bill Clinton, taxes/ big government/jobs, war on West River, mining, timber, federal grazing land	"When I'm governor, we aren't going to let them kick us around anymore."
"Big Job"	Issues (jobs, income tax, crime, property taxes) changed South Dakota; farmers, fight against D.C.	"[Janklow] made America stand up and pay attention to South Dakota like never before."
"My Dad"	Family, personality, compassion	"At heart, dad's a private person, but he values family, friends, and others."
"Across South Dakota"	Property tax, leadership, jobs, government growth	"People are outraged over higher and higher property taxes. They want proven leadership that can solve this crisis."

Source: Audio-Visual Materials, Janklow Personal Papers, USD.

in areas pertaining to soft leadership qualities ("shares my values," "cares about people like me"). Yet, unlike the primary election, those soft leadership qualities were not as important as the issues on which Janklow was perceived as being stronger, such as leadership and execution, providing jobs, and handling the property tax debate. In sum, Bill Janklow was in a much better position in the general election running against Beddow than he had been when running against Miller in the primary.

Janklow's issue agenda for the 1994 general election found expression in his television advertisements (Table 7). Following upon his strategy in the primary election, the Janklow camp sought to play up the character traits and issues their candidate owned, while minimizing issues less salient or owned by Beddow. As Janklow was better situated against his opponent in terms of character traits, only one advertisement was used to bolster his personality (as opposed to three of the four advertisements in the primary). "My Dad" was an advertisement aimed at persuading voters of Janklow's softer side, again using narration by his children, imagery of him playing with grandchildren, and language to promote the idea of the former governor as a family man. More common in the general election were substantive advertisements focused on election issues, such as the property tax debate and the acquisition of jobs. Four of the five advertisements made some mention of Bill Janklow's record of producing jobs in South Dakota.

A prime example of the general election strategy of the Janklow campaign can be seen in the television advertisement "War on West." Using public opinion data compiled by the Wirthlin Group in early November 1994, the Janklow camp sought to understand why their candidate was struggling with West River voters in particular. Through a mix of prompted and open-ended responses taken from an oversampled group of West River voters, the campaign discovered that Janklow's weakness in the region derived from perceptions of several key leadership attributes: creating jobs, doing more for South Dakota, and being best able to prepare South Dakota for the future. While Janklow held a lead against Beddow in all of these survey questions, they were identified as areas of weakness when looking at regional support. As a result of this information, the campaign crafted "War on West":

Black and white images, starting with a clip of the White House, moving to images of prairie, a woman decorating a church sign, a rancher, Main Street, two old women, and then Bill Clinton.

Narrator: Washington's war on the West. From families, to ranchers, to small businesses, to senior citizens. Bill Clinton's team is increasing taxes, expanding government, killing jobs. It's a war West River must win.

Cut to Bill Janklow, in color, moving to images of trucks, trees, and prairie.

Janklow: There really is a Washington war on the West. When you talk about mining, timber, federal grazing lands. Washington is taking a hostile approach. When I'm governor, we aren't going to let them kick us around anymore.

Text on screen: "Janklow. He Can Do More For South Dakota. Image behind text is a prairie sunset.

Narrator: Bill Janklow for Governor[37]

From the public opinion data, West River voters were more likely to be skeptical about Janklow's ability to understand their needs than East River voters and more likely to be responsive to the needs of East River and big business. "War on West" addressed these concerns. First, it reiterated Janklow's ability to create jobs, and not just for the eastern part of the state. Second, it emphasized his ability to get things done. Third, it reinforced the "us versus them" mentality that many South Dakotans harbored with regard to politics in Washington.[38] The advertisement was a successful way to remind voters that Janklow could deliver on jobs, the number one issue in the 1994 election.

According to Rollyn Samp, Janklow was positive that he would lose to Beddow, despite holding a massive lead in the waning weeks of the general election campaign. Many close to Janklow were aware of this kind of self-doubt, but most of the general public were not. To help motivate the candidate, Samp bet Janklow that he would not only win but win specifically in Woonsocket (Beddow's hometown) and in Mitchell (home of Dakota Wesleyan, the college Beddow served as president). The bet motivated Janklow, to the point of obsession, to defeat Beddow on his home turf. Janklow won Sandborn County, housing the city of Woonsocket, with 53.2 percent of the vote. He won Davison County by over 20 percent (58.3 percent to Beddow's 30.2 percent).[39]

While the candidate's response to the bet may have turned a few votes, Janklow's electoral success had largely been written on the wall. His return to the governorship in 1994 resulted from a combination of his familiarity with and his embodiment of South Dakota's unique political culture. Janklow's name recognition in the state was unparalleled. Ask any South Dakotan, and she will give you her Bill Janklow story. It might be about his late night obsessions and retaliation with a political foe or a recollection of some personal gesture he did for a family member, but it was certainly memorable and directly related to how the teller viewed Janklow's success or failure as a politician. Once again in 1994, his ability to embody the values of South Dakotans, regardless of political ideology, had translated to electoral success.

NOTES

1. Rollyn Samp, interview with author, 18 Apr. 2017.

2. Jim Soyer, interview with author, 18 Jan. 2017; Wirthlin Group, "1994 General Election Public Opinion Poll," 22 Sept. 1994, Janklow Personal Papers, I. D. Weeks Library, University of South Dakota (USD), Vermillion.

3. Daniel J. Elazar, *American Federalism: A View from the States* (New York: Thomas Y. Crowell Co., 1966). The term republican used in this context refers to a "small r" republican philosophy, a belief that government closest to the people is most capable of dealing with the citizens who live there. As such, republicanism advocates for a decentralized government power comprised of local political actors.

4. "South Dakota: Past Governors Bios: Governor William J. Janklow," National Governors Association, www.nga.org/cms/home/governors/past-governors-bios /page_south_dakota/col2-content/main-content-list/title_janklow_william .default.html.

5. Ibid.; Cara Hetland and Mark Steil, "He Just Wants to Win," Minnesota Public Radio, 21 Jan. 2004, news.minnesota.publicradio.org features/ 2004/01 /21_hetlandc_janklowtwo/;Marshall Damgaard, "Bill Janklow Biography," 2016, Governor William J. Janklow Archival Project, USD; "Janklow, William J.," *Biographical Directory of the United States Congress, 1774–Present,* bioguide.congress .gov/scripts/biodisplay.pl?index=J000286; John Raimo, *Biographical Directory of the Governors of the United States, 1978–1983,* (Westport, CT: Meckler Publishing, 1985), pp. 287–89.

6. South Dakota, Secretary of State, "1978 Gubernatorial Primary Election Results," "1978 Gubernatorial General Election Results," and "1982 Gubernatorial Election Results," all sdsos.gov.

7. Bob Mercer, "A Political History of Former Governor Bill Janklow," *Aberdeen News,* 17 Jan. 2012.

8. "Crash Kills George S. Mickelson; South Dakota's Governor Was 52," *New York Times,* 20 Apr. 1993, p. B7; Rollyn Samp, interview, 18 Apr. 2017; "1994 General Election Returns: Statewide Offices," sdsos.gov. Electorally, the remainder of Governor Janklow's efforts were largely successful. He did not face a primary challenge for his fourth and final term as governor and won the 1998 general election with 64 percent of the vote. At the end of his fourth term in 2002, Janklow ran for the United States House of Representatives, defeating Democrat

Stephanie Herseth-Sandlin with 53.4 percent of the vote. Scandal marred the latter days of his career. On 20 January 2004, Janklow resigned from the House after his conviction for second-degree manslaughter in the death of a motorcyclist while speeding and running through a stop sign on a rural highway. He served one hundred days in the Minnehaha County Jail, received four more speeding tickets, and never ran for public office again. In 2012, Governor Janklow died of brain cancer at the age of seventy-two. "1998 General Election Returns: Statewide Offices," sdsos.gov; Denise Ross, "Janklow Resigns after Manslaughter Conviction," *Rapid City Journal*, 7 Dec. 2003; Richard Goldstein, "Bill Janklow, a Four-Term Governor of South Dakota, Dies at 72," *New York Times*, 12 Jan. 2012, p. B16.

9. Hagan, interview with author, 19 July 2017.

10. Interviews with campaign staffers Marshall Damgaard, Jim Hagan, Rolly Samp, and Jim Soyer all confirmed the endorsements.

11. Hagan, interview, 19 July 2017.

12. Quoted in Wirthlin Group, "South Dakota Cross Sectional Public Opinion Poll," 22 Sept. 1994, Janklow Personal Papers, USD.

13. Public Opinion Strategies, "Statewide Survey," 20–22 May 1992, ibid.

14. Rollyn Samp, interview with author, 7 Feb. 2017.

15. Daugaard, "Remembering Bill Janklow," *South Dakota State News: Governor's Column*, 18 Jan. 2012, news.sd.gov/newsitem.aspx?id=12428.

16. Hagan, interview, 19 July 2017.

17. Susan Welch and John G. Peters, "State Political Culture and the Attitudes of State Senators toward Social, Economic Welfare, and Corruption Issues," *Publius* 10 (1980): 59–67; Richard A. Joslyn, "Manifestations of Elazar's Political Subcultures: State Public Opinion and the Content of Political Campaign Advertising," ibid., 37–58; Russel H. Hillberry and William D. Anderson, "From Policy Preferences to Partisan Support: A Quantitative Assessment of Political Culture in South Dakota," 2012, Department of Economics, Working Papers Series 1156, University of Melborne; Jon K. Lauck, John E. Miller, and Edward Hogan, "Historical Musings: The Contours of South Dakota Political Culture," *South Dakota History* (Summer 2004): 157–78; Joel Lieske, "Regional Subcultures of the United States," *Journal of Politics* 55 (Nov. 1993): 888–913.

18. Public Opinion Strategies to Janklow (campaign memo), 8 Feb. 1993, Janklow Personal Papers.

19. Marshall Damgaard, "A History of Taxes in South Dakota" (working paper) 2016, Janklow Archival Project.

20. Wirthlin Group, "South Dakota Brushfire Analysis," 21 Apr. 1994, Janklow Personal Papers.

21. "About Us: History," South Dakota Lottery, lottery.sd.gov/about/history/;

Rollyn Samp, interview with author, 7 Aug. 2017; Marshall Damgaard, interview with author, 7 Aug. 2017.

22. Wirthlin Group, "South Dakota Brushfire Analysis."

23. Ibid.

24. Public Opinion Strategies, "Statewide Survey."

25. Quoted ibid.

26. Samp, interview, 7 Feb. 2017.

27. *See* Joe McGinniss, *The Selling of the President 1968* (New York City, N.Y.: Penguin Books).

28. Wirthlin Group, "South Dakota Brushfire Analysis."

29. Ibid.

30. Samp, interview, 7 Feb. 2017; Wirthlin Group, "Memorandum to Bill Janklow," 21 Apr. 1994, Janklow Personal Papers; Hagan, interview, 19 July 2017.

31. Samp, interview, 7 Feb. 2017.

32. David Damore, "The Dynamics of Issue Ownership in Presidential Campaigns," *Political Research Quarterly* 57 (Sept. 2004): 391–97; Janklow, talking points used in speeches, Rollyn Samp Collection.

33. Jim Hagan, interview with author, 7 Feb. 2017.

34. Wirthlin Group, "Memorandum to Bill Janklow"; "1994 Statewide Primaries," sdsos.gov.

35. Samp, interview, 7 Feb. 2017; Hagan, interview, 7 Feb. 2017.

36. Hagan, interview, 19 July 2017; Samp, interview, 7 Feb. 2017.

37. "War on West" (tape), Audio-Visual Materials, Janklow Personal Papers.

38. Wirthlin Group, "West River Oversample," 1 Nov. 1994, Janklow Personal Papers; Jon K. Lauck, John E. Miller, and Donald C. Simmons, Jr., eds., *The Plains Political Tradition: Essays on South Dakota's Political Tradition,* [Vol. 1] (Pierre: South Dakota Historical Society Press, 2011).

39. Samp, interview, 7 Feb. 2017; Hagan, interview, 7 Feb. 2017; "South Dakota Official Election Returns and Registration Figures," sdsos.gov.

COMPILED BY MICHELE CHRISTIAN,

DANIEL L. DAILY, LISA E. DUNCAN, AND

CHELLE SOMSEN

APPENDIX

SOUTH DAKOTA'S GOVERNORS,

UNITED STATES SENATORS, AND UNITED

STATES REPRESENTATIVES: A GUIDE TO

THE RESEARCH COLLECTIONS

. . .

In 1968, Dr. Herbert Schell, historian and professor at the University of South Dakota, wrote the following to Joe Foss, twentieth governor of South Dakota, "We sincerely hope you will find it possible to place your private papers with the University as a part of our growing manuscripts collection." Schell continued, "You might wonder what kind of materials make up a manuscript collection. The answer briefly is everything—your own letters, letters received, clippings, photographs, documents, pamphlets, etc."[1] Schell, who wrote and published widely on the history of South Dakota, knew the value of primary source materials and the need to ensure their preservation and access through the state's libraries and archives. The research guide assembled here is a testimony to the diligence of Schell and many others who have strived to ensure that the official records and private papers of South Dakota political figures are available to the public and scholars alike.[2]

Public office holders such as Joe Foss have worked with public servants such as Schell to deposit political papers in the state's libraries and archives. The South Dakota State Historical Society (SDSHS) in Pierre, specifically the State Archives, has led the effort and is the primary repository for the papers of the territorial and state governors. Moreover, a number of United States senators and congressmen have deposited their papers in the State Archives Collection as well. A majority of South Dakota's public university and independent college libraries are also home to collections of papers from governors, congressmen, or senators. Several private historical museums around the state likewise care for the papers of some of South Dakota's most notable political figures. Finally, as the guide shows, the papers of South Dakota's political figures are found outside the state as well. Remarkably, the papers of most of the state's governors and United States representatives and senators who served between 1861 and 2014 reside in a library or archives.

The following guide draws upon the list of elected officials as presented in Volume One, Appendixes A and B of *The Plains Political Tradition: Essays on South Dakota Political Culture*.[3] Hence, it is limited to those who served as governor, representative to Congress, and/or United States senator. This scope is not to diminish the importance of state-level, elected officials and private individuals that have shaped the state's political culture. Governors and those elected to the United States House and Senate, however, hold a unique place in South Dakota's political culture. Their papers are fundamental to understanding both the history of the state and its role in our national history.

To locate the collections of political papers, the compilers consulted guides maintained at the state's various archives and libraries, as well as online tools such as ArchiveGrid and the *Biographical Directory of the United States Congress, 1774–Present*.[4] While South Dakota politicians' letters may be found in other individuals' papers, such collections are not listed here. The scope of such a project is beyond this guide, which focuses on collections deposited by the office holder or his/her estate at a library, archives, or museum.

The order of the guide follows the list of elected officials as presented in Volume 1 of *Plains Political Tradition* and, therefore, begins with territorial governor and state governors' papers, followed by entries for United States delegates, senators, and representatives. The list has been brought up to date through 2017. Each entry includes a biographical sketch, a brief description of the collection(s), and the location of the papers. Unless specifically stated, all collections are open for research. Biographical sketches for each entry are purposively brief; for more complete information, readers will find it convenient to consult the SDSHS homepage, the National Governors Association homepage, and the *Biographical Directory of the United States Congress, 1774–Present*. The abbreviations for the locations of the collections correspond to the following libraries, archives, and museums:

ALPLM	Abraham Lincoln Presidential Library & Museum
	212 North Sixth Street
	Springfield, IL 62701
AU	Augustana University, Center for Western Studies
	2121 S. Summit Ave.
	Sioux Falls, SD 57197
BHSU	Black Hills State University
	E. Y. Berry Library
	1200 University St.
	Spearfish, SD, 57799
DSU	Dakota State University
	Karl E. Mundt Library
	820 N. Washington Ave.
	Madison, SD 57042
DU	Duke University
	Rubenstein Rare Book and Manuscript Library
	316 Perkins Library
	Duke Box 90185
	Durham, NC 27708
DWU	Dakota Wesleyan University
	McGovern Library
	1200 W. University Ave
	Mitchell, SD 57301
MHM	Mellete House Museum
	421 5th Ave. NW
	Watertown, SD 57201
MNHS	Minnesota Historical Society
	345 W. Kellogg Blvd.
	St. Paul, MN 55102
NAHA	Norwegian-American Historical Association
	1510 St. Olaf Avenue
	Northfield, MN 55057
NL	Newberry Library
	60 West Walton Street
	Chicago, IL 60610

PU	Princeton University
	Seeley G. Mudd Library
	65 Olden Street
	Princeton, NJ 08540
SDSHS	South Dakota State Historical Society
	900 Governors Dr.
	Pierre, SD 57501
SDSU	South Dakota State University
	H. M. Briggs Library
	1300 N. Campus Dr.
	Box: 2115
	Brookings, SD 57007
SHM	Siouxland Heritage Museums
	Pettigrew Home and Museum
	131 N. Duluth
	Sioux Falls, SD 57104
SHSM	State Historical Society of Missouri
	University of Missouri-Columbia
	1020 Lowry St.
	Columbia, MO 65201
SHSND	State Historical Society of North Dakota
	612 East Boulevard Ave.
	Bismarck, ND 58505
USD	University of South Dakota
	I. D. Weeks Library
	414 East Clark St.
	Vermillion, SD 57069
YCHS	Yankton County Historical Society
	610 Summit
	Yankton, SD 57078
YU	Yale University
	Beinecke Rare Book and Manuscript Library
	New Haven, CT 06511

Jayne, William, 1826–1916, Republican. Born in Springfield, Ill. First territorial governor, 1861–1863; U. S. delegate, 1863–1864.

ALPLM: Correspondence primarily from Jayne's brother-in-law Lyman Trumbull, political appointments, and records of land transactions.150 items.

SDSHS: Proclamation for Home Defense, 1862; an autobiography of Jayne; governor's message; copies of territorial records on microfilm, including correspondence, proclamations, and appointments, 1861–1863 (originals in SHSND). 0.75 cubic ft.

SHSND: Correspondence, proclamations, memorials, appointments, and official oaths. 0.5 linear ft.

Edmunds, Newton, 1819–1908, Republican. Born in Hartland, N.Y. Territorial governor, 1863–1866.

SHSND: Correspondence, proclamations, applications and resignations, recommendations, oaths, and bonds. 0.25 linear ft.

Faulk, Andrew J., 1814–1898, Democrat, Republican. Born in Milford, Pa. Territorial governor, 1866–1869.

SDSHS: Appointments, copies of correspondence, messages to the legislature, and a proclamation regarding troops to suppress Indian hostilities, as well as Faulk's letter to President Andrew Johnson concerning Justice Peter Shannon. 0.3 cubic ft.

SHSND: Correspondence, proclamations, appointments, notarial bonds, and applications. 0.25 linear ft.

YU: Correspondence, accounts, receipts, and official documents related to Faulk's duties as governor, superintendent of Indian Affairs, and clerk of the U. S. District Court; family papers. 1.8 linear ft.

Burbank, John A., 1827–1905, Republican. Born in Centerville, Ind. Territorial governor, 1869–1873.

SDSHS: Correspondence, messages, and resolutions. 0.3 linear ft.

SHSND: Correspondence, proclamations, appointments, notarial bonds, and applications. 0.5 linear ft.

Pennington, John L., 1829–1900, Republican. Born in New Berne, N.C. Territorial governor, 1874–1878.

SDSHS: Copies of correspondence, addresses, and messages. 0.3 cubic ft.

SHSND: Correspondence, appointments, treaty documents, notarial bonds, and applications. 0.5 linear ft.

Howard. William A., 1813–1880, Republican. Born in Hinesberg, Vt. U. S. representative (Mich.), 1854–1862; territorial governor, 1878–1880.

SDSHS: Report to secretary of the interior, 1878; message to the legislature, 1879; copies of correspondence; and miscellaneous proclamations and appointments. 0.2 cubic ft.

SHSND: Correspondence, notarial bonds and applications, and recommendations. 0.5 linear ft.

Ordway, Nehemiah G., 1828–1907, Republican. Born in Warner, N.H. Territorial governor, 1880–1884.

SDSHS: Letters, including one to President Chester Arthur; copies of memorials; copies of correspondence; a report to secretary of the interior; messages to the legislature; oaths, notarial bonds and applications; recommendations; and extradition requisitions. 0.4 cubic ft.

SHSND: Correspondence, notarial bonds and applications, and recommendations. 2.0 linear ft.

Pierce, Gilbert A., 1839–1901, Republican. Born in East Otto, N.Y. Territorial governor, 1884–1887.

SDSHS: Proclamations, photograph, reports to secretary of the interior, messages to legislature, copies of correspondence, applications and recommendations, oaths and bonds, and extradition requisitions. 0.55 cubic ft.

SHSND: Correspondence, proclamations, applications, recommendations, and notarial oaths. 2.0 linear ft.

Church, Louis K., 1846–1897, Democrat. Born in Brooklyn, N.Y. Territorial governor, 1887–1889.

SDSHS: Copies of correspondence relating to Yankton Bond, railroads, and Indian affairs; notarial oaths and bonds; message to the legislature; and reports to secretary of the interior (originals in SHSND). 0.6 cubic ft.

SHSND: Papers include correspondence, proclamations, appointments, and applications. 1.5 linear ft.

Mellette, Arthur C., 1842–1896, Republican. Born in Henry County, Ind. Last territorial governor, 1889; first governor of South Dakota, 1889–1893.

MHM: Family correspondence, political ephemera, information relating to Samuel Elrod, scrapbooks, Civil War correspondence, and family Bible.

SDSHS: Territorial governor's papers consist of proclamations, Jonathon Brock Play House program, report to secretary of the interior, applications and petitions for pardons, and letters. 0.4 cubic ft.

SDSHS: Copies of Mellette's Civil War diary, copies of family papers, correspondence, proclamations, manuscripts, and speeches. 5.2 cubic ft.

SHSND: Oaths and bonds, petitions, recommendations, and proclamations. 8.25 linear ft.

USD: Personal notes, correspondence, and journals that pertain to travels in the West and time in Dakota Territory. 0.5 linear ft.

Sheldon, Charles H., 1840–1898, Republican. Born in Johnson, Vt. Territorial council, 1886; governor, 1893–1897.

SDSHS: Inaugural address; messages to the legislature; letters and proclamations; documents relating to S. A. Wheeler, state ommissioner of labor; and an 1892 certificate of election. 0.7 cubic ft.

Lee, Andrew E., 1847–1934, People's Party, Fusion Party. Born near Bergen, Norway. Governor, 1897–1901.

SDSHS: Message to secretary of state; Arbor Day Proclamation; address to anti-trust conference in Chicago, 1900; inaugural addresses; newspaper clippings; photographs; personal papers; scrapbook relating to Andrew and Myrtle Lee and Burl Anderson, 1895–1963, and incoming and outgoing correspondence, 1896–1902. 4.7 cubic ft.

SHSND: Eight reels of microfilm consisting of incoming and outgoing correspondence from Lee's governorship that pertain to land use, the South Dakota National Guard, war with Spain, and state funds.

USD: Executive and personal correspondence as well as letter books. 2.0 linear ft.

Herreid, Charles, N. 1857–1928, Republican. Born in Dane County, Wis. Lieutenant governor, 1892–1896; governor, 1901–1905.

SDSHS: Proclamations, speeches, inaugural address, selected veto messages, messages to the legislature, correspondence relating to the last buffalo hunt, appointments, pardons, the Rosebud reservation, the Pan-American Exposition, and the Good Roads Association. 2.8 cubic ft.

Elrod, Samuel H., 1856–1935, Republican. Born in Coatesville, Ind. Governor, 1905–1907.

SDSHS: Inaugural address, Thanksgiving Day proclamations, messages to the legislature, correspondence relating to National Guard activities and a new capitol building, and documents relating to the State Soldiers Home, agricultural issues, and the railroad commission. 1.55 cubic ft.

Crawford, Coe I., 1858–1944, Republican. Born in Volney, Iowa. Governor, 1907–1909; U. S. senator, 1909–1915.

SDSHS: Photograph of Crawford and Charles E. Deland in their Pierre law office, 1885; message to the legislature; speech delivered at Eureka, S.Dak.; inaugural address to the legislature; and other official papers. 16.2 cubic ft.

Vessey, Robert S., 1858–1929, Republican. Born in Winnebago County, Wis. State senator, 1905–1908; governor, 1909–1913.

    SDSHS: Proclamations; photographs of Vessey, staff, and new capitol; correspondence; messages to legislature; inaugural address. 10.9 cubic ft.

    USD: Three state holiday proclamations. 0.1 linear ft.

Byrne, Frank M., 1858–1927, Republican. Born in Volney, Iowa. State senator, 1889–1910, 1907–1910; lieutenant governor, 1909–1913; governor, 1913–1917.

    SDSHS: Proclamations; correspondence relating to military affairs and service on Mexican border; messages to the legislature; and family papers consisting of photographs, news clippings, and correspondence. 1.2 cubic ft.

Norbeck, Peter, 1870–1936, Republican. Born in Vermillion, D.T. State senator, 1909–1915; lieutenant governor, 1915–1916; governor, 1917–1921; U. S. senator, 1921–1936.

    NAHA: Collection of speeches, 1910–1936. 0.2 linear ft.

    SDSHS: Photograph, certificates, messages to legislature, and other records relating to the Council of Defense, exempt boards, coal, highways, Roberts County (S.Dak.), and budgets. 4.4 cubic ft.

    SHSM: Correspondence concerning Republican Party politics at the national and state levels, 1921–1936. 0.1linear ft.

    USD: Bills, correspondence, speeches, clippings, plans, reports, correspondence related to Norbeck's time as a U. S. senator and governor of South Dakota, books related to his career, photographs, and map collection; of note is material related to Mount Rushmore. 84.0 linear ft.

McMaster, William H., 1877–1968, Republican. Born in Ticonic, Iowa. State representative,1911–1912; state senator, 1913–1916; lieutenant governor,1917–1920; governor, 1921–1925; U. S. senator, 1925–1931.

    SDSHS: Inaugural messages, proclamations, correspondence, and petitions. 0.45 cubic ft.

    USD: Speeches, news clippings, correspondence, photographs, and bills. 3.0 linear ft.

Gunderson, Carl, 1864–1933, Republican. Born in Clay County, D.T. State representative, 1893–1919; lieutenant governor, 1921–1925; governor, 1925–1927.

> SDSHS: Inaugural address, message to legislature, Arbor Day proclamation, and papers relating to state finances and the South Dakota National Guard; Gunderson's field notes while working as engineer for U. S. Indian Service on South Dakota reservations. 0.6 cubic ft.

Bulow, John W., 1869–1960, Democrat. Born in Moscow, Ohio. State senator, 1899–1901; governor 1927–1931; U. S. senator, 1931–1943.

> SDSHS: Inaugural addresses and messages to legislature, postcards of Bulow and President Calvin Coolidge, photograph of Bulow and Charles Lindbergh, campaign broadside, and letter to Brook Howell. 0.7 cubic ft.

Green, Warren E., 1870–1945, Republican. Born in Jackson County, Wis. State senator, 1907–1908, 1923–1926; governor, 1931–1933.

> SDSHS: Inaugural address and scrapbooks. 0.7 cubic ft.

Berry, Tom, 1879–1951, Democrat. Born in Paddock, Nebr. Governor,1933–1937.

> SDSHS: Inaugural messages, Thanksgiving Proclamation, stratosphere balloon photographs, and correspondence. 0.5 cubic ft.

Jensen, Leslie, 1892–1964, Republican. Born in Hot Springs, S.Dak. Governor, 1937–1939.

> SDSHS: Inaugural message, message to legislature, correspondence, and recording he made while serving in Australia in 1944. 0.4 cubic ft.

Bushfield, Harlan J., 1882–1948, Republican. Born in Atlantic, Iowa. Governor, 1939–1942; U. S. senator, 1943–1948.

> SDSHS: Inaugural messages, correspondence, biennium supplementary budget, radio interview transcript between Lawrence K. Fox and Bushfield (KGFX radio), and a photograph of First Lady Bushfield christening the battleship *South Dakota*. 0.6 cubic ft.
>
> USD: Speeches and radio addresses (typescripts). 1.0 linear ft.

Sharpe, Merrell Q., 1888–1962, Republican. Born in Marysville, Kans. Governor, 1943–1947.

SDSHS: Inaugural address, messages to legislature, brochure promoting Black Hills as site for United Nations headquarters, and papers concerning Missouri River development. 4.2 cubic ft.

USD: Gubernatorial records, including correspondence and other materials, and files related to public service, including service as attorney general of South Dakota. 54.25 linear ft.

Mickelson, George T., 1903–1965, Republican. Born in Selby, S.Dak. State representative, 1937–1941; governor, 1947–1951.

SDSHS: Addresses to legislature; biennium budget; files on state agencies, boards and committees, offices, and universities; and a family scrapbook. 2.4 cubic ft.

USD: Correspondence, subject files and files on government agencies, speeches, clippings, memorabilia, and photographs. 9.75 linear ft.

Anderson, Sigurd, 1904–1990, Republican. Born in Webster, S.Dak. Governor, 1951–1955.

SDSHS: Correspondence; files on state agencies, committees, offices, universities, and boards; subject files; inaugural address; and messages to legislature. 11.85 cubic ft.

USD: Governor's files, state agency and department files, correspondence, photographs, and memorabilia. 96.5 linear ft.

Foss, Joseph Jacob, 1915–2003, Republican. Born near Sioux Falls, S.Dak. State representative, 1948, 1952; governor, 1955–1959.

SDSHS: Inaugural message, messages to legislature, photographs (with John Headley), budget, report titled "The South Dakota Survival Plan," *Life Magazine* article, legislative correspondence, minutes and correspondence relating to public welfare, meeting minutes of State Pardons Board, and copies of commutation orders. 1.35 cubic ft.

USD: Correspondence and manuscript and print materials. 21.0 linear ft.

Herseth, Ralph, 1909–1969, Democrat. Born near Houghton, S.Dak. State senator, 1951–1952, 1955–1956; governor, 1959–1961.

SDSHS: Materials concerning Deadwood fire of 1959, inaugural address, scrapbook, newspaper clippings, and photographs. 0.5 cubic ft.

USD: Speeches, minutes of state meetings, departmental files, clippings, legislative research files, and correspondence. 24.75 linear ft.

Gubbrud, Archie M., 1910–1987, Republican. Born in Lincoln County, S.Dak. State representative 1950–1960; governor, 1961–1965.

SDSHS: Thanksgiving Proclamation, Theodore Roosevelt Centennial Proclamation, certificate relating to 1913 Panama-Pacific Exposition, inaugural message, and message to 1963 legislature. 0.2 cubic ft.

Boe, Nils A, 1913–1992, Republican. Born in Baltic, S.Dak. State representative, 1950–1958; lieutenant governor, 1962–1964; governor, 1965–1969.

AU: Correspondence, speeches, subject files, photographs, personal and family papers, scrapbooks, and artifacts. 7.0 linear ft.

SDSHS: Files on state agencies, committees, offices, universities, and boards; audit reports and fact sheets, 1967–1968; records relating to Black Hills flood of 1965; records relating to March 1966 blizzard; scrapbook; and messages to legislature. 9.2 cubic ft.

USD: State agency and department files, administrative files, and subject files. 12.0 linear ft.

Farrar, Frank L., 1929–. Republican. Born near Britton, S.Dak. Governor, 1969–1971.

SDSHS: Files on state agencies, committees, offices, universities, and boards; executive orders; inaugural message and message to legislature; governor's office guest register; and audits and reports. Collection is partially open per SDCL 1-27-1.20 and 1-27-1.21. 1.3 cubic ft.

USD: Speeches, budgets, clippings, correspondence, and radio addresses. 1.75 linear ft.

Kneip, Richard F., 1933–1987, Democrat. Born in Tyler, Minn. State senator, 1964–1970; governor, 1971–1978; U. S. ambassador to Singapore, 1978–1980.

    SDSHS: Speeches, photographs, cabinet meeting minutes, proclamations, reports, messages to legislature, and correspondence addressed to both Kneip and Harvey Wollman, 1978. 2.65 cubic ft.

    USD: Gubernatorial records include department and agency files, general correspondence, state issue files (including American Indian Movement activities), schedules, news clippings, and bills. 109.0 linear ft.

Wollman, Harvey, 1935–. Democrat. Born in Frankfort, S.Dak. State senator, 1969–1974; lieutenant governor, 1974–1978; governor, 1978–1979.

    SDSHS: Democratic Party correspondence between Wollman and gubernatorial candidate Roger McKellips; postcards of Wollman in front of South Dakota capitol; correspondence with federal agencies and members of U. S. Congress; speeches; general correspondence; state agency correspondence; and 1978 inaugural address. Collection is partially open per 1-27-1.20 and 1-27-1.21. 0.5 cubic ft.

Janklow, William J., 1939–2012, Republican. Born in Chicago, Ill. Governor, 1979–1987, 1995–2003; U. S. representative, 2003–2004.

    USD: State agency files, subject files, news clippings, reports, state senate and house records, notes, and photographs. Collection is open, except for files closed per SDCL 1:27. 375.0 linear ft.

    USD: Personal and political papers consisting of correspondence, photographs, interviews, campaign records, audio-visual materials, publications, and memorabilia. 160.0 linear ft.

Mickelson, George S., 1941–1993, Republican. Born in Mobridge, S.Dak. State representative, 1975–1981; governor, 1987–1993.

    SDSHS: Executive proclamation; photographs; slides and photographs of funeral; outgoing correspondence, 1987–1989; videos; press releases and clippings; general files; documents on topics such as China Trade Council, Charlottesville Education Summit, Crazy Horse Mountain, and the USS

Rushmore christening; tapes of interviews for Mickelson Project; awards; correspondence of George and Linda Mickelson, 1987–1993; inauguration address and photographs, 1987; memorials; social calendar and menus, 1983–1992; public schedule, 1987–1993; maps concerning Super Conducting Supercollider, 1987; speeches; videotapes; general files relating to boards and commissions; family photographs; strategic plan for South Dakota; and Centennial Education Summit Files, 1989. 165.1 cubic ft.

Miller, Walter Dale, 1925–2015, Republican. Born in Viewfield, S.Dak. State representative, 1967–1986; lieutenant governor, 1987–1993; governor, 1993–1995.

SDSHS: Files relating to processes of state and federal government; speeches; photographs; correspondence of Miller and executive staff; and material related to Governor's Planning Council on Developmental Disabilities. 8.9 cubic ft.

Rounds, M. Michael, 1954–. Republican. Born in Huron, S.Dak. State senator, 1991–2000; governor, 2003–2011; U. S. senator 2015–.

SDSHS: Gubernatorial papers consisting of monthly reports, correspondence, proclamations, speeches, oaths of office, financial statements, inmate files, senate and house bills, journals and reports, inauguration materials, agency files, executive proclamations, slides, prints, negatives and digital photos. Collection is partially open as per 1-27-1.20 and 1-27-1.21. 74.0 cubic ft.

Daugaard, Dennis, 1953–. Republican. Born near Dell Rapids, S.Dak. State senator, 1997–2002; lieutenant governor, 2002–2011; governor, 2011–2019.

Official papers in custody of the Office of the Governor.

Todd, John Blair S., 1814–1872, Democrat. Born in Lexington, Ky. U. S. delegate, 1861–1863, 1864–1865; territorial representative, 1866–1867.

> MNHS: Papers,1849–1855, consisting of one field journal containing drawings of the journey from Fort Leavenworth to the Black Hills and a topographical description of the Battle of Ash Hollow, along with accounts of buffalo herds, military life, scenery, and a trip to Sioux City, Iowa. 0.1 linear ft.

> SDSHS: Publication entitled "Views of the Minority," John B. S. Todd vs. William Jayne, 1864. 0.1 cubic ft.

> USD: Biographical materials such as articles and news clippings. 0.25 linear ft.

Jayne, William, 1826–1916, Republican. *See* listing under governors above.

Burleigh, Walter A., 1820–1896, Republican. Born in Waterville, Maine. U. S. delegate, 1865–1869; territorial council, 1877; state senator, 1893.

> SDSHS: "Reports Concerning S. L. Spink and Walter Burleigh vs. M. K. Armstrong," 1870–1872. 0.1 cubic ft.

Spink, Solomon L., 1831–1881, Republican. Born in Whitehall, N.Y. Territorial secretary, 1865–1869; U. S. delegate, 1869–1871.

> SDSHS: "Reports Concerning S. L. Spink and Walter Burleigh vs. M. K. Armstrong," 1870–1872. 0.1 cubic ft.

Armstrong, Moses, K., 1832–1906. Democrat. Born in Milan, Ohio. Territorial representative, 1861–1863; territorial council, 1866, 1867, 1869; U. S. delegate, 1871–1875.

> MNHS: Correspondence, scrapbooks, and diaries of a trip from Minnesota to Dakota and journeys with the U. S. Indian Commission. 0.5 linear ft.

> SDSHS: "Reports Concerning S. L. Spink and Walter Burleigh vs. M. K. Armstrong," 1870–1872. 0.1 cubic ft.

> NL: Ledger in which Armstrong recorded business of the Historical Society of Dakota, 1862–1871. 1 item.

Kidder, Jefferson P., 1815–1883, Republican. U. S. delegate, 1875–1879.
> SDSHS: Family papers; correspondence, maps; newspaper articles and other papers relating to the death of Lt. Lyman S. Kidder (1842–1867); political material concerning Kidder's career. 0.4 cubic ft.

Bennett, Granville, G., 1833–1910, Republican. U. S. delegate, 1870–1881.
> No official papers located.

Pettigrew, Richard F., 1848–1926, Republican. Born in Ludlow, Vt. Territorial representative, 1872; territorial council, 1877, 1879, 1885; U. S. delegate, 1881–1883; U. S. senator, 1889–1901.
> AU: Microfilm copies of Richard F. Pettigrew Papers held at Pettigrew House and Museum, Sioux Falls, S.Dak. 38 reels.
> SDSHS: Congressional speeches, 1894–1901. 0.2 linear ft.
> SHM: Correspondence, letters, and miscellaneous files from his political, legal, and business career from the 1880s, with bulk pertaining to service in U. S. Senate. 12.0 linear ft.

Raymond, John B., 1844–1886, Republican. U. S. delegate, 1883–1885.
> No official papers located.

Gifford, Oscar S., 1842–1913, Republican. U. S. delegate, 1885–1889.
> No official papers located.

Matthews, George A., 1852–1941, Republican. U. S. delegate, 1889.
> No official papers located.

Pettigrew, Richard F., 1848-1926, Republican. U. S. senator, 1889-1901. *See* listing under delegates above.

Moody, Gideon C., 1832-1904, Republican. U. S. senator, 1889-1891.
No official papers located.

Kyle, James H., 1854-1901, Populist, Republican. Born near Xenia, Ohio. State senator, 1890; U. S. senator, 1891-1901.
SDSHS: Copies of newspaper clippings about Kyle. 1.0 microfilm reel.

Gamble, Robert J., 1851-1924, Republican. U. S. senator, 1901-1913.
No official papers located.

Kittredge, Alfred B., 1861-1911, Republication. U. S. senator, 1901-1909.
No official papers located

Crawford, Coe I., 1858-1944, Republican. U. S. senator, 1909-1915. *See* listing under governors above.

Sterling, Thomas, 1851-1930, Republican. U. S. senator, 1913-1925.
No official papers located

Johnson, Edwin S., 1857-1933, Democrat. U. S. senator, 1915-1921.
No official papers located

Norbeck, Peter, 1870-1936, Republican. U. S. senator, 1921-1936. *See* listing under governors above.

McMaster, William H., 1877-1968, Republican. U. S. senator, 1925-1931. *See* listing under governors above.

Bulow, John W., 1869-1960, Democrat. U. S. senator, 1931-1943. *See* listing under governors above.

Hitchcock, Herbert E., 1867-1958, Democrat. U. S. senator, 1936-1938.
No official papers located

Pyle, Gladys, 1880–1989, Republican. Born in Huron, S.Dak. State representative, 1923–1927; U. S. senator, 1937–1938.

SDSU: Research material from Jeanette Kinyon and Jean Walz for biography titled *The Incredible Gladys Pyle*, including manuscripts, letters from Pyle noting corrections, letter from Sigurd Anderson praising Pyle, audiocassettes, transcripts, and notes from an oral history interview with Pyle. 0.4 linear ft.

USD: Personal files, clippings, videocassette commemorating Pyle; scrapbooks pertaining to Pyle's life, education, and service. 4.0 linear ft.

Gurney, John C. ("Chan"), 1896–1985, Republican. Born in Yankton, S.Dak. U.S senator, 1939–1951.

YCHS: Scrapbooks containing clippings, especially regarding Armed Services Committee; photographs; and memorabilia; senatorial papers destroyed upon defeat in 1950. See *Biographical Directory of the United States Congress*.

Bushfield, Harlan J., 1882–1948, Republican. Born in Atlantic, Iowa. U. S. senator, 1943–1948, died in office. *See* **listing under governors above.**

Bushfield, Vera Cahalan, 1889–1976, Republican. Born in Miller, S.Dak. Appointed U. S. senator to fill husband's term, Oct.-Dec. 1948. *See* **Bushfield, Harlan under governors above.**

Mundt, Karl E., 1900–1974, Republican. Born in Humboldt, S.Dak. U. S. representative, 1939–1948; U. S. senator, 1949–1973.

DSU: Materials related to Mundt's congressional career, including correspondence, diaries, manuscript on the Army-McCarthy hearings, resolutions, hearings, reports, bills, speeches, agendas, memoranda, minutes of meetings, research papers, drafts of legislation, voting records, campaign material, published material, newspaper clippings, and television and motion-picture film and recordings. 640.0 linear ft.

Case, Francis H., 1896–1962, Republican. Born in Everly, Iowa. U. S. representative, 1937–1950; U. S. senator, 1951–1962.

DWU: Papers, 1936–1962, include correspondence, memoranda, constituent mail, legislative files, speeches, newsletters, scrapbooks, cartoons, clippings, and photographs; strengths include work on American Indian issues, interstate highways, and development of the Missouri River basin. 300.0 linear ft.

SDSHS: Papers, 1936–1962, include correspondence; congressional papers, including weekly newsletters; correspondence with Will G. Robinson (1948–1962); legislative documents; campaign materials; newspaper clippings; and reports. 0.5. cubic ft.

Bottum, Joseph H, 1903–1984, Republican. Born in Faulkton, S.Dak. Lieutenant governor, 1960–1962; appointed U. S. senator to fill vacancy on death of Francis Case, July 1962–Jan. 1963.

SDSHS: Constituent newsletters. 0.1 cubic ft.

McGovern, George S., 1922–2012, Democrat. Born in Avon, S.Dak. U. S. representative, 1957–1961; U. S. senator, 1963–1981.

DWU: Personal and political files containing speeches, articles, news clippings, research materials, campaign files, seven thousand photographs, and campaign memorabilia; extensive materials from McGovern's post-congressional career. 16.0 linear ft.

PU: Legislative materials, campaign items, correspondence, speeches, and agency files; photographs and multimedia covering McGovern's congressional career. 838.0 linear ft.

SDSHS: Newsletters, 1959. 0.2 cubic ft.

Abourezk, James G., 1931–. Democrat. Born in Wood, S.Dak. State senator, 1956–1968; lieutenant governor, 1969–1970; U. S. representative, 1971–1973; U. S. senator, 1973–1979.

SDHS: Reports, 1972–1976. 0.1 cubic ft.

USD: Congressional records include correspondence, speeches, photographs, interviews, news releases, and administrative files, along with materials relating to occupation of Wounded Knee in 1973. Access requires prior approval from Abourezk or designee. 480.0 linear ft.

Pressler, Larry L. 1942–. Republican. Born in Humboldt, S.Dak. U. S. representative, 1974–1978; U. S. senator, 1979–1997.

SDSHS: Newsletters. 0.1 cubic ft.

USD: Congressional records include correspondence, legislative files including committee work, speeches, news releases, press files, subject files, bills, photographs, and audio-visual materials. Closed. 300.0 linear ft.

Abdnor, James, 1923–2012, Republican. Born in Kennebec, S.Dak. Lieutenant governor, 1969–1970; U. S. representative, 1973–1981; U. S. senator, 1981–1987.

SDSHS: Congressional records containing newspaper clippings, newsletters, publications, speeches, bill and subject files, election campaign records, correspondence, schedules, photographs, video and audio recordings, microfilm, and electronic files of Abdnor's activities in Congress and as administrator of U. S. Small Business Administration; records from Huron Field Office; campaign materials; and prints documenting professional appearances. Open for research with restrictions on records protected by FERPA and correspondence containing confidential information about individuals. 410.0 cubic ft.

Daschle, Thomas A., 1947–. Democrat. Born in Aberdeen, S.Dak. U. S. representative, 1979–1987; U. S. senator, 1987–2005.

SDSU: Papers, 1949–2015, include correspondence, photographs, audiotapes, videotapes, and other materials that document, among other things, the September 11 tragedy, anthrax attack on Daschle's office, and impeachment of President William Clinton. 2,200 linear ft. and 0.5 Tb of digital objects.

Thune, John, 1961–. Republican. Born in Pierre, S.Dak. U. S. representative, 1997–2003; U. S. Senator, 2005–.

No official papers deposited as of 2017.

Johnson, Timothy P., 1946-. Democrat. Born in Canton, S.Dak.
State representative, 1979–1983; state senator, 1983–1986; U. S.
representative, 1987–1997; U. S. Senator, 1997–2015.
  SDSHS: Certificate of election, 1986; *Congressional Record* Capitol
    Centennial, 2010. 0.2 cu. ft.
  USD: Papers documenting political career in South Dakota and
    Washington, D.C., include reports, correspondence, committee
    files, subject files, case files, and audio-visual materials. Closed.
    200.0 linear ft. and 4.0 Tb of digital objects.

Rounds, M. Michael, 1954-. Republican. U. S. senator, 2015-. *See*
listing under governors above.

UNITED STATES REPRESENTATIVES FROM SOUTH DAKOTA

Gifford, Oscar S., 1842–1913, Republican. U. S. representative,
1889–1891.
  No official papers located.

Pickler, John A., 1844–1910, Republican. Born near Salem,
Ind. Territorial legislator, 1884–1885; U. S. representative, 1889–1897.
  SDSHS: Congressional papers include committee assignments
    files, especially related to Civil War veterans' pensions, and
    letters of appreciation from fellow congressmen; other papers
    relate to woman suffrage support in territorial legislature, as
    well as family and business correspondence. 65.1 cubic ft.

Gamble John R., 1848–1891, Republican. U. S. representative, 1891.
  No official papers located.

Jolley, John L., 1840–1926, Republican. Born in Montreal, Canada.
Territorial representative, 1878–1881; state senator, 1889–1890;
U. S. representative, 1891–1893.
  AU: Correspondence, departmental files, and photographs.
    1.0 linear ft.
  USD: Correspondence, financial materials, legal materials,
    photographs, printed materials, and ephemera. 0.5 linear ft.

Lucas, William V., 1853–192, Republican. U. S. representative, 1893–1895.
No official papers located.

Gamble, Robert J., 1851–1924, Republican. U. S. representative, 1895–1897, 1899–1901.
No official papers located.

Kelley, John E., 1853–1941, Populist. U. S. representative, 1897–1899.
No official papers located.

Knowles, Freeman T., 1846–1910, Populist. U. S. representative, 1897–1899.
No official papers located.

Burke, Charles H., 1861–1944, Republican. U. S. representative, 1899–1907, 1909–1915.
SDSHS: Family papers, 1897 resolution proposing the removal of the capital from Pierre and 1933 letter regarding the resolution, photographs, correspondence, and papers relating to 1931 Exposition of Overseas Countries in Paris. 3.6 cubic ft.

Martin, Eben W., 1855–1932, Republican. U. S. representative, 1901–1907, 1909–1915.
No official papers located.

Hall, Philo, 1865–1938, Republican. U. S. representative, 1907–1909.
No official papers located.

Parker, William H., 1847–1908, Republican. U. S. representative, 1907–1908.
No official papers located

Dillion, Charles H., 1853–1929, Republican. Born near Jasper, Ind. State senator, 1903–1911; U. S. representative, 1913–1919.
USD: Scrapbook including congressional bills, programs, clippings, letters, and memorabilia. 0.25 linear ft.

Gandy, Harry L., 1881–1957, Democrat. U. S. representative, 1915–1921.
No official papers located.

Johnson, Royal C., 1882–1939, Republican. U. S. representative, 1915–1933.
No official papers located.

Charles A. Christopherson, 1871–1951, Republican.
Born in Amherst Township, Minn. State representative, 1912–1916; U. S. representative, 1919–1933.
USD: Diaries, 1899–1913; scrapbooks of speeches and news clippings; photographs; correspondence; and material related to prohibition. 4.0 linear ft.

William Williamson, 1875–1972, Republican. Born near New Sharon, Iowa. U. S. representative, 1921–1932.
DU: Correspondence concerning mining interests in South Dakota and the passage of Smith-McNary Bill. 46 items.
USD: Correspondence, personal diaries, news clippings, speeches, and materials relating to Indian jurisdictional legislation, reclamation, and Mount Rushmore National Memorial. 51.0 linear ft.

Hildebrandt, Fred. H., 1874–1956, Democrat. U. S. representative, 1933–1939.
No official papers located.

Werner, Theodore B., 1892–1989, Democrat. U. S. representative, 1933–1937.
No official papers located.

Case, Francis H., 1896–1962, Republican. U. S. representative, 1937–1950. *See* listing under senators above.

Mundt, Karl E., 1900–1974, Republican. U. S. representative, 1939–1948. *See* listing under senators above.

Lovre, Harold O., 1904–1972, Republican. U. S. representative, 1949–1947.
No official papers located.

Berry, Ellis Y., 1902–1999, Republican. Born in Larchwood, Iowa. State senator, 1939–1941; U. S. representative, 1951–1971.

    SDSHS: Newsletters, 1951–1962. 0.25 cubic ft.

    BHSU: Correspondence, department and legal files, and other material related to committee assignments; photographs; motion-picture film; sound recordings; and memorabilia. 240.0 linear ft.

McGovern, George S., 1922–2012, Democrat. U. S. representative, 1957–1961. *See* listing under senators above.

Reifel, Benjamin, 1906–1990, Republican. Born on Rosebud Indian Reservation, S.Dak. U. S. representative, 1961–1970.

    SDSU: Memorabilia, scrapbooks, campaign items, photographs, audio recording, and materials relating to Reifel's career in Bureau of Indian Affairs and U .S. House; materials related to his post-congressional career. 19.8 linear ft.

Abourezk, James G., 1931–. Democrat. Born in Wood, S.Dak. U. S. representative, 1971–1973. *See* listing under senators above.

Denholm, Frank E., 1923–2016, Democrat. Born in Day County, S.Dak. U. S. representative, 1971–1975.

    SDSU: Press releases, newspaper clippings, correspondence, calendars, photographs, audio and video recordings, and campaign artifacts. 17.39 linear ft.

Abdnor, James, 1923–2012, Republican. U. S. representative, 1973–1981. *See* listing under senators above.

Pressler, Larry L. 1942–. Republican. U. S. representative, 1974–1978. *See* listing under senators above.

Daschle, Thomas A., 1947–. Democrat. U. S. representative, 1979–1987. *See* listing under senators above.

Roberts, Clint R., 1935–. Republican. U. S. representative, 1981–1983.

    No official papers located.

Johnson, Timothy P., 1946–. Democrat. U. S. representative, 1987–1997. *See* listing under senators above.

Thune, John, 1961–. Republican. U. S. representative, 1997–2003.
No official papers deposited as of 2017.

Janklow, William J., 1939–2012, Republican. U. S. representative,
2003–2004. *See* listing under governors above.

Herseth Sandlin, Stephanie, 1970–. Democrat. Born near Houghton,
S.Dak. U. S. representative, 2004–2011.
No official papers deposited as of 2017.

Noem, Kristi, 1971–. Republican. Born in Watertown, S.Dak. State
representative, 2007–2010; U. S. representative, 2011–.
No official papers deposited as of 2017.

NOTES

1. Schell to Foss, 11 June 1968, Control File, Joe Foss Papers, Archives and
Special Collections, University of South Dakota, Vermillion.

2. In this essay, "Papers" refer to collections of official records and/or private
papers.

3. Richard Loftus, comp., "Appendix A: Governors of Dakota Territory and
South Dakota" and "Appendix B: Members of Congress Representing Dakota
Territory and South Dakota," in *The Plains Political Tradition: Essays on South
Dakota Political Culture*, [vol. 1], ed. Jon K. Lauck, John E. Miller, and Donald C.
Simmons, Jr. (Pierre: South Dakota Historical Society Press, 2011), pp. 341–45.

4. AchiveGrid, beta.worldcat.org/archivegrid/; *Biographical Directory of the
United States Congress, 1774–Present*, bioguide.congress.gov/biosearch/biosearch
.asp.

Contributors

Ryan Burdge is an alumnus of University of Wisconsin-Milwaukee with degrees in history, religious studies, and library science. His interest is in Midwest and Great Lakes regional history, digital preservation, and community archives. Since 2014, he has worked as the administrator and manager of the Karl E. Mundt and university archives at Dakota State University in Madison, South Dakota.

Michele Christian is archivist and special collections librarian at Hilton M. Briggs Library, South Dakota State University, Brookings. She has also been collections archivist for the Special Collections Department of the Iowa State University Library and labor archivist at the State Historical Society of Iowa. She received her M.A. in history and MLIS from the University of Wisconsin–Milwaukee and her B.A. in history from the University of Northern Iowa. Christian has written on such topics as managing artifacts in archives, applying social media for outreach, and using oral histories in collection development.

Linda M. Clemmons is a professor of history at Illinois State University in Normal, Illinois. She specializes in American Indian and nineteenth-century American history. Her first book, *Conflicted Mission: Faith, Disputes, and Deception on the Dakota Frontier* (2014), examined the interaction of Protestant missionaries with the Dakota of Minnesota. She is currently working on a book about the exile of the Dakota from Minnesota following the United States–Dakota War of 1862.

Daniel L. Daily is the dean of libraries, University of South Dakota, Vermillion. Previous positions include library director, Northwestern College; project archivist, Dartmouth College; and assistant university archivist, Duke University. Daily holds a B.A. from the University of Southern Maine; an M.T.S. from Duke University; and an MLIS from the University of North Carolina at Chapel Hill.

Lisa E. Duncan is the collections management archivist at the University of Arizona Libraries. Previously, she worked as the archivist and special collections librarian at the University of South Dakota and as a project archivist at the University of Arizona

Libraries. She received her B.A. and M.A. from the University of Arizona and is a certified archivist.

Cory M. Haala is a Ph.D. candidate at Marquette University. He is writing a dissertation on upper midwestern liberalism and political history during the 1980s.

Kurt Hackemer is professor of history and chair of the History Department at the University of South Dakota, Vermillion, where he specializes in American military and naval history as well as nineteenth-century United States history. His books include *The U. S. Navy and the Origins of the Military-Industrial Complex, 1847– 1883* (2001) and *To Rescue My Native Land: The Civil War Letters of William T. Shepherd, First Illinois Light Artillery* (2005). Hackemer's current research explores the world of Civil War veterans who moved to the frontier.

Jon K. Lauck received his Ph.D. in history from the University of Iowa and his law degree from the University of Minnesota. He is the author of several books, including *From Warm Center to Ragged Edge: The Erosion of Midwestern Literary and Historical Regionalism, 1920–1965* (2017). He is the past president of the Midwestern History Association, associate editor of *Middle West Review*, and an adjunct professor at the University of South Dakota.

Art Marmorstein has been teaching at Northern State University in Aberdeen, South Dakota, since 1988. He did his undergraduate work at Stanford, earning his B.A. in drama in 1974. After teaching high-school English and drama, he returned to graduate school, earning a Ph.D. in history at the University of California, Davis, in 1988. Marmorstein writes regular columns for the *Aberdeen American News*, and he is a frequent lecturer for various on-campus and off-campus groups.

John E. Miller received his B. A. in history from the University of Missouri and his M.A. and Ph.D. from the University of Wisconsin. He taught twentieth-century American history and other courses at the University of Tulsa and at South Dakota State University, Brookings, for thirty years before becoming a fulltime writer in 2003. His eight books include *Looking for History on Highway 14*, *Small-Town Dreams: Stories of Midwestern Boys Who Shaped America*, and three books on Laura Ingalls Wilder.

Paula M. Nelson is professor emeritus in the Department of History at the University of Wisconsin-Platteville, where she taught for twenty-six years. Her research interests include agricultural settlement in the Great Plains and upper Midwest, rural life and culture, rural women's history, and small towns. Nelson is the author of *After the West Was Won* and *The Prairie Winnows Out Its Own*, books about West River South Dakota, and the editor of *Sunshine Always*, a book of courtship letters from Dakota Territory.

Matthew Pehl is an associate professor of history at Augustana University, Sioux Falls, South Dakota. His book *The Making of Working-Class Religion* was published in 2016 by the University of Illinois Press.

Matthew Remmich received his B.A. from Northern State University, Aberdeen, and is currently a graduate student in history at the University of South Dakota, Vermillion. In 2017, he received the James Madison Graduate Fellowship for the state of South Dakota, an award designed for those who wish to become outstanding teachers of the American constitution at the secondary school level.

Kenneth L. Smith grew up in western Colorado and attended college in Ellendale and Dickinson, North Dakota. He taught high school in suburban Grand Rapids, Michigan, before earning an M.A. and D.A. in history at the University of North Dakota. Smith subsequently taught history and social science courses at Trinity Bible College in Ellendale and graduate courses at the University of North Dakota's School of Education. He is currently completing a Ph.D. in Great Plains History at North Dakota State University.

Chelle Somsen is the South Dakota State Archivist with the South Dakota State Historical Society. She holds degrees from South Dakota State University and Mankato State University. She received the Digital Archives Specialist Certificate in 2013. Somsen is the chair of the South Dakota State Historical Records Advisory Board, an alumnus of the Archives Leadership Institute, and a member of the American Institute for Conservation–National Heritage Responders.

Emily O. Wanless earned her Ph.D. in political science from the University of Georgia and is currently an assistant professor of government and international affairs at Augustana University in

Sioux Falls, South Dakota. Her teaching and research interests focus on American politics, specifically political ambition, institutions, and state elections. Most recently, she has authored book chapters on the 2014 South Dakota senate slection and the 2016 presidential nomination season.

Jeff Wells is an associate professor of history at the University of Nebraska at Kearney and an associate editor of *Middle West Review*. A native of Joplin, Missouri, Wells received his B.A. in history summa cum laude from Missouri Southern State University, M.A. in history from Missouri State University, and Ph.D. in history from Texas Christian University. Prior to pursuing his doctoral degree, he served as a reporter at daily newspapers in Missouri and Kansas and as editor of a business journal.

Eric Steven Zimmer is a senior historian at Vantage Point Historical Services, Inc., in Rapid City, South Dakota, and a research fellow at the Center for American Indian Research and Native Studies on the Pine Ridge Indian Reservation. After completing his Ph.D. at the University of Iowa in 2016, he has focused on American Indian history, the fields of museum design and development, business history, history of philanthropy, and Jewish American history. He earned the 2017 Rachel Carson Prize for best dissertation from the American Society for Environmental History.

Index

102, 110n59; wheat marketing
agreements, 189
Canfield, George S., 75
Canton Dakota Farmers' Leader, 66, 72
Carleton College, 142
Carter, James E. ("Jimmy"), 183, 189
Case, Francis H., 144, 147, 250, 254
Catholic missionaries, 5, 33–37, 48–49
Cavalier, L. E., 71
Chase, Salmon P., 25
Chicago, Milwaukee & Saint Paul
Railroad, 82n45
Chicago & North Western Railroad,
100
Chicago Tribune, 90, 93
Chivington, John, 35
"Christianity and Citizenship"
(Crawford), 97, 108n44
Christianity and the Social Crisis
(Rauschenbusch), 110n56
Christianity/Christian tradition:
Indian conversions, 51;
interdenominational conflict,
44–46, 51; Jewish relationship
with, 113, 123–24, 130; missionary
work with the Indians, 32–37; and
S.Dak. political culture, 6, 215t;
Swing/Patton heresy trial, 91–93
Christopherson, Charles A., 254
Church, Frank, 203n15
Church, Louis K., 238
Civil War: beginning secession,
13; influence on S.Dak. political
culture, 4–5, 10–11, 17–18; political
philosophy of Lincoln and,
12–13; post-war Indian policy, 5,
32–34, 50–51; post-war Populist
movement, 59; preservation of the
Union, 16–22; territorial politics
and, 13–14
Clanton, Gene, 59

Clark Honest Dollar, 64
Clem, Alan, 183, 186
Clemmons, Linda M., 5, 32–51, 257
Clinton, William J. ("Bill"), 226t, 227
Cochrane, Stacey A., 70, 73, 80n19,
81n31
Codington County, 153
Collins, Lorraine, 167
Collins, W. T., 95
Colman, Nathan, 116
Colussy, Gil, 173
Commission on the Status of
Women (CSW). *See* South Dakota
Commission on the Status of
Women
Commission on Balanced Economic
Development, 150
Common Sense Rural Credits (Loucks),
77
Community Action Program, 148
Comprehensive Operational Planning
System, 153
Congregation B'nai Isaac, 115, 119,
121–25, 131, 136n42
Congressional Gold Medal, 118
"Consciousness Razor" (CSW
newsletter), 170
Conservative politics: Commission
on the Status of Women and, 7–8;
Democratic Party decline and,
182–202; gender and abortion
issues, 130–31, 159–60, 174; S.Dak.
political culture and, 3–4
*The Conspiracy of the House of Morgan
Exposed and How to Defeat It*
(Loucks), 77
Cook, Joseph W., 40, 43
Cook, Joy, 176
Coyler, Vincent, 39
Crandall, Lona, 163, 167
Crawford, Coe I.: beginnings of

political career, 96–106; death of, 102; 1896 Senate bid, 98; 1914 Senate bid, 102; 1909 Senate bid, 101–2; 1906 gubernatorial election, 100–101; 1902 Senate bid, 100; papers, 239, 248; political philosophy, 110n56; skill as orator, 96, 105n6; social attitude, 110n59; S.Dak. political culture and, 4, 6; success as governor, 85–87, 102–6; work as railroad attorney, 100, 109n53

Crawford, Robert Dean, 102

Credit discrimination, 7, 169–70

Crow Creek Indian Reservation, 35–36, 42, 44, 48, 55n45

Culver, John, 203n15

Cummings, E. B., 64, 65

Cummins, Albert B., 85

Cunningham, George V., 184, 186, 192–94, 206n57

Daily Capital Journal, 176

Daily Huronite, 73

Dakota Catholic American, 65

Dakota Council of B'nai B'rith, 121

Dakota Education Association, 85

Dakota Farmer, 61

Dakota Farmers' Alliance, 79nn7–8

The Dakota Republican (Vermillion), 15

Dakota Ruralist, 61, 64, 65, 67, 76

Dakota State University (formerly Eastern State Normal School), 142–43

Dakota Territorial Farmers' Alliance, 58, 61–62

Dakota Territory: Civil War southern sympathies, 23; creation as territory, 19; 1860 census, 15; formation of National Union Party, 25–26; immigration and

settlement, 10–11, 14–15, 20; People's Union convention, 21–23; Sioux relocation following Dakota War, 35–36, 42, 44, 48, 55n45; statehood, 25–26, 51, 52n2, 61–62. *See also* South Dakota

Dakota Territory, 1861–1889: A Study of Frontier Politics (Lamar), 4, 11

Dakota Union (Yankton), 23, 26

Dakota War of 1862, 35, 55n45, 257

The Dakotian (Yankton), 15–17, 19–20, 23–26

Daschle, Thomas A.: 1980 congressional election, 185; 1982 congressional election, 186, 188–92, 205n47; 1984 election campaign, 193–94; 1986 Senate election, 8, 194–97, 207n64, 208n78; papers, 251, 255; political philosophy, 130; 2004 re-election defeat, 201

Daugaard, Dennis, 131, 214, 245

Davison County, 198–99, 228

Dawes Act of 1887, 50

Deadwood, S.Dak.: Jewish community, 116–17, 125; rebuilding Highway 14A, 147

Deadwood Black Hills Daily Times, 68

Deadwood Daily Pioneer, 69

Deadwood Independent, 67, 69

Deadwood Lantern, 77

Democratic-Farmer-Labor Party (DFL), 148

Democratic Party: appeal during economic stress, 4; East River/West River, 184, 186; formation as political party, 18; 1980 election losses, 183–86; 1984 election campaign, 192–94; 1986 election campaign, 194–202, 207n74;

Feinstein, Manley, 121, 125
Feinstein Brothers, Inc. (Mitchell), 115, 121
Feinstein's Ready-to-Wear (Aberdeen), 121
The Feminine Mystique (Friedan), 163
Feminism, 7–8, 159–67, 171–78
FirstBank South Dakota, 119
Flandreau Herald, 67
Florida Times-Union, 63
Ford, Gerald, 126
Ford, Lee Ellen, 164
Fort Pierre Times, 185
Foss, Joseph Jacob, 7, 232, 242
Freeman, Orville, 148–49
Free silver, 62, 66–67, 69–70, 72–74, 78, 81n42
Frémont, John C., 24–25, 31n63
Friedan, Betty, 163

Galler, Robert, 48
Gamble, John R., 252
Gamble, Robert J., 248, 253
Gandy, Harry L., 253
Gay rights movement, 174, 216t, 217
Gender equality, 162, 165, 174
George, Milton, 79n8
Georgia, Cherokee removal, 41
Gerner, Karl, 81n31
Gifford, Oscar S., 247, 252
Gird, Arthur W., 83n65
God is Not One (Prothero), 113
Goldberg, Jacob, 116
Goldwater, Barry, 126–27, 129
Goodwyn, Lawrence, 59, 81n42
Grams, William, 176
Grand Forks Herald, 95
Grand River (D.T.). *See* Standing Rock Indian Reservation
Grant, Ulysses S., Indian "Peace Policy," 32–51

Great Society program, 140–41, 148
Green, Warren E., 241
Gubbrud, Archie M., 128, 243
Gunderson, Carl, 241
Gurney, John C., 249

Haala, Cory M., 8, 182–209, 258
Hackemer, Kurt, 4, 10–27, 258
Hagan, Jim, 212
Haire, Robert (Fr.), 64–65, 73–74, 76, 80nn19–20
Hall, Philo, 253
Hanford, F. F., 83n61
Hanna, Mark, 109n49
Hanover College (Ind.), 88
"The Hanukkah Song" (Sandler), 113
Hare, William Hobart (Bishop), 42–43
Harlow, Bryce, 152
Harrison, Benjamin, 66
Head Start program, 148
Henkin, Joe, 118
Henkin, Mort & Sylvia, 118–19, 131
Herreid, Charles N., 239
Herseth, Lars, 8, 187, 194–97, 199–201
Herseth, Ralph, 128, 243
Herseth-Sandlin, Stephanie, 229n8, 256
Hildebrandt, Fred H., 143, 254
Hill City Harney Peak Mining News, 83n67
Hinman, Samuel, 39–40
Hiss, Alger, 144
"A History of Dakota" (Blackburn), 99
History of Dakota Territory (Kingsbury), 29n34
Hitchcock, Herbert E., 248
Hodge, Charles, 88
Hoffman, LeRoy G., 211
Hogan, Edward P., 1
Holt, Kathleen, 173
Holy Rosary Mission, 49

Johnson, Edwin S., 248
Johnson, Lyndon B., 7, 126, 140–41,
  148–52, 155
Johnson, Royal C., 142, 254
Johnson, Timothy P., 8, 197, 199–201,
  252, 255
Jolley, John L., 252

Kadoka, S.Dak., 117
Kane, George, 185, 196
Karim, Ruth, 173–74
Katus, Tom, 184
Kelley, John E., 67–68, 70, 74, 76, 253
Kelly, Frank, 80n19, 81n31
Kennedy, John F., 160
Kertes, Abraham A. (Rabbi), 122–23
KFSY-TV (station), 118, 119
Kidd, William E., 64, 67–70, 76,
  80n19, 83n61
Kidder, Jefferson P., 247
Kimball Graphic, 69
King, Frank G., 73
Kingsbury, George W., 11, 19–24, 61,
  73, 82n54
Kipp, J. H., 67
Kittredge, Alfred B., 248
Kneip, Richard F.: defense of ERA,
  175; 1986 gubernatorial campaign,
  197; papers, 244; political
  appointments, 121; rebuilding
  the Democratic Party, 186, 188,
  192–93, 195, 201; resigned, 211;
  rural development projects, 153;
  stance on abortion, 173; support of
  women's issues, 163–64, 166
Knights of Labor, 60, 62, 64–65,
  109n48
Knock, Thomas J., 110n56
Knowledge activism, 7, 160
Knowles, Freeman T., 67–70, 74,
  76–77, 253

Korean War, 146
KSOO Radio (station), 118
Ku Klux Klan (KKK), 203n17
Kyle, James H., 62–63, 67–68, 70–71,
  82n44, 248

Labor movement, 61, 65, 73
LaFollette, Robert ("Fighting Bob"),
  82n57, 85
LaFollette, William T., 74, 75, 82n57
Lake County, 153
Lake Mohonk Conference of the
  Friends of the Indians, 50
Lamar, Howard Roberts, 4, 11, 18–19,
  26, 27n3, 58
Lamont, Frances ("Peg"), 165–67
Landers, Isaac, 64, 80n19
Lattim, G. W., 81n31
Lauck, Jon K., 1–9, 33, 59, 79n7, 87,
  182, 200–201, 258
Lawrence County, 116–17, 128
Lead, S.Dak., 147
Lee, Andrew E., 60, 70–72, 74, 76–78,
  80n20, 109n49, 239
Lee, R. Alton, 58–59, 78nn2–3
Legalization of marijuana, 216t, 217
Leslie, Jensen, 241
Lincoln, Abraham, 12–13, 15–27
Lincoln, Mary Todd, 21
Lindau, Moses, 119–20, 125
Linn, Arthur, 72
Litke, Ina, 166
Loetscher, Lefferts, 106n13
"Logroller" (pseudonym), 30n60
Lord, Willis, 89
Loriks, Emil, 143
Loucks, Henry Langford: death of,
  77; founding of SDPRA, 80n19;
  Populist Party and political
  aspirations, 4–6, 60, 68–69, 71,
  74; Republican politics and, 6,

76–77; return to Republican Party, 74, 77; role in Farmers' Alliance, 61–62, 79n8; role in Independent (People's) Party, 62–71
Lovre, Harold O., 254
Lucas, William V., 253
Lukes, C. W., 82n46
Lyng, Richard, 190

McCarthy, Joseph, 144
McCaughey, Robert, 152
McCormick, Cyrus Hall, 89–90, 94, 106n15, 106n18, 107n27
McCormick Hall (Pierre University), 96
McCosh, James, 93
McEldowney, Mary Ellen, 168
McGovern, Eleanor, 185
McGovern, George S.: 1980 Senate reelection loss, 8, 155, 182–86, 189–90; 1956 congressional campaign, 121; 1974 Senate reelection, 155; 1972 presidential nomination, 121; papers, 250, 255; political philosophy, 110n56, 163, 185, 192, 195, 200; post-Senate political activities, 186–89, 204n30
MacGregor, Scott, 191
McKellips, Roger, 186, 194, 196, 211
McManima, J. C., 61
MacMaster, Erasmus D., 89
McMaster, William H., 240, 248
McMath, Robert C., 59
Macune, Charles W., 59, 63, 78n4
Madison, S.Dak., 142
Madsen, RoJean, 169–70
Magnuson, Warren, 203n15
Marmorstein, Art, 6, 112–32, 258
Martin, Eben W., 253
Martinsky, Bertha, 117
Marty, Martin (Bishop), 65

Masons/Freemasonry, 125, 136n42
Matthews, George A., 247
Maynard, C. J., 82n54
Mazakutemani, Paul, 42
Mellette, Arthur C., 238
Melton, Orrin, 119
Mendel, David, 117
Mental health issues, 120–21
Messing, Joel (Rabbi), 125
Mickelson, George S., 199–200, 212–13, 222, 244–45
Mickelson, George T., 120, 242
Mid-America Conservative Political Action Committee, 188
Middle Border (newspaper), 142
Mill, John Stuart, 91
Miller, John E., 1–9, 258
Miller, Linda, 167, 176
Miller, Walter Dale, 212–13, 218, 220–26, 245
Miller, Worth Robert, 59, 79n7
Minnehaha County, 22, 119, 127, 201, 230n8
Minnesota: Democratic-Farmer-Labor Party, 148; Interstate highway program, 147; Jewish immigration/settlement, 114; missionary efforts with the Indians, 40; Reform Press Association, 75–76; Republican political dominance, 20; Sioux removal, 35, 55n45
Minnesota (Farmers') Alliance, 61, 79n8
Missionaries, role in Grant's Indian "Peace Policy," 32–51
Missouri River: Mundt and development projects, 7, 140; Pick-Sloan project, 144–46; territorial settlement, 15
Mitchell, S.Dak., 115, 121
Mitchell Capital, 75

Mobridge, S.Dak., 145

Mobridge Tribune, 145

Model Rural Development program, 152–54, 156

Monkman, W. S., 83n65

Moody, Gideon C., 248

Moody County, 153

Mormons, 37

Mound City Campbell County Courier, 67

Mountain-Plains Federal Regional Council, 152–53

Mount Pleasant Cemetery, 116

Mount Zion Cemetery Society, 116

Mount Zion Synagogue, 116, 117, 131

Muchmore, Lynn, 152

Muenster, Ted, 166

Mulle, Walter, Mrs., 173

Mundt, Karl E.: achieving success in S.Dak. politics, 4; childhood and education, 142; 1948 Senate election, 143–44; 1938 congressional election, 143; 1936 election defeat, 142–43; papers, 249, 254; political philosophy and activities, 143–44; role in Interstate highway program, 146–48; role in Pick-Sloan project, 144–46; and rural economic development, 148–56; teaching career, 142

Mundt, Mary Moses, 142

Murphy, William Beverly, 151

Muslims, 124, 130

Myers, Mary Lynn, 163, 164, 167, 169, 175

National Advisory Council on Economic Opportunity, 126

National Association for Community Development, 148–49

National Conservative Political Action Committee (NCPAC), 184–85

National Farm Crisis Day, 190

National Farmers' Alliance and Industrial Union, 65, 79n8

National Organization of Women (NOW), 161, 163, 167, 169

National Press Reform Association (NRPA), 63–64

National Union Party, 25–26

Nebraska Reform Press Business Association, 82n54

Neill, Henry, 80n19

Nelson, Gaylord, 203n15

Nelson, Paula M., 1–9, 162, 259

Neth, Mary, 162

Newspapers: defining public opinion, 16–17; help wanted notices, 168; influence in the Western U.S., 10, 14, 59–61; numbers of publishers in D.T., 15, 60, 79n7; political reporting, 185, 189. *See also* South Dakota Press Reform Association

The New York Times, 1, 159

Niobrara, Neb., 55n45

Nixon, Richard M., 7, 121, 128, 152–56

Noem, Kristi, 256

Nonpartisan League, 76

Norbeck, Peter, 102, 240, 248

Norris, Kathleen, 178

North Dakota: Blackburn as university president, 85, 95, 104; Indian reservations, 49, 52n2; Jewish presence, 114, 121; statehood, 51, 52n2, 62

Northern State University, 122–24

Northwest Seminary (Theological Seminary of the Northwest), 89–94, 107n27

Noyes, George C., 94, 108n32

Pred, Isaac & Dan, 115
Premack, Bernice ("Bea"), 123–24, 131
Premack, Herschel, 123, 125
Premack, Julius, 136n42
Presbyterianism: Blackburn influence on, 83–87, 103–4; conservative influence of McCormick on, 89–90, 103, 106n15; influence on settlement and education, 87–88; Old School Calvinism wing, 88–90, 103–4, 106n13, 106n18; Swing/Patton heresy trial, 90–94, 103, 107n22, 110n63
Presho, S.Dak., 186
Presidential Commission on the Status of Women, 160
Pressler, Larry L.: 1978 Senate election, 155, 182; papers, 251, 255; political philosophy, 209n92; political popularity, 192, 206n57; support of Roberts' 1980 campaign, 191
Princeton College, 93, 103–4, 111n64
Princeton Seminary, 88, 90
Principle over Party: The Farmer's Alliance and Populism in South Dakota, 1880–1900 (Lee), 59, 78nn2–3
Prohibition, 62, 65
Property taxes, 212, 214, 217, 219–27
Protestant missionaries, 5, 32–51
Prothero, Steven, 113
Prucha, Francis Paul, 50
Public Works and Economic Development Act of 1965, 149
Pyle, Gladys, 249

Quakers, 36, 46
Quinn, S.Dak. (aka "Jew Flats"), 117

Racism/racial discrimination, 121, 124, 218t
Rahill, Peter J., 33
Railroads: economic benefits, 17; government regulation, 66, 69, 71, 82n45, 85, 101, 104; impact on settlement, 146–47; political corruption and, 100–101, 109n53; Populist policy, 67; S.Dak. purchases tracks, 188
Rapid City, S.Dak.: employment of women, 177; flood (1972), 127; Janklow political support, 222; Jewish community, 6–7, 113–14, 132; political influence of Stan Adelstein, 112, 125–27, 129
Rapid City Black Hills Union, 67, 82n54
Rapid City Chamber of Commerce, 193
Rapid City Journal, 129, 200
Rapid City Press, 173
Rapid City Regional Hospital, 127
Rauschenbusch, Walter, 101, 110n56
Raymond, John B., 247
Reagan, Ronald: endorsement of Abdnor, 198–99; influence on S.Dak. politics, 182, 189–90, 192–93, 201, 203n15; 1980 presidential election, 126; political philosophy, 129; support of farm legislation, 196; tax and economic policies, 155, 187–88; visits S.Dak., 191
Recall votes, 99
Redfield, S.Dak., 70
Reed, E. B., 67
Referendum and initiative, 74, 76, 80n20, 99, 109n48, 146, 159
Reform Press Association of Minnesota, 75

Reform Press Association of South Dakota. *See* South Dakota Reform Press Association

Reform Press Association of the Black Hills, 75, 83n65

Reform Press Bureau, 71–73, 77

Religious Society of Friends. *See* Quakers

Remmich, Matthew, 6, 112–32, 259

Renville, Antoine, 42

Renville, Daniel, 49

Republicanism: ideology, 11–14, 229n3; influence on D.T. politics, 20–21, 25–26; politics over principle, 18, 27n8; Populist identification with, 58–59, 79n7. *See also* Unionism

Republican Party: conservative politics and, 3–4; formation as political party, 18; 1986 election campaign, 198–99; 1960 presidential nomination, 128; Silver Republican faction, 69–70, 73–74, 78

Riggs, Alfred, 32, 50, 57n95

Riggs, Martha, 39

Riggs, Stephen, 39, 42–48

Riggs, Thomas L., 32, 39, 42, 45–46, 49–50, 57n95, 95, 103

Roberts, Clint R., 186, 191, 205n47, 211, 255

Robinson, Duane, 11

Robinson, Will, 23

Rockefeller, Nelson, 127, 129

Roe v. Wade (1973), 7, 159, 173

Roosevelt, Franklin D., 118, 143

Roosevelt, Theodore, 109n49

Root, Elihu, 85

Rosebud Indian Reservation, 49, 112, 211

Rosenthal, Joel, 119, 198

Rounds, M. Michael, 130, 159, 245, 252

Rural development: flood control and irrigation projects, 144–46; Indian education programs, 154; industrializaton and rural population decline, 140–41, 149–51, 174; Interstate highway system and, 146–47; record of Mundt's efforts toward, 148–56; and S.Dak. political culture, 7; unemployment and poverty, 148–49

Rural education, 142

"Rural identity," 143

Saint Elizabeth's School for Indian Girls, 49

Saint Mary's School for Indian Girls, 49

Saint Paul Pioneer Press, 68

Samp, Rollyn, 220, 223, 225, 228

Samuelson, Bob, 193

Sanborn County, 228

Sand Creek Massacre (1864), 34–35

Sandler, Adam, 113

Santee Indian Reservation, 43–44, 46–47, 55n45

Santee Normal Training School, 49

Sawyer, H. W., 75

Schaff, Jon D., 183

Schell, Herbert, 18, 27n3, 232

Schlafly, Phyllis, 175

Schuette, Nancy, 167

Schumaker, Larry, 184

Scovel, Sylvester, 88, 105n11

Seventeenth Amendment, United States Constitution, 85, 102

Sexual and domestic abuse, 7, 160–61, 171–72

Shannon County. *See* Oglala Lakota County

Sharpe, Merrell Q., 242

Sheldon, Charles H., 97, 238

Sherrin, A., 83n62

Shields, Laurie, 169

Shockley, A. S., 83n65

Silver, politics/economic policy, 62, 66–67, 69–70, 72–74, 78, 81n42

Sim, David, 39

Sioux City Register, 15, 24

Sioux Falls, S.Dak.: employment of women, 169, 177; Janklow political support, 213, 219, 222; Jewish community, 6–7, 114–16, 118–19; NOW chapter, 163, 167; Populist Party convention (1900), 109n49; recruitment of Citibank, 188, 214; State Fair (1895), 68; support for forming D.T., 14, 61; women in government, 192, 204n26

Sioux Falls Argus Leader, 98, 173, 191

Sioux Falls Chamber of Commerce, 119

Sioux Falls Fremad, 83n67

Sioux Falls Press, 72, 82n46

Sloan, Glenn, 145

Social gospel, 110n56

Socialist Party, 76–77

Social Security, 169, 218t

Socrates (Greek philosopher), 91

Sons of Israel (synagogue), 116

South Dakota: decline in rural population, 140–41, 149–51, 174; East River/West River, 189, 191, 194–95, 197–200, 212–13, 222, 226t, 227–28; gender roles/ wages, 177; implementation of political reform, 99; Interstate highway program, 146–48; Jewish population/contributions,

114–32; Pick-Sloan Missouri Basin Program, 144–46; political culture of, 1–9, 210–11; statehood, 25–26, 51, 61–62. *See also* Dakota Territory

South Dakota Board of Charities and Corrections, 80n20

South Dakota Board of Regents, 80n20

South Dakota Broadcasters Association, 118

South Dakota Commission on the Status of Women (CSW): domestic and sexual abuse and, 171–72; economic equality and, 169–71; establishment and objectives of, 7–8, 160–61; gender equality and, 161–69; and rise of antifeminism, 161–62, 172–74; support of the ERA, 7, 165–67, 174–77. *See also* Women's issues

South Dakota Department of Transportation, 129

South Dakota Farmers' Alliance, 5, 62, 65

South Dakota Historical Collections, 99

South Dakota Historical Society Press (SDHSP), 2

South Dakota History (journal), 1

South Dakota insurance commissioner, 71, 73–74

South Dakota Reclamation Association, 145

South Dakota Reform Press Association (SDRPA): beginnings of, 58–60, 79n7; challenge to Republican Party establishment, 68–73; founding of, 60, 64, 80n19; fusion politics and, 72–73; membership decline, 76; Populist movement and, 5–6, 73–78; selection of officers, 80n19, 81n31, 83n62

United States Federal Housing
Administration (FHA), 154
United States Postal Service, 82n54
United States Supreme Court, 7,
82n45, 113, 159, 173
U. S. News and World Report, 149

Vermillion, S.Dak., 15, 19, 21, 70
Vermillion Plain Talk, 72
Vessey, Robert S., 240
Video lottery, 216t, 217, 219–20
Vietnam War, 152, 155
Volkmar, H. S., 73, 75

Wall Street Journal, 198
Wanless, Emily O., 8, 210–31,
259–60
War on Poverty, 140–41, 148–49,
155–56
Watertown, S.Dak., 142, 185
Watson, Tom, 81n42
Webster, Daniel, 88
Weekly Dakotian, 10
Welles, Gideon, 31n63
Welsh, William, 37, 39, 41, 45, 57n95
Werner, Theodore B., 118, 254
Werthmann, Kitty, 175–77
Whipple, Henry, 40–41, 44–45, 50
Whitaker, R. S., 80n19
Whitton, Rex, 147
Wilder, Frank, 64, 80n19
Wilder, Laura Ingalls, 2
Williams, Bob, 8, 192, 193–94
Williams, Ora, 83n61
Williamson, Andrew, 46
Williamson, John, 40, 42–43, 48, 50,
57n95
Williamson, William, 254
Wilson, Woodrow, 93, 111n64

Winship, George, 95
Wohrman, C. Von, 83n65
Wollman, Harvey, 184, 186–87, 190,
192, 196, 201, 206n57, 211, 244
Women's issues: birth control/
abortion, 130–31, 159, 161,
173–77, 185, 190, 216t, 218t, 225;
credit discrimination, 7, 169–70;
documenting women's heritage,
170–71; Equal Rights Amendment,
7, 165–67, 174–77; feminism, 7–8,
159–67, 171–78; gender equality,
162, 165, 174; sexual and domestic
abuse, 7, 160–61, 171–73; and
S.Dak. political culture and, 4,
7; suffrage, 65, 162, 171. *See also*
South Dakota Commission on the
Status of Women
Women's Liberation Movement, 163,
166–67, 170–72, 178
Woonsocket, S.Dak., 68, 81n31, 228
World War I, 102, 142
Wright, Fred, 83n62

Yankton, S.Dak., 21, 61, 68–69
Yankton Agency, 42–44, 48–49
Yankton County, 22
Yankton Press and Dakotan, 184
Young Men's Christian Association
(YMCA), 119
Young Women's Christian
Association (YWCA), 122
Your Washington and You (Mundt
newsletter), 143

Zelinsky, Wilbur, 20
Zenker, Marion, 195
Zimmer, Eric Steven, 6, 112–32, 133n6,
260